A *Conservative* and *Compassionate*
Approach to Immigration Reform

A *Conservative* and *Compassionate* Approach to Immigration Reform

Perspectives from a Former U.S. Attorney General

Alberto R. Gonzales
and David N. Strange

Foreword by Gordon Morris Bakken

Texas Tech University Press

This book is typeset in Minion Pro. The paper used in this book meets the minimum requirements of ANSI/NISO Z39.48-1992 (R1997). ∞

Designed by Kasey McBeath

Library of Congress Cataloging-in-Publication Data
Gonzales, Alberto R.
    A conservative and compassionate approach to immigration reform : perspectives from a former US Attorney General / Alberto R. Gonzales and David N. Strange ; foreword by Gordon Morris Bakken.
        pages cm — (American liberty and justice)
    Includes bibliographical references and index.
    ISBN 978-0-89672-896-7 (hardback) — ISBN 978-0-89672-897-4 (e-book)
1. Emigration and immigration law—United States. 2. Emigration and immigration—United States. 3. Law reform—United States. I. Strange, David N., author. II. Title.
    KF4819.G569 2014
    342.7308'2—dc23

2014024584

14 15 16 17 18 19 20 21 22 / 9 8 7 6 5 4 3 2 1

Texas Tech University Press
Box 41037 | Lubbock, Texas 79409-1037 USA
800.832.4042 | ttup@ttu.edu | www.ttupress.org

CONTENTS

Contents

Foreword

There is something for everyone to hate in *A Conservative and Compassionate Approach to Immigration Reform*. This is a book that conservatives and liberals will find compelling in its arguments and the depth of careful, comprehensive research. Yet the issues are so divisive that advocates for change will be taking copious notes from the text and sources. The authors have crafted arguments so skillfully that politicians of every stripe must deal with the implications for revision of the statutes.

Yet the immigration reform issues are complex. Clearly, mass deportations would hurt certain service industries, such as the undocumented work of cooks and other restaurant workers, construction labor, maids and housekeepers, grounds maintenance, and agricultural workers. Some ask why so many of the undocumented risk deportation rather than simply securing lawful status through an employment visa. The answer is in the nature of their work and the visa process. The authors fill in the procedural impediments for the undocumented, particularly the kind of work they perform. The answers may surprise some readers.

Some may debate the costs of illegal immigrants in our schools and hospital emergency rooms. Others may question the costs of uninsured motorists and wonder about the rise of hit-and-run accidents. The authors explore both and provide deeply researched discussions. They then move to federalism issues and the Tenth Amendment to the Constitution. Why do some states issue driver's licenses to the undocumented and others do not? California moved a license bill sponsored by Senator Kevin de Leon of Los Angeles after he was "told by Gov. Jerry Brown that he was willing to sign the bill to goad Congress into immigration reform."[1] The bill evoked expected comment. One Garden Grove resident thought the people should "recall Gov. Jerry Brown and the state senators and representative who voted to give illegal immigrants California driver's licenses." A Huntington Beach resident asked of the undocumented, "If they see no problem in breaking two of our laws, can we trust them to buy insurance or even stop when they are involved in an accident?"[2] An exercise in federalism evoked strong opinions.

Akhil Reed Amar argues, "We must once again read the Constitution not merely as a text, but also as a deed."[3] He also has some observations regarding the Tenth Amendment and federalism, and readers will find the present book more cogent on the subject. On immigrant equality Amar supported a constitutional amendment to make naturalized citizens eligible for the presidency.[4] After reading this book, ponder the possibility of how such an amendment would expand the spirit of the Constitution. This book pushes the mind as well as the heart because the issues are so evocative of emotion.

Border security is another contested area. The authors suggest that border security is possible with limited fencing, the use of natural barriers, legal "virtual fences," technology, and training for border patrol personnel. Enforcement of the law is a critical issue and employment compliance is a necessity, yet the obstacle to reform is money. Congress must pay for the tools of border security. The federal government spends more than it receives in revenue and border security requires spending. Liberals and conservatives both will clearly find something to hate in the proposals for reform. Readers must have their pens out and ready to take notes. The complex issues have comprehensive proposals in this book. Read the book with care.

Gordon Morris Bakken
California State University, Fullerton

PREFACE

Initially, we think it is important to state that we do not believe that all aspects of our immigration system are "broken." In fiscal year 2010 alone, there were over 159 million nonimmigrant lawful admissions into the United States (counting multiple admissions of persons).[1] These admissions include, but are not limited to, temporary workers and their families (roughly three million), students (roughly 1.6 million), exchange visitors (roughly five hundred thousand), diplomats and other representatives (roughly four hundred thousand), visitors for pleasure, i.e., tourists (roughly thirty-five million), visitors for business (roughly five million), and transit aliens (roughly three hundred thousand).[2]

From fiscal years 2000 to 2009, over ten million immigrants acquired lawful permanent resident (LPR) status in the United States, and an additional one million acquired LPR status in fiscal year 2010 alone.[3] Over seventy thousand refugees arrived in the United States in fiscal year 2010, and this country granted over twenty thousand asylum cases in the same year.[4] There were over seven hundred thousand applications for naturalization filed in fiscal year 2010 and over six hundred thousand persons naturalized.[5]

Moreover, our government makes available to non-U.S. citizens many forms of "immigration relief" outside the channels referred to above. These include, but are not limited to, cancellation of removal, asylum, withholding of removal, relief pursuant to the United Nations Convention against Torture, stay of removal, temporary protected status, U-visa relief for survivors of domestic violence and other crimes, humanitarian parole, protection under the Violence Against Women Act, trafficking victims relief, and deferred action. Some of these forms of relief from removal, or deportation, lead to lawful permanent residency and eventual U.S. citizenship, while others do not.

In fiscal year 2011 the U.S. Immigration and Customs Enforcement (ICE) removed 396,906 individuals, which was the largest number in the agency's history to date.[6] In fiscal year 2012 ICE removed another 409,849 individuals, which once again became a record high.[7] The number of removals for fiscal year 2013 dropped to 368,644 but remained robust.[8] We have in place an intricate system of review and appellate procedure that allows non-U.S. citizens to seek redress before the immigration administrative system and before the U.S. courts. There are also available a myriad number of waivers available to both intending immigrants and nonimmigrants that forgive past conduct, making admission to the United States possible. Our civil servants in the Immigration Courts, the Department of Homeland Security, and abroad are consummate professionals, and they deserve to be recognized for the outstanding work they perform.

The point is that the United States has a functioning immigration system designed to deal with a global economy where we compete with other countries for goods and services. But in a post-9/11 world our government must have a much better understanding of what people are in our country and why they are here.

The dynamics of immigration necessitates that policymakers reexamine existing programs and design brand-new programs. Meanwhile, the regulation of immigration is a federal responsibility; however, because of our federal leaders' failures, our state and local governments, along with the private sector, are left struggling at the forefront of the social, economic, and civic integration of immigrants. Arguably, these entities have been forced to be at the forefront, often at severe costs to their budgets.

In this book we propose a compassionate, conservative approach to immigration reform, one that focuses on protecting our national security and supporting our economy. Our approach is built upon two fundamental truths: America is a nation of laws and a nation of immigrants. While the executive branch has discretion in the enforcement and execution of our laws, to suspend enforcement of the law against large groups of individuals breeds disrespect for the law and anger among law-abiding citizens. As a nation of immigrants, our country is stronger because of our diversity. We acknowledge that there are some in this country who support instant citizenship for the majority of the millions of undocumented immigrants currently present. We also recognize that there are those who believe we should remove the same millions of undocumented immigrants and build a three-thousand-mile fence on our southern border. We reject both approaches and instead suggest a more pragmatic alternative.

In general, we support greater border security and workplace enforcement. We also support tougher penalties for visa violations. We believe our visa process needs to be substantially revised in order to better address current and future immigration pressures, as well as to attract the necessary skilled and unskilled workers. We do not support mass deportations of the estimated eleven million undocumented immigrants presently within the United States.[9] We support placing those who are eligible and without a criminal record into temporary lawful status after paying a fine and back taxes. We do not oppose their becoming eligible for lawful status so long as those who followed the law are not disadvantaged. We also support placing eligible children into temporary lawful status and giving them a realistic opportunity for more permanent lawful status. We understand that many immigrants come to America to escape poverty and violence in their home countries and that we will never fully contain unlawful migration until conditions improve beyond our borders.

We believe that comprehensive immigration reform is good policy; however, we recognize that this issue has been politicized by certain factions of both political parties and that there is little realistic chance of comprehensive legislation any time soon. Nevertheless, we believe in the reforms outlined in this book and are hopeful that the American public will insist that their federal elected officials do what is right and necessary for America by enacting some level of meaningful reform.

While we certainly have a strong, working immigration system, this is not to say that we cannot improve. We can improve, and we should.

Alberto R. Gonzales
David N. Strange
May 2014

ACKNOWLEDGMENTS

The authors thank Valerie Finella (J.D., 2012, Texas Tech University School of Law), Bradley Parkin (J.D., 2013, Texas Tech University School of Law), Chloe Evans (J.D., 2013, Texas Tech University School of Law), Robert "Derek" Pennartz (J.D., 2012, Texas Tech University School of Law), Eric Reyna (J.D., 2013, Texas Tech University School of Law), Mischeka Nicholson (J.D., 2013, Texas Tech University School of Law), Tatiana Dennis (J.D., 2013, Texas Tech University School of Law), Elias Garcia (J.D., 2012, Texas Tech University School of Law), Michael Salas (J.D., 2014, BYU Law), Arslan Umarov (J.D., 2011, Texas Tech University School of Law), Niel Alden (J.D., 2014, Belmont University College of Law), and especially Christina Woods (J.D., 2012, Texas Tech University School of Law).

The authors also thank Shellie Handelsman (J.D., 2014, Belmont University College of Law) for her valuable assistance.

Mr. Strange also thanks George Whittenburg for his invaluable support in the study and practice of law, as well as Professors Calvin Lewis and Joseph A. Vail for freely giving of their time and energy in service to others.

Selected Abbreviations

DHS: U.S. Department of Homeland Security

ICE: U.S. Immigration and Customs Enforcement

USCIS: U.S. Citizenship and Immigration Services

CBP: U.S. Customs and Border Protection

DOS: U.S. Department of State

BIA: Board of Immigration Appeals

INA: Immigration and Nationality Act

IIRAIRA: Illegal Immigration Reform and Immigrant Responsibility Act of 1996

IRCA: Immigration Reform and Control Act of 1986

DACA: Deferred Action for Childhood Arrivals

LPR: Lawful Permanent Resident

RPI: Registered Provisional Immigrant

A *Conservative* and *Compassionate* Approach to Immigration Reform

Chapter One
Basics of U.S. Immigration Law

Introduction

Aliens[1] entering into the United States are generally divided into tempo-rary[2] and permanent[3] categories.[4] Aliens within the temporary categories are nonimmigrants; all other aliens present in the United States, including lawful permanent residents (LPRs), are immigrants.[5]

The nonimmigrant[6] categories are nicely laid out in Immigration and Nationality Act[7] (INA) § 101(a)(15).[8] With some exceptions every alien seeking to enter the United States is presumed to be an immigrant until he[9] establishes that he is entitled to nonimmigrant status under INA § 101(a)(15).[10] Nonimmigrant admissions[11] into the United States are by no means insignificant. There were approximately 165.5 million nonimmi-grant admissions into the United States in fiscal year 2012 alone.[12] By comparison, there were just slightly over one million immigrant admis-sions in that same year.[13] Immigration reform typically focuses extensively on immigrant admissions into the United States,[14] and nonimmigrant is-sues are largely overlooked by the mainstream media. We think both are deserving of significant consideration.

Immigrant Admissions and the Quota System

In order to immigrate to the United States, an alien must fit into one of the categories established by Congress[15] that allow for immigrant status.[16] Moreover, an alien seeking admission into the United States may not be subject to any of the inadmissibility grounds found in INA § 212(a).[17]

The immigrant categories are the family-based,[18] employment-based,[19] diversity-based,[20] and "miscellaneous other" categories.[21] These catego-ries, in turn, are further divided into subcategories.[22] Most of these subcategories are numerically limited, with some exceptions discussed below, and may not exceed an annual quota set by Congress.[23]

The annual worldwide quota for family-based immigration is 480,000, minus the number of immediate relatives who were admitted in the preceding fiscal year, plus any employment-based immigrant visas that were available in the preceding fiscal year but not used.[24] However, this number may not be less than 226,000 in any fiscal year.[25]

The annual quota for employment-based immigration is 140,000, plus any family-based immigrant visas that were available in the preceding fiscal year but not used.[26] The annual quota for diversity-based immigration is 55,000.[27] The "miscellaneous other" category is subject to quotas specific to the miscellaneous forms of relief available therein,[28] and those quotas will not be specifically addressed in this book.

Per-Country Limits within the Quota System[29]

The worldwide quotas are also subject to numerical limitations on individual foreign states.[30] For purposes of the quota system, a person seeking to immigrate is charged, or allocated, to the foreign state (including any colony or territory of the foreign state) in which he or she was born.[31] Moreover, the number of immigrant visas available in the family-based and employment-based categories to aliens charged to any particular foreign state in any fiscal year may not exceed 7 percent (or 2 percent in the case of chargeability to the colony or territory of a foreign state) of the combined worldwide limits.[32] The effect of these per-country limits is that the quotas may fill faster for aliens charged to particular countries than for aliens charged to other countries, resulting in longer waiting times for people from certain countries.[33] Similarly, under the diversity-based immigrant program, the percentage of visas available to aliens charged to any particular foreign state may not exceed 7 percent in any fiscal year.[34]

Immigration to the United States

Family-Based Immigration

Immediate Relatives

The family-based provisions are principally found at INA §§ 201(a)(1), 201(b)(2), 201(c), 203(a), and 203(d).[35] These provisions play a huge role in lawful immigration to the United States and account for approximately two-thirds of all lawful immigration.[36] Accordingly, it is reasonable to assume that any focus on immigration reform should, at a minimum, include some consideration of family-based immigration.[37]

The family-based category consists of immediate relatives and preference relatives.[38] Immediate relatives are the children,[39] spouses,[40] and parents[41] of U.S. citizens.[42] If an alien fits into one of these described groups, a U.S. citizen may file an immigrant petition on behalf of that alien.[43] In the case of an alien parent, the U.S. citizen who is filing a petition for the alien parent must be at least twenty-one years old.[44] An alien child born abroad to an alien lawfully admitted for permanent residence is also considered an immediate relative for classification purposes.[45] Immediate relatives are not subject to numerical limitations and as a result are exempt from the quota system.[46]

Preference Relatives

Preference relatives, on the other hand, are subject to the quota system and have numerical subceilings.[47] There are four preference categories, identified as first through fourth preferences.[48] These preference categories describe the people who fit therein (i.e., for whom an immigrant petition may be filed),[49] and each preference category has a numerical cap.[50] If an alien fits into one of these described preference groups, a U.S. citizen or LPR may file an immigrant petition on behalf of that alien.[51]

First Preference Category: The first preference category is limited to unmarried adult sons and daughters of U.S. citizens.[52] This preference category is allocated a number of immigrant visas not to exceed 23,400, plus any visas not required by the fourth preference.[53]

Second Preference Category: The second preference category allows for two subgroups of intending immigrants.[54] The first subgroup permits aliens lawfully admitted for permanent residence to file immigrant petitions for their spouses and children.[55] The second subgroup permits aliens lawfully admitted for permanent residence to file immigrant petitions for their unmarried sons and daughters.[56] The two subgroups in this preference category are allocated a number of immigrant visas not to exceed 114,200, plus the number (if any) by which the worldwide family-based level exceeds 226,000, plus any visas not required by the first preference.[57] Moreover, Congress has specifically mandated that at least 77 percent of the immigrant visas allocated to this preference category must be allocated to the first subgroup described therein.[58]

Third Preference Category: The third preference category is limited to married sons and daughters of U.S. citizens.[59] A married son or daughter may be one who has not yet attained twenty-one years of age but is no longer a child for immigration purposes by virtue of marriage.[60] This preference category is allocated a number of immigrant visas not to exceed 23,400, plus any visas not required by the first and second preferences.[61]

Fourth Preference Category: The fourth preference category is limited to brothers and sisters of U.S. citizens.[62] For this preference category the U.S. citizen sibling filing an immigrant petition must be at least twenty-one years old.[63] This preference category is allocated a number of immigrant visas not to exceed 65,000, plus any visas not required by the first, second, and third preferences.[64]

Employment-Based Immigration[65]

The employment-based provisions are principally found at INA §§ 201(a)(2), 201(d), 203(b), and 203(d)[66] and are generally related to professional or occupational credentials or to employment creation.[67] These provisions account for approximately 13 percent of all lawful immigration.[68] Immediate relatives do not exist in the employment-based category,[69] and all employment-based immigrants are subject to the quota system.[70]

There are five employment-based preference categories, identified as first through fifth preferences.[71] These preference categories describe the people who fit therein (i.e., for whom an immigrant petition may be filed),[72] and each preference category has a numerical cap.[73]

First Preference Category ———————————————

The first preference category is reserved for (1) aliens with extraordinary ability[74] in the sciences, arts, education, business, or athletics;[75] (2) outstanding professors and researchers; and (3) certain multinational executives and managers.[76] This preference category is allocated a number of immigrant visas not to exceed 28.6 percent of the worldwide employment-based annual quota, plus any visas not required by the fourth and fifth preferences.[77]

Second Preference Category

The second preference category is reserved for aliens who are members of the professions holding advanced degrees or aliens of exceptional ability.[78] This preference category is allocated a number of immigrant visas not to exceed 28.6 percent of the worldwide employment-based annual quota, plus any visas not required by the first preference.[79]

Third Preference Category

The third preference category is reserved for skilled workers, professionals, and other workers.[80] This preference category is allocated a number of immigrant visas not to exceed 28.6 percent of the worldwide employment-based annual quota, plus any visas not required by the first and second preferences.[81] No more than 10,000 of the immigrant visas in this preference category may be allocated to the other workers described therein.[82]

Fourth Preference Category

The fourth preference category is reserved for certain special immigrants described in INA § 101(a)(27).[83] This preference category is allocated a number of immigrant visas not to exceed 7.1 percent of the worldwide employment-based annual quota.[84] Unlike most other preference categories, this preference category may not include unused visas that other preference categories do not require.[85]

Fifth Preference Category

The fifth preference category is reserved for employment creation.[86] This preference category is allocated a number of immigrant visas not to exceed 7.1 percent of the worldwide employment-based annual quota.[87] Like the employment-based fourth preference category, this preference category may not include unused visas that other preference categories do not require.[88]

Diversity-Based Immigration

The diversity-based provisions are principally found at INA §§ 201(a)(3), 201(e), 203(c), and 203(d)[89] and authorize immigrant visas to aliens from foreign states or regions of the world from which the United States has received low percentages of immigration during the previous five years.[90] The diversity-based provisions account for approximately 4 percent of all lawful immigration.[91] The diversity-based category, while subject to the quota system, does not have preference categories; instead, the distribution of diversity-based immigrant visas is based on a series of formulas designed to further enhance the allocation of visas to underrepresented foreign states and regions of the world.[92] A more complete discussion of the diversity-based category is beyond the scope and purpose of this book and will not be undertaken here.[93]

"Miscellaneous Other" Immigration

U.S. immigration law allows immigration based on provisions other than the three broad categories (family-based, employment-based, and diversity-based) found initially at INA § 201(a).[94] For example, immigration is possible through the refugee and asylum provisions of the INA;[95] certain longtime residents may be able to immigrate;[96] and other humanitarian grounds may allow for immigration based on exceptional and extremely unusual hardship standards[97] through a form of relief known as "cancellation of removal."[98] These and other miscellaneous provisions account for approximately 16 percent of all lawful immigration.[99] Again, a more complete discussion of this "miscellaneous other" category is beyond the scope and purpose of this book and will not be undertaken here.[100]

Nonimmigrant Admissions

Nonimmigrants are aliens who have a residence in a foreign country that they have no intention of abandoning and who seek to enter the United States temporarily for business or temporarily for pleasure.[101] The provisions for nonimmigrant admissions are principally found at INA §§ 101(a)(15)(A) through 101(a)(15)(V).[102] The visa designations are labeled with their corresponding subsections under INA § 101(a)(15). As noted previously, nonimmigrant admissions are substantial in number, with approximately 165.5 million nonimmigrant admissions into the United States in fiscal year 2012 alone. A brief overview of the full panoply of nonimmigrant visas can be found in appendix 1 at the end of this book.

Grounds of Inadmissibility

It is clear that an alien must fit into a specific category authorized by Congress in order to be admitted into the United States as a lawful immigrant or nonimmigrant.[103] Fitting into any particular category, however, is not enough.[104] The alien must also clear the various grounds of inadmissibility described in INA § 212(a).[105] The classic example is that a known alien terrorist will not be permitted to immigrate to the United States even though married to a U.S. citizen spouse who has properly filed an immigrant petition for the alien terrorist spouse.[106] And, of course, there are other less extreme grounds of inadmissibility.[107] An intending immigrant or nonimmigrant must clear the grounds of inadmissibility under INA § 212(a) in order to be admitted into the United States.[108]

Conclusion

The Second Circuit Court of Appeals once observed:

> We have had occasion to note the striking resemblance between some of the laws we are called upon to interpret and King Minos's labyrinth in ancient Crete. The Tax Laws and the Immigration and Nationality Act . . . are examples we have cited of Congress's ingenuity in passing statutes certain to accelerate the aging process of judges. In this instance, Congress, pursuant to its virtually unfettered power to exclude or deport natives of other countries, and apparently confident of the aphorism that human skill, properly applied, can resolve any enigma that human inventiveness can create, has enacted a baffling skein of provisions for the I.N.S. and courts to disentangle.[109]

In this chapter we have attempted to simplify U.S. immigration law in a bare-bones sort of way in order to assist the reader with the remaining chapters of this book, and we hope this brief overview is helpful as we later discuss our ideas on U.S. immigration laws and policies.

Chapter Two
Strategy for Success

Introduction

During the 2012 presidential campaign, President Barack Obama and former Massachusetts Governor Mitt Romney understandably focused their campaigns on issues related to the economy and jobs—issues most important to American voters. Relatively little was said about immigration reform. Although President Obama failed to deliver on his promise to push for immigration reform during his first term, Hispanics overwhelmingly voted for him in 2012 by a 71–27 percent margin.[1] Some political experts believe the level of Hispanic support was the difference in the outcome in certain key electoral states.[2] Governor Romney took a very conservative position on immigration policy during the Republican state primaries. For example, he advocated self-deportation, and he expressed support for Arizona Senate Bill 1070 (discussed later). In contrast, during the closing days of the campaign, President Obama told the Iowa media that he would deliver immigration reform early in a second term.[3]

Given Governor Romney's moderate record as governor of Massachusetts, his immigration stance may have been motivated by politics, and while his position on immigration during the Republican primaries positioned him to win the nomination, unfortunately it hurt him among some Hispanic voters in the general election. Following Governor Romney's poor showing among Hispanics, some Republicans who opposed immigration reform now appear willing to approach the issue from a more practical perspective. Although they may be motivated by political survival, the important fact is that the stage appears as receptive as it has ever been for some type of legislative action. We turn first, however, to a brief recap of recent legislative failures.

Previous Legislative Efforts

The last major comprehensive legislative change in immigration law occurred in the 1980s.[4] Since that time the size of the unauthorized immigration[5] population has swelled, fueling claims by some that undocumented immigrants[6] are taking jobs away from citizens and costing state and local governments millions of dollars in the form of services and benefits. Initially, immigration reform ranked high on the agenda of President George W. Bush. President Bush, owing primarily to his popularity with the Latino electorate and a good working relationship with Mexican president Vicente Fox, appeared poised and equipped to initiate reform. Both favored a combination of tougher border controls and conditional legalization (not necessarily citizenship) of undocumented immigrants residing on American soil.

Unfortunately, momentum for broad immigration reform stalled after 9/11.[7] In the atmosphere of national angst and political turmoil, immigration reform was recast as primarily an issue of national security. Comprehensive immigration reform was placed on the shelf due to the demand to secure the borders, and as a result, no significant immigration bills emerged from Congress for some time after 9/11.

Several years passed before immigration reform again received serious attention; however, this time instead of liberalization of our policies, steps were taken to deny access to the border, remove undocumented immigrants, and restrict foreign nationals' access to the United States.[8] For example, in 2005 Congress passed the REAL ID Act, which tightened immigration enforcement and imposed federal requirements on the states. Reestablishing momentum in favor of durable immigration reform requires a return to rational discourse and an acknowledgment that reform is consistent with protecting our national security.

In 2006 President Bush directed an effort in the White House to pass immigration legislation. The president recognized the need, in a post-9/11 world with a sluggish economy, for legislation producing a policy that would meet our national security needs and bolster our economy. President Bush wanted to achieve a comprehensive solution, and he worked for months to get legislation passed. In the end, however, he was unable to pass a bill, in large part because of opposition from members of his own party. Republicans, fearful of another amnesty program similar to the one passed under President Reagan, insisted on a staggered approach. Many Republicans were unwilling to consider (1) reform unless the border was secure and (2) legalization for the millions already here unless they returned first to their home countries.

After this failed effort, separate bills were introduced to address different aspects of immigration policy. The most notable was a revised version of the DREAM Act,[9] which focused on extending lawful status to qualified immigrant children brought unlawfully to the United States by their parents. Republicans, fearing this legislation would encourage further unauthorized immigration and reward parents for their unlawful actions, blocked this legislation. Many of the objectives of the DREAM Act, however, have now been achieved through the executive order issued by President Obama in June 2012, authorizing Deferred Action for Childhood Arrivals (DACA), discussed more fully in chapter 10.[10]

Aside from the Gang of Eight's Senate bill (discussed below), there have been over sixty immigration-related bills introduced in Congress.[11] Topics include border security, unlawful immigration, citizenship and naturalization, foreign labor, immigration status and procedures, and visas and passports.[12] While this legislative effort may appear promising for changes in immigration law, every one of these immigration-related bills has only been referred to committee and not made any further progress toward passage.[13]

Comprehensive Legislation

Immigration policy affects our national security and foreign policy. It touches our economy, jobs, and commerce. Our policy affects families and communities. It relates to the very essence of who we are as a country of immigrants. There are many constituents, interest groups, and organizations with a vested interest in the outcome of the immigration debate.

Because of the complexities of the issues and the very nature of the democratic process, all interested parties will need to compromise. No one will get exactly what he wants on every issue relating to immigration policy. Achieving that compromise will be virtually impossible in our judgment unless all issues are put on the table so all parties can make intelligent decisions on the various components of immigration policy. For example, a hardliner on border security may be willing to support a pathway to lawful status for children brought here unlawfully by their parents if he sees an effective plan to provide more resources to the border. We believe this effort should be done through one comprehensive bill, if possible, although we acknowledge that because of the scope of the challenges, implementation of the policy may have to occur in stages.

Some lawmakers will continue to push for immigration reform in smaller bills, and the House leadership has announced that it will not consider the Gang of Eight's Senate bill (discussed below), instead electing to consider several smaller bills. House Republicans have blamed President Obama for selectively enforcing laws he supports and not enforcing laws he does not support. Republicans fear that in passing a comprehensive bill the president will ignore border security requirements and pursue legalization. We believe the failure by the president to do his job does not excuse members of Congress from doing their jobs.

The danger of separate bills is that the Republican-controlled House will pass only bills focused on border security, ignoring our economic needs and the potential danger posed by those who overstay their visas. Respectfully, unless members of the House are more disciplined than they have been, and are committed to passing legislation to deal with security and our economy, efforts to deal with immigration in small bills would be a mistake. Similarly, we believe that unilateral executive action that only addresses relief from removal is a mistake. The recent influx of immigrant children following the news that the Obama Administration will stop deporting certain immigrant children demonstrates clearly our need for greater border security. It is an example of the disastrous effects of trying to address only one aspect of immigration policy. We believe a far more effective approach is a comprehensive solution that involves both tougher enforcement and some remedial measures providing relief from removal.

For example, following the 2012 presidential election, Republican members began introducing legislation to deal with immigrant children and to award more high-tech visas.[14] Not only is this approach of separate legislative bills likely to be viewed as self-serving and political, it may actually work against the goal of addressing all the problems related to immigration. Immigrant children brought here unlawfully by their parents present a sympathetic story. Even some hardliners on border security feel that something should be done to help these children.[15] However, if legislation similar to the DREAM Act is passed, this may relieve political pressure on some members to address the other difficult issues related to immigration.

Gang of Eight's Proposed Immigration Legislation—The Border Security, Economic Opportunity, and Immigration Modernization Act of 2013 (S. 744)

On April 17, 2013, a "Gang of Eight" senators introduced S. 744, seeking comprehensive change to our immigration laws.[16] The Gang of Eight includes John McCain (R), Chuck Schumer (D), Michael Bennet (D), Marco Rubio (R), Lindsey Graham (R), Jeff Flake (R), Robert Menendez (D), and Dick Durbin (D). On June 27, 2013, the Senate passed S. 744 by a bipartisan vote of 68–32,[17] and it immediately became the most promising vehicle for comprehensive immigration reform. However, in the ensuing months it became clear that the bill lacked sufficient support in the House of Representatives. Nevertheless, various provisions are illustrative in highlighting the political nature of the immigration debate, as well as the public sentiment over immigration policy. For these reasons, we believe it helpful to understand the key provisions of S. 744.

Title 1 of the Proposed Bill

The bill's top priority is to secure the border,[18] a goal that it aims to achieve through persistent surveillance in "high-risk" areas along the southern border and by achieving a 90 percent effective rate every year in these areas.[19] The Gang of Eight calculates this rate by dividing the number of apprehensions and turn-backs by the total number of unlawful entries during one year.[20] However, it may be difficult, if not impossible, to determine a 90 percent effective rate. If immigrants are entering the United States without being detected, it is difficult to understand how the government can accurately calculate the effective rate.

The legislation defines a "high-risk" area as one where "apprehensions are above 30,000 individuals per year."[21] Within 180 days after the legislation is enacted, the DHS Secretary must submit two strategies to Congress, the "Comprehensive Southern Border Security Strategy" (Security Strategy) and the "Southern Border Fencing Strategy" (Fencing Strategy).[22] The Security Strategy will implement additional border patrol agents and custom officers, surveillance and detection capabilities, and drones through a 3-billion-dollar budget.[23] The Fencing Strategy will implement fencing and other technology to secure the border through a 1.5-billion-dollar budget.[24] We believe in the importance of effective, cost-efficient border security, including limited fencing (discussed later). Whatever new legislation is implemented, we understand the political considerations in passing legislation and the need for tough border security measures in order to garner sufficient Republican support for the legislation.

The bill also requires a mandatory E-Verify, obligating all employers to verify the identity and certify the eligibility of their workers and to ensure that each worker has a biometric work authorization card.[25] We support the limited use of an E-Verify program as a safe harbor for employers but reject the notion that an American worker needs permission from the government to obtain a job and caution against the expansion of E-Verify "into a comprehensive national identity system that would be used to track and control Americans."[26]

Hoeven-Corker Amendment

The Hoeven-Corker Amendment was adopted into the proposed Senate bill on June 26, 2013.[27] With the aim to placate conservatives, the amendment attempts to ensure that the bill's Registered Provisional Immigrants (RPIs) cannot obtain LPR status until certain "tangible, concrete triggers" are met.[28] These triggers mandate that RPIs cannot receive LPR status until at least ten years after enactment of the bill and until the DHS Secretary, in consultation with the Attorney General, the Secretary of Defense, the DHS Inspector General, and the U.S. Government Accountability Office, certifies that the triggers have been met.

In addition to the ten-year requirement,[29] five other requirements must be fully implemented and operational.[30] First, twenty thousand additional Border Patrol agents must be hired, which more than doubles the current patrol.[31] Second, the Security Strategy must be implemented and operational.[32] Third, the Fencing Strategy must have been implemented, in addition to the completion of 700 miles of additional fencing along the southern border.[33] Fourth, the electronic visa entry and exit system must be fully operational.[34] Finally, all U.S. employers must use E-Verify.[35] Once all five requirements are operational, RPIs who have been in that status for ten years may apply for LPR status.[36]

Additionally, the Hoeven-Corker Amendment modifies the Gang of Eight proposal by requiring DHS to initiate removal proceedings for at least 90 percent of the visa overstayers identified by the newly implemented entry and exit system.[37] Furthermore, the amendment restricts some nonimmigrant visa holders from using health-care benefits, such as Medicaid, the State Children's Health Insurance Program, and the Affordable Care Act; prevents immigrants who used a fraudulent Social Security number from getting Social Security credits; and prohibits the U.S. Department of Health and Human Services from providing cash assistance benefits to needy RPIs.[38]

While we applaud the Hoeven-Corker Amendment and support its objectives of greater border security, we question whether such triggers are realistic and can ever be met.[39] If they cannot, will RPIs remain in such status perpetually? Will they be subject to deportation at some point, and will this create another underclass of people living in the shadows in America? If Congress were to pass legislation that introduced provisions similar to the Hoeven-Corker Amendment, members should level with the American people and inform them that we may have simply "kicked the can" down the road and punted on these questions to future generations.

Title 2 of the Proposed Bill

Until the two strategies are submitted, no undocumented immigrant may begin the process of acquiring lawful status.[40] The bill provides an escape clause in two situations: (1) when litigation or *force majeure* prevents implementation or implementation is found to be unconstitutional, and (2) when ten years have passed since the bill was enacted.[41] However, if and when the two strategies are submitted after enactment of the bill, or the escape clause is activated and has vested, undocumented immigrants may apply for RPI status.[42]

Additional requirements to apply for RPI status include that the applicant (1) has resided in the United States prior to December 31, 2011, and has been continuously present since that date; (2) pays a $500 penalty, plus

taxes and fees, (3) has not been convicted of a felony, three or more misdemeanors, an offense in a foreign country, or has unlawfully voted, and
(4) is not otherwise inadmissible for national security or public health
reasons.[43] Spouses and children may apply for derivative status based on
the principle beneficiary.[44] An RPI may work for any employer and travel
outside the United States.[45] The application period is one to two years, and
RPI status lasts for six years and is renewable with payment of another
$500 penalty.[46] An RPI will be considered to be lawfully present in the
United States.[47]

An RPI may then apply for LPR status after DHS certifies the following: the two strategies have been substantially completed, the E-Verify
system has been implemented, and an electronic exit system is in place.[48]
Moreover, an RPI may only apply after ten years and if (1) he has continuously resided in the United States, (2) he has paid taxes, (3) he has worked
regularly in the United States (with some exceptions), (4) he can demonstrate a basic knowledge of American civics and English, (5) he pays a
$1,000 penalty, and (6) backlogs in other categories have been eliminat-
ed.[49] Exceptions are made for DREAM Act children and agricultural
workers, who may apply for LPR status after only five years.[50] Additionally,
DREAM Act children become eligible for citizenship immediately after
receiving LPR status.[51]

We believe the RPI provision, with no other meaningful relief to the
millions of undocumented immigrants present in the United States, is unlikely to be effective in substantially reducing, much less eliminating, the
present undocumented population. The legislation forces this population
to wait ten years or longer, a period that may or may not lead to LPR status.[52] Thus, they pay taxes and forgo benefits hoping to achieve a status
that for many is virtually impossible to attain. Supporters of the RPI provision may argue that those who breach our laws are not entitled to fair
treatment. That may be so, but Congress should be forthcoming in advis-
ing the American people that we may continue to have a significant undocumented population even with the passage of this or similar legislation.

Many undocumented immigrants who are already waiting for a traditional visa to become available will undoubtedly elect to skip the whole
RPI process altogether. Some attorneys might even advise them to do so—

if a traditional visa leading to LPR status is only a short way off, it might be better to just bypass the RPI provision and continue to remain unlawfully in the United States until a permanent visa becomes available, unencumbered with the baggage of RPI status. In the meantime, if ICE apprehends the undocumented immigrant, the RPI option becomes a fallback provision. Moreover, by some estimates, nearly half of the undocumented immigrant population will never qualify for LPR status. That number, obviously, will be higher if the border security triggers are not met. Accordingly, many undocumented immigrants will be in no better position than they are now. In ten to fifteen years we could be facing the same immigration issues once again.[53] Therefore, we believe proposals that include significant but simple amendments to the current INA (amendments we discuss later) may be more effective and easier to achieve politically.

S. 744 also redrafts the family preference system to include only unmarried adult children, married adult children with petitions filed before age thirty-one, and unmarried adult children of LPRs.[54] The fourth preference sibling category would not be eliminated.[55] Importantly, a new V visa nonimmigrant category would be created to allow beneficiaries of approved petitions to enter the United States to work while waiting for LPR status to become available.[56] Spouses and children of LPRs would be considered immediate relatives and no longer subject to the quota system.[57] We believe that bringing back the V visa nonimmigrant category is sound policy because it allows for greater family unity. The new V visa, in turn, would largely render unnecessary any need to switch spouses and children of LPRs into the immediate-relative category because the new V visa would already address these concerns.[58] In our opinion, only close family members of U.S. citizens should be treated as immediate relatives. This further serves our general policy of granting greater immigration benefits to U.S. citizens over noncitizens.

Additionally, under Title 2 of S. 744, employment-based visas would be allocated in the following proportions: 40 percent to people holding advanced degrees in the sciences, arts, professions, or business of a U.S. employer and those with a master's degree or higher in science, technology, engineering, or mathematics; 40 percent to skilled workers and other professionals; 10 percent to special immigrants; and 10 percent to those who foster employment.[59] Additionally, foreign entrepreneurs coming to the United States would be given a start-up visa.[60] Moreover, after five years a merit-based visa system will be created and given to those with the most points based on education, employment, length of residence, and other considerations.[61] This cap will begin at 120,000 visas and may increase up to 250,000. These proposals appear to be sound policy, but we should consider unintended consequences in supporting a merit-based system. Many educated professionals will certainly seek to immigrate, and brain drain from poor, developing countries might become an issue for our foreign allies struggling to develop their own economies to do business with the United States.

Title 3 of the Proposed Bill

S. 744 requires E-Verify to be fully implemented within five years and punishes companies that don't comply.[62] Within this same section the bill eliminates the one-year filing requirement for asylum applications, and it authorizes asylum officers to grant asylum during credible-fear interviews.[63]

S. 744 also increases Immigration Court personnel, as well as training and resources for the Immigration Courts.[64] Controversially, the bill provides access to counsel at no expense to alien children and incompetent adults.[65] The bill also tightens the grounds of inadmissibility relating to document fraud, DWI convictions, gang-related activities, domestic-violence convictions, child abuse, stalking, violations of protective orders, and failure to register as a sex offender.[66]

Title 4 of the Proposed Bill

Under title 4, S. 744 seeks to reform the H-1B nonimmigrant visa category. The cap will be raised to 110,000 and 25,000 for advanced-degree holders.[67] The caps will increase or decrease based on a specific formula set forth in the legislation.[68] We support these efforts to increase the H-1B cap.

To protect American workers, employers must pay significantly higher wages and fees for H-1B workers.[69] If an employer has fifty or more employees and 30–50 percent are H-1B workers, the employer must pay a $5,000 fee per worker.[70] If more than 50 percent are H-1B workers, the employer must pay a $10,000 fee per additional worker.[71] The new legislation also prohibits companies from obtaining additional H-1B workers when their workforce already largely consists of foreign workers.[72] In subsequent years companies will be banned from adding H-1B workers if they had more than 75 percent in 2014, 65 percent in 2015, and 50 percent in 2016.[73] We think these are fair considerations, and we support this section of the proposal as well.

Increasing the H-1B numbers is sound policy and serves the U.S. economy. Under current law before any employer may hire or recruit an H-1B worker, the employer must first try to recruit an American worker, and the employer may not give preference to an H-1B worker over an American worker; this wise policy will continue under the proposed bill.[74]

A new W visa program will be implemented for lower-skilled workers. A newly created Bureau of Immigration and Labor Market Research (Bureau) will determine the annual cap, in addition to declaring work shortages and expanding the list of proper recruitment methods.[75] However, for the first four years, the caps will be twenty thousand, thirty-five thousand, fifty-five thousand, and seventy-five thousand respectively.[76] If there is a work shortage, the Bureau may make additional visas available.[77] No more than 33 percent of the registered positions available per year may be in the construction industry.[78] We support this section of the proposed bill as strongly as we support increasing the H-1B caps. Both will beneficially serve our economy, while protecting American workers.

To be eligible for a W visa, the immigrant must pass a criminal background check and only accept registered positions from employers.[79] The W visa may be granted for three years and may be renewed for three additional years.[80] The W worker may not be required to waive any legal rights or protections or be treated as an independent contractor, unless the employer operates solely as an independent contractor.[81] We believe these are reasonable requirements.

Employers will also have strict requirements for hiring W workers. First, the employer must submit an application for registration and be accepted.[82] The employer must pay a registration fee and then may register for a three-year term, in addition to renewing for an additional three years.[83] Once the employer is registered, it may hire W workers, as long as it pays an additional fee for each approved registered position it posts.[84] The employer must estimate the number of W workers it will seek per year, describe the type of work the position entails, and list the anticipated dates of employment.[85] We believe these requirements are also reasonable.

The wage requirements for W workers are strict as well. The wages must be equal to the higher of (1) the actual paid wage to other employees with similar experience and qualifications or (2) the prevailing wage in the geographic area for the occupation.[86] The employer must state that the W worker's position will not replace a current U.S. worker or adversely affect another U.S. worker.[87] The employer must also prove that it has posted the job for thirty days and could not find an available, qualified U.S. worker for the position.[88] Finally, if the unemployment rate is above 8.5 percent, no W workers may be hired unless the Bureau determines that a shortage exists.[89]

House Democrats Introduce Their Version of Senate Bill 744

On October 2, 2013, House Democrats introduced their version of an immigration bill: the Border Security, Economic Opportunity, and Immigration Modernization Act.[90] It is very similar to S. 744 but removes the Hoeven-Corker "border surge" amendment and replaces it with the McCaul-Thompson bill, which the House Homeland Security Committee unanimously passed in May 2013.[91] Significantly, the McCaul-Thompson bill requires more extensive accountability, including regular reports to DHS on border control, a strategy to control the southern border within five years, and a plan for a biometric entry-exit system at all ports.[92] However, with the federal government shutdown, worry about the government reaching its borrowing limits, and concerns in Ukraine, Syria, and elsewhere, the House bill did not immediately gain very much traction.[93]

The press has also leaked some immigration proposals of President Obama.[94] Overall, his suggestions are similar to the Gang of Eight's bill. His recommendations include a pathway to citizenship for undocumented immigrants after an eight-year journey, allowing undocumented immigrants to become LPRs only after a visa has become available for someone who lawfully entered the United States, requiring employers to check the immigration status of their workers, increasing penalties for those who break the law, increasing border protection and patrol, and offering a path to residency for soldiers and students brought to the United States unlawfully as children. While President Obama's suggestions have support, he has repeatedly asserted that he will only offer his proposal for consideration if the Gang of Eight proposal is defeated.[95]

Conclusion

While S. 744 has the most support of any proposed comprehensive immigration proposal in years, there appears to be sufficient opposition to defeat it and the bill itself is subject to sunset. Some conservatives believe that S. 744 will grant amnesty, and thus they oppose it. Additionally, some media outlets have reported a "Gang of Six" in the House who may be an impediment to the Senate bill.[96] It now appears that if the House takes up immigration reform, it will do so in separate bills.

However, proponents of immigration reform should not be discouraged. The Senate proposal is just the beginning of this process. Whatever the vehicle, we need immigration reform. If the Senate bill is unacceptable, then we should improve it. If it cannot be fixed, then we should insist on other legislative solutions. The reality is that we need reform for our national security and our economy because the status quo is unacceptable. Members of Congress should continue to work together to pass a law that meets our national security and economic needs.

Chapter Three
The Known and Unknown Challenges
of Unauthorized Immigration

Introduction

Most immigrants come to the United States seeking a better life for themselves and their families. However, long wait times and confusing immigration procedures often encourage unlawful immigration. Without a system to track accurately the number of undocumented immigrants entering the United States, estimating the growing or falling trend of unauthorized immigration is difficult. Consequently, the numbers vary according to which researcher is reporting the statistics. The difficulty in tracking highlights the problem of using benchmarks to trigger new legislation. If we cannot track unlawful migration now, how can we track it in the future?

As of January 2006, DHS estimated that approximately 11.6 million undocumented immigrants resided in the United States.[1] Subsequently, in 2007, scholars estimated the population of undocumented immigrants in the United States to be closer to twelve million.[2] Regardless of which estimate is correct, the unauthorized immigration trend was for some time believed to be declining.[3] In 2008 the Center for Immigration Studies estimated that the number of undocumented immigrants dropped by as much as 1.3 million people, compared to its 2007 estimate.[4] Although the rate of unauthorized immigration may have decreased over the past few years, the numbers remain substantial—and the need for a comprehensive plan remains great.

The American community represents more than 180 different countries of origin for immigrants.[5] The landscape has recently changed with Asian and Latin American immigrants significantly outnumbering European immigrants, previously the predominant group. Patterns of immigrant settlements have also changed. In the past, immigrants settled in major urban areas and common border states, such as California, New York, Florida, Texas, New Jersey, and Illinois. Currently, immigrant communities are flourishing in Arizona, Arkansas, Colorado, Georgia, Idaho, Kentucky, Minnesota, Nebraska, Nevada, North Carolina, South Carolina, Tennessee, and Utah.[6] The changes in settlement areas will ultimately lead to many challenges, some which are now easily discernible, while others may currently be unknown.

As the U.S. population continues to climb, immigration figures predominately in this growth. From 1967 to 2006, the population grew by one hundred million people, with legal immigrants and their descendants largely advancing this increase.[7] The U.S. Census Bureau estimates that during that same period the percentage of foreign-born citizens rose from 5 to 12 percent. For the last ten years approximately one million new lawful immigrants arrived every year.[8] Undocumented immigrants, who either enter unlawfully or enter lawfully but then overstay their visa, also contribute to the increases in the U.S. population.

Outside the United States other nations are concerned with where they will find their future workforce.[9] However, the U.S. population still continues to grow, even during the recession, largely because of lawful and unlawful immigrants. But, to truly benefit our future workforce, the influx of skilled and necessary labor must continue, or the country will experience stagnant growth in the future, as many other countries are currently experiencing.

Documenting the Undocumented

As a start the government needs to implement measures to determine which immigrants are in the United States unlawfully. For our purposes here, an undocumented immigrant is a noncitizen who is currently in the United States unlawfully. We consider such noncitizen to be undocumented in one of the following ways: (1) arriving and entering without inspection, (2) entering by defrauding the inspection process, or (3) arriving lawfully but overstaying the period of lawful stay or admission.

The U.S. population is approximately 316 million people.[10] If approximately 11.5 million immigrants are here unlawfully, that is about one in twenty-seven.[11] It is estimated that nearly two-thirds of those unlawfully present enter surreptitiously, by crossing the U.S.–Mexico border, and the remaining nearly one-third are present after overstaying a temporary visa.[12]

Despite the decline of the unlawful immigrant population due to our struggling economy, the high levels of unlawful entry will likely resume once the economy recovers.[13] We do not believe self-deportation is realistic, but neither is the federal government capable of removing the approximately 11.5 million undocumented immigrants. Even if it could, mass removal would devastate certain service industries, such as food processing, construction, landscaping, and agriculture.[14] Congress should explore allowing those who would qualify to lawfully remain under an expanded temporary-worker program for skilled and unskilled workers based on American economic need. Many who are here and working do not aspire to citizenship; they simply want to work. For the immigrants who want more long-term security, perhaps Congress should consider allowing the newly created W visa to be extended indefinitely (similar to the current E visa), and Congress should certainly afford derivative status allowing for work and study authorization to the spouses and children of long-term W visa holders. Congress might also consider creating a path to nationality, rather than citizenship, as described in chapter 5.

Coming to America Unlawfully

As discussed previously, immigrants have various options for employment and lawful residence in the United States. The number of undocumented aliens, however, still remains high. In 2010 an estimated eight million undocumented workers unlawfully resided in the United States.[15] Undocumented workers accounted for 5 percent of the American workforce in 2010.[16] In January 2011 DHS estimated the number of undocumented immigrants (as opposed to workers) at approximately 11.5 million, down from 11.6 million in 2010.[17] DHS reported that "Mexico continued to be the leading source country of unauthorized immigration to the United States," with 6.8 million in the United States.[18] "[Undocumented] immigrants from El Salvador were a distant second, with some

660,000 believed to be in the United States."[19] But the question remains, why do so many undocumented immigrants risk removal rather than simply obtaining lawful status through an employment visa?

The U.S. government issues some 140,000 employment visas for permanent residency annually.[20] In many instances foreign workers must wait until their prospective employer has obtained a labor certification from the Department of Labor before filing for a visa.[21] The certification attempts to establish that no qualified, available American worker is able and willing to fill the position for a similar wage.[22]

In addition to securing a labor certification for permanent residency, a foreign worker generally must also ensure that his country has a "current" priority date on the visa bulletin.[23] The wait can last for more than ten years.[24] Temporary workers, as well, go through a similar process involving a labor condition application.

Obtaining an employment visa, when possible, can be a lengthy and difficult process.[25] Therefore, many immigrants avoid the visa process, ignore American immigration laws, assume the risks, and enter the United States unlawfully.

Working in the United States

Many believe that undocumented immigrants displace American workers. A 2005 study revealed that of the 56,000 insulation workers in the country at that time, 36 percent were undocumented immigrants.[26] Other common jobs for undocumented immigrants include cooks, construction laborers, maids and housekeepers, grounds and maintenance workers, slaughterhouse workers, and agricultural workers.[27]

It is also widely believed that undocumented immigrants do not pay income taxes. Some reports state that most undocumented immigrants are paid "under the table," meaning they are paid in cash and no taxes are deducted.[28] According to a 2005 Bear Stearns report, undocumented workers held twelve to fifteen million jobs and accounted for 8 percent of the total employed population,[29] and because of these undocumented workers, the United States may be losing an estimated thirty-five billion dollars in uncollected income tax.[30]

In March 2010 the Pew Hispanic Center estimated that undocumented workers comprised about 5.2 percent of the U.S. labor force, which equaled about eight million undocumented immigrants (apparently including unemployed undocumented workers).[31] In 2012 it was estimated that undocumented workers amounted to 75 percent of the more than one million workers in the agriculture industry.[32]

The Internal Revenue Service (IRS) estimates that roughly six million undocumented immigrants file individual income taxes each year, using false or fraudulently obtained social security numbers (SSNs) or IRS-issued tax identification numbers.[33] Even with some undocumented workers filing income tax returns, the United States continues to miss an opportunity for more revenue. The previously mentioned Bear Stearns report, which found that the United States lost an estimated thirty-five billion dollars in 2005 due to the failure to tax undocumented workers, clearly illustrates the need to tackle this problem.[34]

Actual and Perceived Costs of Unauthorized Immigration

Unauthorized immigration expenditures often do not fit neatly into the category of "welfare" expenditures on state budgets.[35] Economists have opined that a massive influx of persons who consume public goods at a moderately high rate, yet pay little to no income taxes, will be costly for the receiving state.[36] Thus, some claim that as the undocumented population within a state increases the financial burden on the taxpayer increases.[37] This is a simplistic explanation that does not take into account the fact that undocumented immigrants pay taxes on purchased goods, property, gasoline, etc., and that many undocumented immigrants do not seek refunds on taxes that their employers have paid to the federal government.

Health care and education are two areas funded by Americans that benefit undocumented immigrants. Over thirteen billion dollars of American taxpayer money is used to provide medical treatment and public education to undocumented immigrants.[38] Additionally, American citizens fund social-service programs that benefit undocumented immigrants.[39] Finally, unforeseen expenses involving undocumented immigrants arise, such as the liability and investigation of automobile accidents caused by undocumented immigrants, who may not carry automobile insurance.

Challenging Education

Educating the children of undocumented immigrants is very costly. These children may either be undocumented themselves or U.S. citizens. The costs are primarily generated from spending on public education and reduced in-state tuition. According to one report in 2006, "[a]t an average annual cost of $7,500 (averages vary by jurisdiction) per student, the cost of providing education to [undocumented] children is about $11.2 billion."[40] But we need growth as a nation, and "[t]o a significant degree, high rates of immigration offset the effect of a declining number of births on school enrollment."[41] A study by the New York Department of Health and Planning revealed that although births declined, there was an increase in school enrollment from 1990 to 2001.[42]

As discussed more fully in the next chapter, in 1982 the U.S. Supreme Court in *Plyler v. Doe* imposed a legal duty upon the states to provide public education to students K–12, regardless of their immigration status.[43] In part, the Court reasoned that eventually some of the undocumented children would acquire lawful status in the United States, and the country would be better served by having an educated population.[44] Whatever the cost of educating an average student in the K–12 curriculum, the cost of educating a child in an English as a Second Language (ESL) curriculum is an additional 10–200 percent per student. The additional costs include the cost of hiring of bilingual teachers to teach ESL. After *Plyler* the five states that incur the greatest burden are California, Texas, Pennsylvania, New York, and Illinois. In 2007 California spent approximately $8.5 billion educating children of undocumented immigrants.[45] This cost amounted to 15 percent of California's total education expenditures for K–12.

Mandates by the federal government impose burdensome tasks on the states, which are required to educate students K–12, primarily at the states' costs. Consequently, the rising costs of ESL classes led California and Arizona to repeal bilingual educational programs.[46] Arizona, for instance, enacted Proposition 203, which mandated that all K–12 classes be taught in English.[47] The only exception was for students characterized as "English learners," who were temporarily placed in English immersion classes. English immersion programs allowed instructors to use the child's native language only when necessary to explain the English lectures or English-only provided materials. Students were limited to a one-year enrollment.

Another challenge to educating undocumented immigrants relates to the transitory nature of migrant work. Transient students miss several days out of the school year, as they shuffle through common migrant routes. ESL classrooms struggle in the same way as students come and go. Despite this inconsistency teachers and other school staff are still tasked with helping these students learn in a steady pattern as they prepare for standardized testing.

An additional challenge for teachers is separating learning disorders from language barriers. Determining whether a student qualifies as learning disabled or has mild to severe mental retardation requires careful testing and methodology. The fear and mistrust of school workers that is shared by many undocumented immigrant parents makes it very difficult to conduct educational assessments for ESL students, a problem that can often leave a child with gaps in reaching educational goals. This remains an issue as ESL students progress to higher grades and are expected to perform at state-mandated levels. The consequence of all of this is that states incur additional costs trying to educate immigrant children, yet they are failing to properly educate them, further perpetuating the cycle of poverty.

Covering the Cost of Emergency Medical Expenses

The Emergency Treatment and Active Labor Act of 1986 (EMTALA) obligates Medicare-participating hospitals with emergency departments to provide emergency medical care to individuals who arrive with an emergency condition without regard to the individual's ability to pay. Pursuant to EMTALA, the hospital is not permitted to transfer the patient until the patient has been stabilized. However, if the hospital is unable to stabilize a patient because the patient's condition requires additional resources that the hospital does not have, the hospital is then permitted to transfer the patient to another hospital. As a result hospitals incur significant unrecoverable costs for treating uninsured, undocumented immigrants. A RAND study shows that in the year 2000 it cost the United States $1.1 billion to provide health-care services to undocumented immigrants.[48]

Many immigrants (documented and undocumented) enter the United States without any type of health insurance. Approximately 59 percent of the nation's undocumented immigrants do not possess health insurance.[49]

The result is that these immigrants rely on public clinics and emergency rooms for health care, and pursuant to EMTALA, many of these facilities are required by federal law to provide a certain level of health care in order to receive funding from the federal government.[50] The federal funding to the health-care facilities is an additional burden undertaken by the government.

The largest U.S. health-care coverage program is Medicaid. While undocumented immigrants as a class are generally not eligible for Medicaid, individual immigrants can qualify if they are part of a class of people otherwise eligible.[51] Such classes include children, pregnant women, families with dependent children, elderly individuals, and disabled individuals.[52] Furthermore, by taking into account loopholes in the recent health-care law reform, the estimated cost of providing Medicaid coverage to an additional approximately eleven million immigrants would be $8.1 billion annually.[53] However, federal funding only covers a portion of the health-care costs, and the states would be forced to bear the remainder.

Public Benefits

Undocumented immigrants benefit from social-service programs. However, undocumented immigrants are generally ineligible to receive many welfare or other social benefits. In 1995 the United States government spent $1.1 billion providing households with food stamps and resources under the Aid to Families with Dependent Children (AFDC) program because undocumented immigrant parents qualified on behalf of their U.S.-citizen children.[54] The majority of households receiving AFDC aid or food stamps resided in just a handful of states. Eighty-five percent of those who received AFDC aid lived in California, New York, Texas, or Arizona.[55] Eighty-one percent of those who received food stamp benefits resided in California, Texas, and Arizona.[56]

In 1996 Congress enacted the Personal Responsibility and Work Opportunity Reconciliation Act (PRWORA), which restricted undocumented-immigrant access to federal, state, and local public benefits.[57] This law requires federal and state agencies to report individuals known to be unlawfully present.[58] Further, under PRWORA states are barred from issuing professional licenses to undocumented immigrants.[59]

States have the ability and political support (in many states) to deny public benefits to undocumented aliens. However, state statutes denying the vast majority of public benefits to undocumented aliens—such as Medicare, Medicaid, unemployment insurance, housing benefits, food assistance, and commercial licenses—merely reinforce federal law.[60] In fact, states that allow public benefits to flow to undocumented immigrants may be in violation of federal laws.[61] PRWORA was designed to ensure that undocumented immigrants do not receive public benefits at the federal, state, or local level.[62] With exceptions made for emergency medical assistance, emergency disaster relief, immunizations, and free K–12 education to undocumented immigrant children, states and municipalities are *required* by federal law to deny all public benefits to undocumented immigrants.[63]

Investigation of Hit-and-Run Crimes

Unauthorized immigration contributes to additional law enforcement costs, including the investigation of hit-and-run crimes. Current laws typically protect drivers in an accident by requiring each driver to carry sufficient insurance to cover the liability of an uninsured or unknown driver. When an accident involving an undocumented immigrant becomes a hit and run, it is most likely due to the immigrant's desire to avoid detection. The undocumented immigrant may feel that he has no other alternative but to run because he may not have the requisite driver's license or car insurance, in addition to his unlawful status.

Another hidden cost of unauthorized immigration is the cost of car-insurance premiums. In 2007 insured drivers paid $10.8 billion to cover the cost of uninsured motorists.[64] Undocumented immigrants, of course, are not alone in lacking automobile insurance, and this just compounds the problem. According to a 2011 study by the Insurance Research Council, 13.8 percent of U.S. citizens did not carry insurance. Add this to the number of undocumented immigrants who are driving, and the potential for significant costs becomes readily apparent.[65]

In order to purchase automobile insurance, the person seeking insurance must have a valid driver's license. While there are no laws prohibiting undocumented immigrants from obtaining insurance, it is usually very difficult to nearly impossible to acquire a driver's license without lawful status. Some insurance companies do not require a potential insured to provide a social security number, while other companies do. There are no direct inquiries into lawful status or citizenship, but the valid driver's license requirement is clearly related, at least indirectly, to lawful status. Licensure is a requirement that an undocumented immigrant cannot avoid. Currently, there are only a handful of states that grant a driver's license to an undocumented immigrant.[66] This overall inability to gain licensure and insurance puts American drivers at risk of bearing the full costs of an accident with an uninsured driver.

Conclusion

Some opponents of immigration reform believe the status quo is preferable to new legislation, that it is more compassionate to allow undocumented immigrants to work wherever they can get a job. However, there is nothing compassionate about forcing people to live in the shadows or to work under conditions that no human should have to endure. Additionally, the status quo is costing American taxpayers millions of dollars in terms of providing an education, certain benefits, and medical care. These are costs that could be minimized significantly with a sound and effective immigration policy that allows the federal government to collect additional income taxes from new documented workers.

We are a great country because of our diversity; that diversity is fueled by immigration. However, our current immigration policy needs improvement. The status quo does nothing to help our economy or protect our country. Furthermore, the status quo is inconsistent with the rule of law and unfair to those immigrants waiting patiently to enter our country lawfully.

Chapter Four
Federalism and the Case for State Action

Introduction

Many people see the failure of the federal government to enhance and enforce immigration laws and policies as an opening—and motivation—for the states to implement immigration legislation.[1] This suggestion is unfortunately true, and we have seen various states pass laws aimed directly at undocumented immigrants. Unfortunately, these state laws will only complicate the dual-sovereignty battle between the federal government and the states.

Since the beginning of our Republic, there has been a struggle for power between the federal government and the states. Although the U.S. Constitution and the courts have directly addressed this issue, the debate continues.[2] This struggle usually occurs over the scope of the Tenth Amendment.

The Tenth Amendment states, "The powers not delegated to the United States by the Constitution, nor prohibited by it to the States, are reserved to the States respectively, or to the people."[3] The Supreme Court clarified this in *United States v. Sprague*,[4] holding that "[t]he Tenth Amendment was intended to confirm the understanding of the people at the time the Constitution was adopted, that powers not granted to the United States were reserved to the States or to the people. It added nothing to the instrument as originally ratified."[5] In a later decision the Court stated that "[w]hile the Tenth Amendment has been characterized as a 'truism,' stating merely that 'all is retained which has not been surrendered,' it is not without significance. The Amendment expressly declares the constitutional policy that Congress may not exercise power in a fashion that impairs the States' integrity or their ability to function effectively in a federal system."[6]

Consistent with the Court's commentary, the most common interpretation of the Tenth Amendment is that if the Constitution does not give a particular power to the federal government, the power falls to the state unless prohibited by the Constitution. In practice, however, the federal government's powers have grown as the courts have granted greater powers as a result of constitutional amendments, including the Fourteenth Amendment. However, given the fact that the federal government has failed in substantially regulating immigration, many states—relying upon their Tenth Amendment authority—have taken immigration regulation into their own hands.

Polls confirm the frustration of many people with the inaction of the federal government. A recent poll showed that 64 percent of Americans are dissatisfied with the current immigration system.[7] With our poor economy many citizens attribute the high unemployment rates and lack of funding for social services to the high percentage of undocumented immigrants. In addition, national security ranks as a top concern for proponents of immigration reform. Our current immigration system has strained local budgets, resulting in a desperate populace eager for accountability and action. This chapter will explore various immigration laws passed at the state level and their effect on the federal immigration system.

State-Level Immigration Concerns

Throughout U.S. history states have taken matters into their own hands when they perceive that the federal government has failed to remedy salient issues. Such efforts have typically led the federal government to respond. National policies on education, racial inequality, health care, and security provide examples of federal action motivated and initiated by state action and concerns. Thus, it is obvious why there is such an uproar regarding immigration.

Unauthorized immigration places a huge burden on state and local governments. Some may argue that the burdens are far more apparent and detrimental than the federal government realizes. A popular perception is that valuable services provided to undocumented immigrants, such as medical treatment and public education, drain state and local budgets; meanwhile, citizens and lawful immigrants are deprived of similar services. Consequently, many Americans believe that the inability to tax undocumented residents unfairly burdens state and local deficits.

State-Funded Education

Education is by far the largest economic burden on state and local governments affected by unauthorized immigration. The cost of educating children of undocumented immigrants nationwide has recently been estimated to be around $137 billion annually.[8]

Understandably, since the early 1980s states, local governments, and school districts have experimented with multiple policies and actions in response to *Plyler*.[9] School boards have attempted to implement additional hurdles for parents of immigrant children, by requiring them to provide their driver's licenses and Social Security numbers, in addition to using separate policies to regulate their registration, safety, college tuition, and undocumented status. Such measures even extend so far as to mandate separate schools for the children of undocumented immigrants.[10]

Despite state efforts to enact legislation to overcome the harsh economic realities associated with *Plyler*, the political process has rebuffed any challenge to the K–12 enrollment of undocumented children at the state and federal levels, despite tightened immigration restrictions in other areas.[11] California's Proposition 187 passed by nearly 60 percent of the vote in 1994 and would have denied virtually all state-funded benefits, including public education, to undocumented Californians; however, nearly all of these provisions were struck down in federal court.[12]

That is not to say that controversy and friction no longer linger on the subject. In March 2006 an Illinois school board denied enrollment to an undocumented student because she and her family were in the United States on long-expired tourist visas. The State Board of Education, using a carrot-and-stick approach, threatened to remove funds, which caused the local school board to reconsider and revise its attendance policies.[13] In the same year a federal suit was settled in New Mexico against the Albuquerque Public Schools. The settlement eliminated the practice of arresting students on school property suspected of being out of status and turning them over to Border Patrol.[14]

Using local examples, the following is a discussion of the overall additional costs relegated to the states from the federal government, which include the cost of hiring additional teachers, ESL programs, and capital expenses that state and local governments incur as a result of educating the children of undocumented immigrants.

ESL in Education

The collateral consequences of unauthorized immigration have been evident to local teachers in Mesa, Arizona. A large number of students who attend Mesa public schools (Title 1 schools) are related to or otherwise connected to undocumented immigrants. Many students live in Spanish-speaking homes and have been essentially segregated from the general English-speaking classroom. The schools, in an attempt to remedy the language barrier, have segregated the Spanish-speaking students from English-speaking students—but at the cost of student interaction and socialization with others.[15] ESL students move as a group from grade to grade. Although these students require extra support in learning to read, write, and comprehend mathematics, the state allows for practically no accommodations, often requiring that students be held to the same standards as English-speaking students on statewide testing scores. We agree that they should be held to the same standard but argue that the state should provide additional resources and appropriate accommodations to prepare them to meet government standards.

Standardized Testing, Transiency, and Learning Disorders

States must meet federal educational benchmarks to receive federal funding. While schools strive to hire imaginative and effective teachers, this goal is tempered by the need to measure student learning. In turn, the educational system, namely the teacher, is held accountable. Given the added accountability, the other obstacles generally associated with educating students, and the federal government's requirements, it is not difficult to understand why schools have a hard time maintaining good teachers.

Although the burdens are heavy, the states are required to meet the federal guidelines. The states, not surprisingly, design programs to reach the desired level of compliance. One such measure, recently implemented by the Mesa public schools, is an incentive-paid bonus program in which teachers receive their yearly bonus payouts according to the success of their students' state standardized testing scores. At first glance this may sound reasonable—even fair; those who teach the best will, as a result, produce the best-prepared students as evidenced by their scores on the standardized tests. However, this places teachers who teach ESL students at a clear disadvantage; they are far from reaching state and national goals. Bonuses and higher pay go to the teachers teaching English-language students, while, unfortunately, teachers of the ESL programs who hope to earn a bonus are forced to put in twice the time and effort to find innovative ways to teach their students.

The States' Medical Bills

In an effort to combat costs, states are taking action to deny certain health care to undocumented immigrants. For example, in Texas, the University of Texas Medical Branch at Galveston, a state-funded institution, has considered denying cancer care to undocumented immigrants.[16] In Oklahoma lawmakers have restricted most undocumented immigrants from access to most public benefits, and Nebraska is not far from implementing the same policy.[17] The effect that unauthorized immigration has had on the states' ability to provide mandatory levels of health care is apparent from the high costs and aggressive state responses.

State Activism

The last several years have witnessed a surge of state legislation related to immigration primarily focused on addressing more localized conditions, rather than on foreign relations or sovereignty concerns.[18] For example, the National Conference of State Legislatures tracked immigration legislation from January 2006 through June 2006, when almost five hundred immigration-related bills were introduced in state legislatures, with nineteen states enacting forty-four bills.[19] The overall state legislation numbers for 2006 were low, however, in comparison to the 2007 state legislative sessions. The legislatures of all fifty states combined introduced 1,562 bills related to unauthorized immigration, up from 570 in 2006.[20] A total of 240 bills were enacted into law, nearly four times the number of immigration-related laws enacted in 2006.[21] Most intended to deter unauthorized immigration in some way; however, not all state action has been anti-immigrant.[22]

The subject matters of these state bills include "education, employment, identification, driver's licenses, law enforcement, legal services, omnibus immigration matters, public benefits, housing and rental, trafficking, voting, and miscellaneous issues such as alcohol and tobacco purchase identification, gun and firearms permits, residency/domicile determinations, and juvenile reporting requirements."[23] Some jurisdictions have enacted legislation or regulations in support of the undocumented immigrant. These include city ID cards, and state-issued driver's licenses. Some jurisdictions have gone further by declaring themselves to be safe havens or sanctuaries for undocumented immigrants.

Federal law arguably preempts many of the previously mentioned state bills. The concept of federal preemption—or the notion that federal law is the supreme law of the land—comes directly from the Supremacy Clause of the U.S. Constitution.[24] State laws cannot supersede federal laws, or have the intent or effect of overriding federal laws, where the federal government is tasked with oversight or responsibility.[25] Beginning with *The Chinese Exclusion Case* in 1889 and its progeny, The Supreme Court has repeatedly held that Congress has plenary power over our nation's immigration laws. Thus, in order to avoid encroaching upon the federal government's plenary power over immigration, states must carefully draft their immigration-related statutes.

Arguably, the policy shift in the 1996 Illegal Immigration and Immigrant Responsibility Act (IIRAIRA) is at the forefront of the friction between the federal and state governments.[26] IIRAIRA created partnerships between federal and local agencies that authorized local law enforcement personnel to investigate and detain persons suspected of violating selected provisions of federal immigration law, assisting in their transfer to ICE facilities and the commencement of removal proceedings.[27] However, the recent federal policy shift—reportedly an effort at standardizing immigration enforcement by focusing efforts upon priority aliens—challenges both federal and local enforcement goals and cultivates an environment that compels local governments to take immigration enforcement into their own hands.[28]

As discussed earlier, it is clear from court decisions that federal preemption prohibits much state action—for example, a state can neither create state-level criteria to determine which aliens are allowed U.S. residency nor impose state criminal penalties on the employers of undocumented immigrants.[29] However, wide latitude exists for states to act without federal preemption, as long as the statute is properly drafted.[30] What follows is a discussion of one well-known state immigration bill and its impact, which led to an important U.S. Supreme Court opinion relating to federal and state authority in the area of immigration.

The Background of Arizona Senate Bill 1070

In 2012 the U.S. Supreme Court heard the case of *Arizona v. United States*.[31] This case involved Arizona's Support Our Law Enforcement and Safe Neighborhoods Act (SB 1070). The events leading up to the passage of SB 1070 and the Supreme Court case are noteworthy and of particular importance to this chapter.

SB 1070's controversial provisions involved the increased authority given to state and local law enforcement.[32] It required state and local law enforcement to make a reasonable attempt to determine the immigration status of a person during routine stops, detentions, or arrests, if "reasonable suspicion exist[ed] that the person [wa]s an alien who [wa]s unlawfully present in the United States."[33] Further, before the person could be released, the arrestee's immigration status had to be determined.[34]

Despite criticism to the contrary, the proposed law prohibited law enforcement personnel from solely considering "race, color or national origin" in carrying out the aforementioned duties.[35] Additionally, local law enforcement was required to contact ICE or Border Patrol when any undocumented immigrant was scheduled to be released from prison or fined upon conviction of a crime.[36] Finally, SB 1070 authorized a warrantless arrest if a law enforcement officer had probable cause to believe that a person had committed a crime that made that person removable under federal immigration law.[37]

Other provisions involved the criminalization of activities that are already federal offenses. SB 1070 "ma[de] it a state crime to willfully fail to complete or carry an alien registration document, provided the alien [wa]s in violation of federal law requiring aliens to register and carry certain immigration documents."[38] It also made it a crime for undocumented aliens to "knowingly apply for work, solicit work in a public place or perform work as an employee or independent contractor."[39]

After signing SB 1070 into law, Arizona Governor Jan Brewer said, "We in Arizona have been more than patient waiting for Washington to act, [b]ut decades of inaction and misguided policy have created a dangerous and unacceptable situation."[40] Governor Brewer's words echoed the sentiments of many citizens in U.S. border states, where the burdens of unauthorized immigration remain particularly heavy. Arizona, "the nation's busiest gateway for human and drug smuggling from Mexico," has an estimated 460,000 undocumented immigrants.[41] Arizona has more unauthorized border crossings than any other state.[42] Even though Arizona and other border states shoulder the burden of unauthorized immigration, attempts to ease their share of the burden have been met with controversy.[43] Perhaps the most-cited complaint against SB 1070 was that its passage authorized racial discrimination against Hispanics.[44] In addition, the Justice Department alleged that SB 1070 unconstitutionally invaded the federal government's exclusive right to regulate the area of immigration law.[45]

Hotly debated for its perceived discriminatory nature, SB 1070 had a more significant potential flaw, which was the focal point of the federal government's position. The federal government argued that the INA preempted SB 1070 in part, if not completely.[46]

Generally, "[a]n act of Congress may preempt state or local action in a given area in any one of three ways: (1) the statute expressly states preemptive intent (express preemption); (2) a court concludes that Congress intended to occupy the regulatory field, thereby implicitly precluding state or local action in that area (field preemption); or (3) state or local action directly conflicts with or otherwise frustrates the purpose of the federal scheme (conflict preemption)."[47] The INA did not expressly preempt state law, so the argument was that either field preemption or conflict preemption served to strike down SB 1070.[48]

Prior to *Arizona*, the Supreme Court had stated that the "[p]ower to regulate immigration is unquestionably exclusively a federal power."[49] It had never, however, "held that every state enactment which in any way deals with aliens is a regulation of immigration and thus *per se* pre-empted."[50] States have successfully enacted laws in the area of immigration without preemption by federal statute.[51] The Supreme Court has held that regulation of immigration involves "a determination of who should or should not be admitted into the country, and the conditions under which a legal entrant may remain."[52] This background is helpful when analyzing the Supreme Court's decision in *Arizona*.

A Tipping Point for Other States

In the weeks and months after Governor Brewer signed SB 1070 into law, conservative state legislators all over the nation announced their intentions to introduce legislation modeled after it.[53] Some legislators even planned to go further.[54] One Republican Oklahoma representative suggested a plan to deport undocumented immigrants in Oklahoma, including American-born children of undocumented immigrants.[55] However, it is one thing to propose legislation; it is quite another to actually pass legislation into law. Many states that introduced laws similar to SB 1070 abandoned them or had to water them down to pass them through their respective state legislatures.[56]

Some attribute the momentum of SB 1070's passage through the Arizona legislature to the conservative campaign fervor of Tea Party–backed Republican campaigns during the 2010 mid-term elections.[57] Reality, however, now appears to have set in.[58] Many states are backing off immigration laws due to uneasiness about defense costs.[59] Arizona spent millions of dollars litigating the lawsuit filed by the Obama administration over SB 1070, and it suffered estimated economic losses of up to $750 million from boycotts against the state due to the provisions of SB 1070.[60] Boycotts, while arguably ineffective, did create an economic stir in Arizona. The San Francisco city government, the Los Angeles City Council, and city officials in Oakland, Minneapolis, Saint Paul, Denver, and Seattle all took specific action, most commonly banning their employees from work-related travel to Arizona or limiting city business done with companies headquartered in Arizona.[61]

Other motivations appear to be causing certain state legislatures to back off immigration laws similar to SB 1070, and a pattern appears to be emerging.[62] Border states, with the obvious exception of Arizona, appear to be backing away from sweeping immigration laws, while non–border states appear to be passing them.[63] This perhaps stems from the experience that border states have had with unauthorized immigration, state laws addressing unauthorized immigration, and large influential Hispanic communities.[64]

For example, California and Texas both experienced surges in unauthorized immigration during the shaky economies and civil wars of South and Central America in the 1980s.[65] Many immigrants who entered unlawfully during that period were granted amnesty by federal law in 1986, contributing to established Hispanic communities in both states.[66]

Arizona, however, appears to have been the perfect storm that allowed SB 1070 to pass through the state legislature with such momentum.[67] The federal government installed fences, lights, and additional border patrol agents to secure the borders in Texas and Southern California in the 1990s but left the border in Arizona largely untouched, thus funneling undocumented immigrants into the United States through Arizona and increasing the burden of unauthorized immigration on Arizona's shoulders.[68] Furthermore, Arizona's Hispanic communities arrived more recently than those in Texas and California. Moreover, Arizona has become a retirement destination for retirees from the Northeast and Midwest, who largely have no experience with and feel no affiliation to Hispanic communities or the countries from which they came.[69] Perhaps in contradistinction to these circumstances and others, the governors of Texas and California, both Republicans, have publicly stated that their states would not attempt to pass SB 1070–type laws.[70]

Non–border states with less experience with unauthorized immigration and with smaller Hispanic communities, however, have sometimes embraced the sentiment commonly held in Arizona and have pursued the passage of similar laws.[71] Increased policy activism by state government reflects the growth of immigration in "new gateway" states that until the 1990s had not encountered immigration issues.[72] Alabama, Indiana, Georgia, South Carolina, and Utah are the only states to have passed immigration laws similar to Arizona's SB 1070, and not one is a border state.[73] The majority of these states are in the Southeast and do not have a substantial Hispanic population. Hispanics lack political clout, and this may explain the passage of such legislation. The influx of undocumented immigrants is new, and these states are reacting quickly and divisively to head off what they perceive to be a serious problem by adopting tough legislation similar to SB 1070. The spike in unauthorized immigration, combined with the failure of federal comprehensive immigration reform proposals in 2006 and 2007, has kindled the fire for a policy response at the state level.[74]

Alabama, in particular, has embraced the principles of SB 1070.[75] Alabama's HB 56, signed into law in June 2011, is more expansive than SB 1070.[76] Like the Arizona law, HB 56 requires a law enforcement official to determine the immigration status of anyone he reasonably suspects is an immigrant during any lawful stop, detention, or arrest. It also prohibits undocumented immigrants from receiving any local or state benefits, enrolling in or attending public colleges, and applying for or soliciting work.[77] Further, HB 56 invalidates any contract in which an undocumented immigrant is a party if the other party to the contract has "direct or constructive knowledge" of the immigrant's unlawful status.[78]

HB 56's most extreme provision requires public-school officials to determine the immigration status of students.[79] This provision does not bar students deemed to be undocumented immigrants from school, but it does require annual reporting from school districts on the number of their undocumented immigrant students.[80] While the state may argue that it merely wants to track state expenditures for undocumented immigrants, it requires no small stretch of the imagination to believe that the state intends to intimidate undocumented parents into pulling their children from a school that asks about immigration status.[81]

Problems with State Action: State Action Further Complicates the Current Immigration System

While the states, in particular the border states, bear most of the burden of unauthorized immigration, and while the urge for state action is understandable, certain state action in immigration law enforcement is counterproductive because it unreasonably complicates the current immigration system.[82] The federal government has a strong interest—as well as a constitutional duty—in retaining control over immigration.[83] Centralized federal control over immigration provides the consistency and efficiency necessary to facilitate admission and removal processes in such a large nation.[84] Without this centralized control, each state could enact its own immigration laws, creating an impractical and unworkable patchwork of laws and procedures that would impede admission into and removal from the United States.[85]

Centralized federal control of immigration also provides for effective observance of the numerous international and diplomatic considerations inherent in such a global issue.[86] One need only look at the Mexican government's public condemnation of SB 1070 for an example of how international relations suffer when states attempt to exert control over immigration enforcement.[87] Federal control over immigration also allows the federal government to better handle the consequences of any discriminatory practices taken on by state or local governments.[88]

State action in immigration law can also affect other states.[89] By enacting its own immigration laws, a state can hinder the economies of other states.[90] For example, due to the uproar that SB 1070 caused, many undocumented immigrants fled Arizona for friendlier jurisdictions, shifting the burden of immigration to other states and disrupting the uniformity provided by federal control.[91]

The key question is how much state action is too much?[92] Does federal law preempt all state action relating to immigration? Or has Congress left room for certain types of state action? As the Court's decision in *Arizona* remained pending, many argued that the right answers take into account the various interests of federal, state, and local governments in mitigating the damages of unauthorized immigration and the heavier burden the states must carry, in addition to acknowledging the overarching control of the federal government that is necessary for the fair and efficient facilitation of immigration.[93]

The Decision in *U.S. v. Arizona*

The constitutionality of SB 1070 was argued before the U.S. Supreme Court on April 25, 2012.[94] At issue were four sections of the statute: 2(B),[95] 3,[96] 5(C),[97] and 6.[98] The federal government argued against SB 1070 on the grounds of federal preemption, while Arizona argued that federal preemption did not apply.[99] A few of the justices seemingly made their opinions known early on during oral arguments. Solicitor General David Verrilli, Jr., had barely begun his argument when Chief Justice John Roberts, having read the briefs outlining each side's argument, interrupted to clarify that none of Mr. Verrilli's arguments involved racial or ethnic profiling, as many critics have complained.[100] Justice Antonin Scalia framed the preemption issue by calling into question the meaningfulness of state sovereignty if a state may not "defend [its] borders."[101] Based on the makeup of the Court, many legal scholars expected a fractured opinion upholding SB 1070's constitutionality against the preemption argument.[102]

However, on June 25, 2012, the Supreme Court surprised many by striking down three of the four challenged provisions of SB 1070.[103] Justice Anthony Kennedy, writing for the majority, held that §§ 3, 5(C), and 6 were preempted by federal law.[104] All of the justices agreed that § 2(B), which allows the Arizona state police with reasonable suspicion to investigate the immigration status of a detained individual, was not preempted and should be upheld. The Court reasoned that based on the present challenges and the lack of interpretation of § 2(B), it would be improper to strike the section down without an express showing of preemption.[105]

Conclusion

The decision in *Arizona* left many people dissatisfied. This decision, while striking down many of the controversial provisions, upholds the "papers, please" portion of SB 1070 and provides to the states the means to develop a better understanding of the scope of unauthorized immigration within their respective jurisdictions.[106] Critics argue that it gives the states latitude to engage in racial profiling and to discriminate in violation of civil-rights laws. Importantly, the Court broached the need for a national "searching, thoughtful, rational civil discourse" of immigration policy.[107] Identifying and understanding the obstacles and objectives of a sound federal immigration policy is a good start, and we will explore these in the next chapter.

Chapter Five
Objectives and Obstacles to Federal Policy

Introduction

Immigration concerns affect every aspect of American life, from individual citizens and families to government and the domestic economy. This impact is especially pronounced at the institutional level. Such a multifaceted and ubiquitous issue requires a comprehensive policy that addresses each of these areas. The United States continues to face many challenges related to immigration that require a modern immigration system to maintain national security efforts and alleviate economic concerns and burdens.[1]

What are the Objectives and Obstacles of the Current Federal Policy

As we saw in chapter 1, immigration law in the United States is very complex. The INA provides the underlying law for federal immigration policy and sets the annual worldwide limits for total permanent immigration into the United States, with certain exceptions for close family members.[2] Historically, the three primary goals of U.S. immigration policy have been the reunification of families, admitting immigrants with skills that are valuable to the U.S. economy, and protecting refugees.[3]

The question is whether these are the desired goals today. To determine the current federal policy regarding immigration and citizenship, one should examine several different sources. Current federal policy includes the desire to reduce, minimize, and mitigate the risks inherent in any immigration system.[4] In addition, federal policy must address possible challenges to the immigration system by various events, such as manmade or natural catastrophes around the world, which would further test the system's ability to ensure timely responses and uphold the integrity of the adjudicative process. Finally, the potential for nefarious exploitation of the immigration system requires a process for detecting identity and benefit fraud through immediate access to accurate, verifiable data.[5]

Objectives

In our judgment, the objectives of federal immigration policy are straightforward, if not intuitive. The first goal is to secure our borders. This arduous task involves completing the necessary background checks effectively and efficiently; working towards collaborative partnerships between federal agencies to achieve optimal immigration security processes; striving to improve other verification tools; improving collaboration between federal, state, and local law enforcement agencies and other public and private entities authorized to verify immigration status; and, ultimately safeguarding the legal privacy rights of individuals. Each of these tasks is outlined more completely in the next chapter.

The second objective should be to foster a stronger workplace enforcement. Properly implemented reform will result in a safer, wealthier, more egalitarian country. We cannot achieve these goals without the cooperation of those who employ undocumented immigrants.

Finally, and more generally, we need a policy that meets our economy's needs and upholds our long tradition of family unity. To be economically feasible, immigration policy must be efficient and flexible. Efficiency in securing our borders and implementing necessary enforcement mechanisms is paramount to creating workable reform. Flexibility is imperative because immigration is an ever-changing issue that must take social and economic changes, domestic concerns, and human ingenuity into account.

Reform legislation must be flexible enough to accommodate special circumstances without hindering decisive enforcement or delaying administrative decisions. Achieving the appropriate flexibility may require giving greater discretion to government officials, however, greater discretion provides more opportunities for abuse. Flexibility, along with checks, such as oversight, will improve our immigration policy's effectiveness. Together, these broad goals of immigration reform lay the foundation for the durable reform U.S. immigration policy requires.

Why Federal Policy?

In our early history, the federal government allowed relatively free and unrestricted immigration, with laws conferring residency rights primarily enacted at the state level.[6] Border and port states promulgated laws regulating entry of immigrants deemed "undesirable." For example, some states adopted entry taxes or bonds to discourage the indigent from settling. Predictably, this type of state-level immigration control resulted in wide policy variance across the country and led to internal friction.[7]

In the 19th century, the U.S. Supreme Court began to clarify who had jurisdiction over immigration by ruling that although the Constitution did not explicitly confer immigration authority to the President or Congress, the power to regulate immigration ultimately rested with Congress.[8] Congress subsequently codified this new understanding, i.e., that immigration regulation is an exclusively federal function, by passing legislation such as the INA.[9] Although Congress has delegated limited immigration authority to the states, federal preemption of state and local laws remains strong.[10]

The Court's decision further reinforces the federal government's predominance in the field of immigration. The *Arizona* Court cited the significance of "prosecutorial discretion,"[11] recognizing that immigration officials may validly choose not to seek the removal or deportation of immigrants who would otherwise be in such proceedings. Justice Kennedy wrote:

> Discretion in the enforcement of immigration law embraces immediate human concerns. Unauthorized workers trying to support their families, for example, likely pose less danger than alien smugglers or aliens who commit a serious crime. The equities of an individual case may turn on many factors, including whether the alien has children born in the United States, long ties to the community, or a record of distinguished military service. Some discretionary decisions involve policy choices that bear on this Nation's international relations. Returning an alien to his own country may be deemed inappropriate even where he has committed a removable offense or fails to meet the criteria for admission.[12]

In emphasizing prosecutorial discretion, the Court's decision acknowledges that the removal of undocumented immigrants is only one of multiple objectives in the enforcement of immigration law and policy, and one that is solely in the hands of the federal government.

Not surprisingly, the Court's decision in *Arizona* reinvigorated the immigration debate. Just months after the decision, the American people re-elected President Obama to a second term. Many believe that President Obama's re-election was made possible by the increasing importance of the Hispanic vote. As mentioned in chapter 2, former Governor Romney, the Republican candidate, received less than a third of the Hispanic votes cast in the election.[13] Hispanics are America's fastest growing minority demographic, and political parties are beginning to understand that their political strategies and proposed policies must take this into account. The 2012 election provided a window into the future of politics and in a sense a mandate to take into account Hispanic priorities when developing national policy. As political parties, candidates, and their constituencies take account of America's new demographic realities, immigration reform is sure to be among the most important topics in the American discourse, assuming of course that Hispanics exercise their power and vote on election day.

The Need for Federal Action

The need for federal action on immigration policy stems from the simple reality that the United States is a singular entity. Arguably, the exclusive constitutional assignment of foreign affairs and naturalization to the President and Congress leaves little room for state immigration regulation.[14] According to the U.S. Supreme Court the Constitution requires a single regulator for immigration, and the Court has determined that our constitutional structure mandates the federal government as the sole regulator.[15]

Undoubtedly, state governments have strong incentives to determine certain immigration policies that address problems unique to their states. However, the federal government is in a better position to monitor large-scale immigration control policies.[16] The purpose of this control is to seek minimal state restrictions on border crossings to ensure free-flowing labor throughout the United States and to address concerns over national security. Ironically, the most touted reason for state involvement in immigration is also the strongest incentive for state governments to defer immigration control policy to the national government—the considerable costs.[17] Fiscal economists perceive the United States as a large marketplace; the faster and more responsive that workers are to geographical labor surpluses or shortages, the more efficient the economy is overall.[18] State-level immigration control is prohibitively expensive because visa checks, waiting periods, administrative fees, border controls, and customs agents are required for each state border.

States can and have passed laws in the realm of immigration without violating areas preempted by the federal immigration regulation.[19] However, a state does not act in a vacuum. Overall, the effect of a state's action may trigger unintended externalities.[20] By enacting its own immigration legislation, a state like Arizona can adversely affect the economy of another state by altering the uniform immigration regulation scheme.[21] Undocumented immigrants may flock to more favorable jurisdictions, thereby shortcutting the purposes of uniformity.[22]

Conversely, a federal policy scheme that requires taxpayers to bear the cost of a single entry attempt provides a comparable level of control far more efficiently and with less overhead expenditures.[23] Moreover, immigration is heavily linked to areas of national security. Through federalism, nation states can use technology to compete with neighbor states successfully.[24] By implication, patrolling a border with armies, police, airplanes, boats, or detection equipment is more efficiently handled by a central entity that can coordinate national security measures and border controls on behalf of all the states.[25] However, even with the federal government's presumptive role in immigration policy and control, the public's fears and concerns with regard to immigration continue to linger, and are particularly dramatic during an election cycle.

The Federal Government Cannot Avoid Reformation of the Immigration System

Overall, some economists have concluded that the federal government enjoys a net financial gain from unauthorized immigration.[26] Federally, the addition of scores of undocumented younger workers underpins the retirement system by paying in an estimated $7 billion a year to Medicare and Social Security. The majority of this contribution will go unclaimed, resulting in a "fiscal windfall" without the burden of providing corresponding services.[27] Some speculate that federal policymakers' reluctance to enforce existing immigration regulations, or to push for reform, is partially because of this windfall.[28] There is evidence of this in states adjoining Alabama after Alabama officials passed tough legislation affecting seasonal workers.[29]

Nevertheless, the federal government's hourglass is running low, as many states—tired of federal inaction—have taken their own steps to reformulate immigration issues. Facing the immediate need to balance the benefits and consequences of the immigrant population, state governments feel compelled to create their own immigration policies.[30] While acknowledging the importance of the federal immigration regulation scheme, the states are placing their "compelling interest" ahead of alleged "attrition through enforcement."[31] The federal government can no longer ignore the need to make further policy changes that address state concerns, while also preserving federal interests.

American Immigration Concerns Linger

In the court of public opinion, many Americans believe that undocumented immigrants negatively affect the economy in a number of ways, such as by not paying taxes while utilizing hospital and school services paid for by tax dollars.[32] Some contend that serious and accurate political discourse on this topic has been lacking, despite the unfair and costly burden on states resulting from lax federal enforcement.[33] In the wake of a dismal performance by Republican candidates among Hispanics in the 2012 elections, hope remains that this discussion will improve, allowing the federal government to work with the states to tailor policy allocating joint responsibility.[34] The increasing impact of the Hispanic vote provides more political motivation than ever to discuss immigration policy.

Obstacles to Federal Policy

There are numerous obstacles to comprehensive immigration reform. Most of the delays to immigration reform can be attributed to one or more of the following political, social, or economic concerns that we will discuss in this chapter. Some obstacles are more problematic than others. For the sake of clarity and conciseness, we have categorized each significant obstacle as political, social, or economic.

Political Obstacles

From a practical standpoint, it makes sense to begin the discussion of federal policy obstacles with politics. America is experiencing a period in which seemingly every issue breeds partisan debate and political opportunism. Republicans and Democrats are digging in and holding fast to their positions, and anyone who gives ground on a contentious issue is labeled a defector by his party, regardless of how prudent his position or compromise may be. This political atmosphere makes bipartisan collaboration on divisive issues such as immigration extremely difficult.

However, the 2012 presidential election demonstrated that adherence to draconian immigration policies has profound consequences in a country undergoing a fundamental demographic shift.[35] The political extremism of the last several years led to a primary season that saw Republican presidential hopefuls engaging in one-upmanship on the issue of unauthorized immigration. Pandering to the far right, the candidates took ever more radical positions, isolating themselves and their party from America's fastest growing demographic. By the time former Governor Romney emerged from the primaries as the Republican presidential candidate, he could only tack to the middle so much, and by then the damage had largely been done.[36] The result was that the Republicans effectively forfeited the Latino vote, and thus the presidency and control of the U.S. Senate.

Presumably having learned from that mistake, Republicans began to craft a new party line on the immigration issue in the months since President Obama's reelection.[37] Pressured by business groups, the clergy, and law enforcement, more Republicans and Democrats now appear to be coming together on this issue, and the country must seize this opportunity to capitalize on increasingly rare bipartisan agreement. Immigration reform seems possible, so it is important to draft legislation that is comprehensive, durable, and effective at securing America's future.

One major obstacle to a final agreement is the issue of amnesty. While we oppose amnesty, we acknowledge that supporters and detractors alike have persuasive arguments on this issue.[38] Among the political consequences of the 2012 election is the belief among many political pundits and Hispanic leaders that a great majority of the Latino vote is likely to be Democratic, at least in the short term. Democrats and liberal organizations appear to want to capitalize on this by achieving complete amnesty for undocumented immigrants, and leading to U.S. citizenship, thereby drastically increasing the potential number of votes for Democrat officials and liberal causes.

Opponents of amnesty and citizenship argue that legalizing the millions of undocumented immigrants already in the United States will only encourage others to circumvent immigration laws as well.[39] Furthermore, they argue that citizenship for those who broke the rules should not occur before citizenship for those who followed the rules. Advocates, on the other hand, believe that a pathway to any form of lawful status is the only answer, and argue that the American economy will benefit through greater tax revenue.

We believe that a vast majority of undocumented immigrants came to America to find work, not to become citizens. They are more concerned about not being deported than about obtaining citizenship. Moreover, two recent surveys from the Pew Research Center found that a majority of Hispanics (55 to 35 percent) and Asian Americans (49 to 44 percent) are more concerned about addressing the threat of deportation than creating a pathway to citizenship for undocumented immigrants.[40] There is no legitimate policy or moral reason to promise citizenship to those who did not follow the rules before making it available to those who did. We do not support amnesty, the complete forgiveness of wrongful action without consequences. We believe that anyone who has entered this country unlawfully must pay a fine before being considered for any type of lawful status. We believe that providing a lawful status for millions of undocumented immigrants should be contingent upon improving border security and enhancing workplace enforcement, lest we simply trade one problem for another. However, the security triggers must either be more realistic (yet effective in protecting our national security and border communities) or our government officials should be honest with the American people and the immigrant population that the triggers likely will never be met. Thus, the undocumented immigrants likely will never become LPRs.

As an alternative to citizenship, and as a means to take this political issue off the table, we propose a pathway to U.S. nationality that would not automatically lead to full citizenship. INA § 101(a)(22) states that all U.S.

citizens are also nationals of the United States; however, not all nationals are citizens. In fact, very few people are nationals while not also being citizens.

INA § 308 confers U.S. nationality, but not U.S. citizenship, on persons born in or having ties with "an outlying possession of the United States." The "outlying possessions" are defined in INA § 101(A)(29) as American Samoa and the Swains Island. No other statute defines any other territories or states as outlying possessions. Section 308 also confers U.S. nationality on those individuals born abroad to two noncitizen national parents, or those born abroad to one alien parent and one noncitizen national parent, and there is a residency requirement placed upon the parents of the child prior to birth in order to transmit U.S. nationality.

In addition to § 308 of the INA, § 302 of Public Law 94-241 provides for certain inhabitants of the Commonwealth of the Northern Mariana Islands, who became United States citizens by virtue of Article III of the Covenant, to opt for noncitizen national status.

INA § 325 allows a noncitizen national who is "otherwise qualified" to seek U.S. citizenship much like an LPR would seek citizenship. If Congress wishes to pass immigration reform leading to nationality short of citizenship, it can simply add the caveat that nationality confirmed through the reform it passes will not otherwise qualify for U.S. citizenship. Relevant sections of law pertaining to U.S. nationality can be found in appendix 2 at the end of this book.

A noncitizen national enjoys many of the same rights as a citizen, but the laws of many U.S. states deny noncitizen nationals the right to vote in federal, state, and local elections, the right to hold public office, the right to serve on a jury, and the right to bear arms.[41] While many people may find it unfair to award only nationality as opposed to citizenship, we must keep in mind that most of the undocumented immigrants in this country came to America to find work, not to become U.S. citizens. We must also remember that they broke our laws and forced themselves ahead of other immigrants who have been waiting in long lines to immigrate lawfully to the United States.[42] We recognize that there is a longstanding American policy to encourage those who enjoy lawful status in our country to become U.S. citizens. We believe an exception to that policy may be appropriate here under the circumstances.

A noncitizen national is treated as an alien admitted for LPR status when filing a petition for a family member,[43] and the petition is placed in a preference category. The INA itself offers little direct guidance on this issue, but the Board of Immigration Appeals (BIA) has spoken to this directly.

In *Matter of Ah San*,[44] in which a noncitizen national of American Samoa petitioned for her daughter, a native and citizen of Western Samoa,[45] the BIA stated that "[a] non-citizen national of the United States does not have the rights of a citizen of the United States. However, as a national, he is accorded certain rights and privileges by reason of being a national which should at least be equal to those of an alien who has been admitted to the United States for permanent residence."[46]

In *Matter of B—*,[47] a case that dealt with three children, all born in the British West Indies to a noncitizen national mother,[48] the BIA explicitly rejected the argument that a noncitizen had the same rights as a citizen and therefore retained the ability to petition for children as immediate relatives.[49] However, the BIA reasoned that because the mother was a national and possessed a valid U.S. passport, she had been granted permission to permanently reside in the United States.[50] Consequently, the U.S. national mother was afforded the rights equal to an LPR and was therefore able to petition for her children in a preference category.[51]

The final political obstacle exists on the local level. Some city and state officials harbor political ambitions that are contrary to federal immigration policy. The most obvious political reason for local officials to eschew federal enforcement policy is to raise name awareness and enhance electability. It may be politically advantageous to be labeled as either "tough on immigration," or conversely, as a compassionate and understanding leader, depending on the audience. These officials stand to benefit politically from taking a line on immigration supported by a majority of local voters. This political incentive may or may not align the interests of elected local officials with the interests of federal immigration policy. This is a difficult obstacle to overcome, especially in light of state sovereignty arguments and widely varying immigration concerns among the states. To move forward with comprehensive immigration reform, to the extent possible, we must align as closley as possible the interests of the states with those of the federal government so that noncooperation is no longer politically advantageous.

Social Obstacles

In addition to political obstacles, there are a number of significant social obstacles to immigration reform. The first and most pronounced is a fear among some white Americans that they are losing control of their country. The demographic reality that America is becoming less white, is a concern for some. That fear, like many xenophobic notions, is founded on irrational conclusions formed on the basis of fundamental misinformation. America has always been a nation of immigrants, but taking the natural evolution of social mores into account, many of the country's core values have remained the same. People come to America because of the opportunities it affords: to be a part of its future and to contribute to its success. We must attempt to deal with the irrational fears accompanying any change to the status quo through education and constructive dialogue if we hope to achieve lasting immigration reform.

Additionally, the INA presents a socio-political obstacle to reform that is difficult to quantify. The INA was passed in 1952 and, although it has been amended several times since then, it is largely structured for America's post-WWII economic and national security needs.[52] Needless to say, America's needs have changed dramatically since 1952, and we believe that amendments to the INA itself should be part of any comprehensive plan for reform.

Another social obstacle to effective immigration reform is the existence of privacy laws that inhibit the ability of the federal government to conduct background checks and to monitor aliens in the United States. The right to be free from unwarranted governmental intrusion into the private lives of its residents is among the most cherished of constitutional protections. Yet effectuating immigration policy requires that federal authorities have the ability to monitor the movements and activities of aliens as they pursue U.S. citizenship or some other type of lawful status. This is a delicate matter, and one that some see as providing the federal government with a chance to diminish constitutional protections to the detriment of all of its citizens. Drafting immigration legislation will require thoughtful consideration of these concerns while providing federal authorities with the authority and flexibility to ensure that aliens comply with the law.

Economic Obstacles

Finally, there are a number of domestic and international economic hurdles that hinder comprehensive immigration reform. The first economic reality is that many countries have no incentive to prevent their poorer citizens from leaving their countries for the United States. Countries like Mexico may be recalcitrant with regard to helping to enforce U.S. immigration policy because of their own economic situation. In other words, from an economic standpoint, Mexico has no incentive to prevent their poorest from leaving the country. From the American perspective, this creates an equally strong incentive to prevent the poorest citizens of other countries from becoming wards of the American federal government. To this end, we must help Mexico find a way to improve its economic situation. Chapter 11 addresses in more detail the importance of strengthening Mexico's economy. This issue speaks to the broader problem of improving Mexico–United States relations.

In chapter 11 we also address the drug-related violence that seeps into the United States from Mexico. From the American perspective, this situation calls for tougher enforcement of immigration policy and greater efforts to secure our borders. From the Mexican perspective, America facilitates drug violence through its lax gun laws that arm Mexican drug lords and with many drug consumers that launder Mexican drug money.

Labor unions also present a significant domestic economic obstacle to immigration reform.[53] Temporary work programs are a staple of proposed immigration reform legislation, but organized labor unions have vehemently opposed these programs as a threat to the workers they represent. Although unionized labor does not have the political clout it once wielded, union labor still has a powerful voice in the immigration debate and with the Obama Administration. This is not to suggest that we should pass immigration reform at the cost of American workers. The livelihood and well-being of American citizens is rightly at the forefront of the debate, but if immigration reform is to provide a path to lawful status for immigrants, we must be able to provide them with a legitimate opportunity to work towards that goal. Therefore, comprehensive immigration reform must address the competing goals of enabling immigrants in their quest for lawful status and protecting the hard fought rights of American workers to their jobs.

Possibly the greatest domestic economic obstacle to immigration reform is the federal deficit. Achieving comprehensive immigration reform is an expensive undertaking, and there are few apparent shortcuts. Even considering the self-evident long-term benefits of immigration reform,[54] the costs of such legislation is a tough sell to the American public given the delicate state of the economy.[55] Many of the necessary measures for successful immigration reform, taken together, could be prohibitively expensive. There will be short-term costs associated, for example, with greater border technology and increased workplace enforcement.[56] There will also be long-term costs, such as Medicare and Medicaid, associated with caring for those immigrants who ultimately achieve citizenship. That is why we must start with every option on the table and find creative solutions to the difficult financial problems this endeavor presents. The president and Congress should level with the American people regarding the overall costs of reform.

Conclusion

The political significance of the growing immigrant community should be apparent in light of the 2012 presidential election. The number of naturalized citizens in the United States is rapidly increasing, meaning that the electoral power of "New American" voters who have a direct, personal connection to the immigrant experience is also rising.[57] Achieving a comprehensive solution will not be easy in light of the numerous obstacles presented by social, political, and economic circumstances. A central element common to each obstacle is the cost of reform in light of the national deficit. In drafting reform legislation, we must make prudent and durable decisions with taxpayers' money. Negotiations over these issues will be tough, and it is therefore incumbent upon everyone involved to compromise in the best interest of the country. Based on what we observed in the 2012 presidential election, we believe this now more than ever. Immigration reform is good policy, and good policy makes good politics. We now turn to our remaining major suggestions for immigration reform.

Chapter Six
Securing Our Borders

Introduction

Borders delineate the boundaries of a nation's territory, and sometimes, walls mark those boundaries. Nevertheless, from Hadrian's Wall along the ancient Roman frontier in modern day England to the Great Wall of China to the Berlin Wall, physical barriers have been unsuccessful in completely eliminating traffic across borders. Human will and desire have been impossible to thwart throughout history. People will always desire a better life, which will continue to motivate them to come to America. Regardless of what security measures and strict policies we put in place, people will continue to come. Moreover, walls send a clear message saying, "Stay out!" Walls separate, control access, and deny opportunity. The fence between Mexico and the United States is indicative of an antagonistic relationship, and we have every reason to foster a more collaborative and amiable alliance with our southern neighbors. Mexico is a friend, ally, and customer, not a competitor or enemy.

This is not to suggest that we should leave our borders unsecured, allowing a free-for-all into America. There are other important steps to alleviate the inevitable influx of immigrants, such as addressing the issues of their home countries, which we discuss in a later chapter. These issues and the methods we should use to address them are highly important to any comprehensive immigration reform legislation. In this chapter, we focus on the measures we can take to make our southern border more secure.

In a post-9/11 world, we have to know what people are in this country and why they are here. The recent Boston bombings highlight the need for our government to better evaluate whether someone who seeks to enter this country is a threat to national security. We may never achieve perfect safety, but we can do better protecting against those who seek to come to American to do harm or engage in criminal activities.

If we were to ask the average American what should be done to help curb unauthorized immigration, the answer would most likely relate to securing U.S. borders. Securing our borders has always been an important focus of the U.S. government. The enormously important task of monitoring our borders primarily belongs to the U.S. Customs and Border Protection (CBP), which is part of DHS. The CBP monitors our northern and southern borders and the coastal waters. We acknowledge that the northern border has similar unauthorized immigration risks as the southern border; however, this chapter primarily focuses on the southern border because that is where the majority of border security strategies are employed in response to unauthorized entry into the United States.

The focus and resources allotted to securing our borders increased significantly after 9/11. We acknowledge that an overwhelming majority of undocumented immigrants are not terrorists. A relatively small number may have terrorist motives, or are hardened criminals, or traffic in people, guns, and drugs. Nevertheless, the extent of serious damage one terrorist could inflict on American interests necessitates our government's full attention. Since the 9/11 attacks, the fear of another catastrophic terrorist attack has led to heightened interest in border security. The threats that terrorist groups pose to our national security are real, and thwarting the efforts of those who would attack America is the first priority in securing our borders. Nonetheless, other important goals of border security must be taken into account when drafting reform legislation. These include detecting, intercepting, and prosecuting groups of undocumented immigrants of varying culpability. Although often thought of as a homogenous group with common characteristics and motivations, the undocumented immigrant population consists of many different groups, with varying culpability and threat of harm to America. One of the challenges of immigration reform is to address groups separately so as not to punish a less culpable immigration violator with the same severity as the most culpable.

Many Americans support additional border security measures that reduce the flow of undocumented immigrants and thwart potential terrorists. Proposed suggestions have included building additional perimeter fences, deploying more border agents and greater military presence, and spending on increased technology. We believe we can secure our borders with limited fences, natural barriers, "virtual fences," improving technology, and increasing and training border personnel. The remainder of this chapter will focus on providing a comprehensive immigration policy related to securing the border with these methods.

Placing Barriers

The United States currently uses two main physical barrier types: the pedestrian fence and the vehicle barrier.[1] Pedestrian fencing and vehicle barriers were created to prevent individuals and vehicles from crossing over into the United States through a non-designated checkpoint.[2] DHS, in taking steps to secure the borders, has completed at least 350 miles of pedestrian fencing and 299 miles of vehicle barriers.[3] In October 2006, President Bush signed The Secure Fence Act of 2006 (2006 Act), which authorized the construction of hundreds of miles of fencing and sanctioned the use of increased technology to secure the southern borders.[4]

The 2006 Act is an attempt at immigration reform, and its purpose is to decrease the numbers of undocumented immigrants, terrorists, and traffickers unlawfully crossing the border.[5] Some Americans believe we have sufficient border security and point to the reduction in the number of undocumented immigrants as proof. Although the 2006 Act has been the subject to much criticism, one of the best ways to address the current unauthorized immigration problem is to cut off the flow of new undocumented immigrants. Quite simply, the nation can never effectively address the millions here unlawfully if their numbers keep growing.

The appropriate required level of fencing going forward will depend, we believe, in part on policies the United States adopts for those immigrants unlawfully in the country. Although the current flow of undocumented immigrants appears to have declined, the numbers may increase if the United States grants blanket amnesty or its equivalent to those here now or if the economy in America improves while conditions in Mexico and Central America deteriorate. As alluded to earlier, providing amnesty to the millions of undocumented immigrants in the United States may encourage others to enter unlawfully.[6] Providing total forgiveness without some penalty would give the inescapable impression that we are cutting corners, unwilling to face the tough tasks immigration reform presents. More importantly, however, the resulting pressure on American enforcement mechanisms might overwhelm our already overworked personnel. Whether tightening border security or providing amnesty, we must be prepared for an increase in pressure at our southern border.

As we have consistently maintained, the United States is in need of some additional border barriers. We support additional limited fencing discussed in S. 744; however, we must be wise about where fencing is placed. We do not support spending money on fencing just because fencing has been authorized. Keeping America's taxpayers in mind, we would also advocate the additional, cost-mitigating measure of conducting an in-depth assessment of the existing barriers before increased spending in that area. Immigration reform legislation will be expensive, and policy-makers must keep in mind that sensible and economical decisions are critical. No one wants to build another Bridge to Nowhere, spending tax-payer dollars on expensive, ineffective, or unnecessary measures. Instead, the focus should be on improving existing barriers through smart construction of additional limited fencing at targeted locations and the efficient use of existing structures and better technology.

By improving the existing barriers before starting new projects, the United States could decrease social costs and perhaps boost public opinion associated with barrier usage. Certain groups oppose the notion of additional barriers altogether.[7] Homeowners, environmentalists, and wildlife protectionists are concerned about their land being taken away, the environmental impact of the structures, the extinction of animals, and plant life restriction due to the barriers.[8] On the other hand, some groups may support physical barriers, but are concerned about their effectiveness.[9] Regardless of how many barriers we build, if undocumented immigrants are still able to climb over, dig under, or otherwise breach the structures, then taxpayers' money is wasted.[10] Consequently, measures in addition to fencing are necessary for border security.

Increasing Technology

The 2006 Act also authorized an increase in technology to secure our borders.[11] Terrorists and criminals use technology to avoid detection; therefore, the government must too. The technology employed by CBP has improved the detection of undocumented immigrants, terrorists, smugglers, drugs, and weapons.[12] For example, CBP programs allow agents to scan the identification cards of potential entrants pursuant to the REAL ID Act and to engage the use of ever-improving infrastructure and technology.[13] Currently, DHS and CBP agents employ motion detectors, radars, scanners, thermal imaging systems, mobile surveillance units, integrated fixed towers, and other technology that help prevent unlawful items and prohibited individuals from entering the United States.[14] There appears to be universal agreement to take advantage of new technologies in securing our border since they serve as "force multipliers" that improve CBP efficiency and capabilities, allowing agents to shift their focus from detection duties to interdiction and resolution of unlawful activity.[15]

More time and energy should be used to extend existing technology to improve our security efforts, such as adding additional night vision technology, unmanned surveillance drones, and motion detectors.[16] This would allow border agents to perform their duties more effectively and safely. As a result, regardless of the time of day or unfavorable conditions, the border agents would still have an advantage over unlawful entrants. As stated earlier, the CBP utilizes a variety of devices at all U.S. ports to prevent prohibited items such as guns, drugs, and radioactive materials from entering the country.[17] Increasing the use of these devices will allow border agents to detect movement safely, particularly during unfavorable times of day in which foot or vehicle patrol is impossible. S. 744 highlights the use of this mandatory technology, and we support this use.

Another advantageous alternative is to reduce the human element from the front lines, thereby lowering the risk of injury to American personnel. In the war on terror, unmanned drones have successfully carried out hundreds of missions related to gathering intelligence and eliminating targets without risking the lives of American soldiers. Since 2005, this same technology has been used to secure our own borders.[18] CBP has ten unmanned drones as of early 2013, a fleet which logged almost 6,000 hours in 2012.[19] Realistically, the use of drones for the entire border would be cost prohibitive; however, drones, based on verified or credible intelligence, are helpful in high traffic areas. Drones can play a critical role in preventing the unlawful crossover of identified terrorists, weapons, and drug and human traffickers. Additional resources will continue to be critical in developing enhanced technology in the war on terror. Further, border security will surely benefit from these advancements.

The use of unmanned drones will not be without controversy. Aside from the costs associated with equipment, personnel, and training, any new surveillance technology inevitably and rightly raises Fourth Amendment concerns. The Fourth Amendment provides that the people shall be free from unreasonable searches and seizures.[20] As technology progresses, the Supreme Court is periodically faced with redefining what constitutes an unreasonable search.[21] Ultimately, the Fourth Amendment question with regard to surveillance is whether there has been a search. If there is no search under constitutional standards, then no warrant is required. With unmanned drones, the question is whether surveillance of activity along the border, either by foot soldiers or by vehicles, constitutes a search under the Fourth Amendment, and if so, whether that search is reasonable.

To answer this, we must look to Supreme Court jurisprudence, which tells us a search is unreasonable if it violates a person's reasonable expectation of privacy.[22] The Court has consistently held that the privacy of the home receives the greatest protection under the Fourth Amendment. However, most of the activities in which CBP would use a drone occur in open spaces or in vehicles, both of which the Court has held provide lesser expectations of privacy for Fourth Amendment purposes.[23]

The touchstone of the Fourth Amendment is that a search be reasonable. Normally, this is satisfied with a finding of probable cause and a warrant. However, the Court has repeatedly found that when "special needs" exist beyond law enforcement, the constitutional requirements can be satisfied without resort to a warrant. In the case of border and national security, we believe the use of drones would normally fit within this exception.[24] Nevertheless, while increasing our use of drone technology, we must be ever vigilant to ensure that constitutional safeguards are always a high priority. After all, the possibility of inadvertent surveillance of American citizens is a real possibility where surveillance is being conducted within our borders. The realities of any Fourth Amendment controversy involving drones are unlikely to be simple as constitutional issues never are.

The border patrol efforts should continue to utilize another nonhuman tool—"war dogs," or border dogs. Dogs have assisted in various law enforcement roles, including use as K-9 dogs by police officers, war dogs in the Middle East, and airport drug dogs. Dogs have been and are currently being used to assist the CBP in their detection efforts. The pilot program, started in 1986, initially trained four dogs to detect humans and narcotics. In 2009 two distinct programs merged into today's current CBP Canine Program (CBPCP). In addition to the detection of humans and narcotics, the CBPCP is responsible for training over 1,500 canine teams, handlers, and instructors on how to detect firearms and currency, conducting search and rescue missions, and processing passengers for narcotics.[25] The dogs selected for the CBPCP are chosen from the CBPCP's own breeding program. This decades-old program should remain part of border patrol efforts. Like technology, the use of dogs has not only proven effective but also has allowed greater control while minimizing risks to American lives.

If the United States can improve the technological aspects of securing the borders, there will be less need for costly additional physical fencing structures. However, such an increase in technology will undoubtedly require an increase of personnel, such as border agents, equipment instructors and monitors, and local law enforcement.

Diversifying Personnel

The final and arguably largest component of this proposed three-prong solution is the personnel aspect of border security. Immigration personnel can be divided into three groups: primary, which includes border patrol agents; support, which includes the National Guard and the regular military; and enforcement, which includes prosecutors and judges (legal personnel) as well as detention facilities and prison personnel (institutions). These three groups are critical in controlling our immigration problems. Therefore, we should ensure that we provide these groups with the money and support they require to be effective.

Border Patrol

Over the past eight years, the number of border patrol agents increased by approximately 85 percent, and today we have approximately 21,000 agents,[26] about 18,500 of which are responsible for the southern border. Since 9/11, the northern border agent presence has increased from a force of 500 to approximately 2,200 agents.[27] Due to geography and a number of other factors, the southern border is arguably more difficult to secure than the northern border. As such, the southern border has always required more agents. Local law enforcement also plays a significant role in the security efforts of the southern border.

The CBP currently works reasonably well with local enforcement officers, but this relationship should be strengthened. We can only win the battle against unauthorized immigration with reliable intelligence and the ability and capacity to react quickly. The border agents need the assistance of local law enforcement officers who possess invaluable localized information. The local officers are often in a better position to "learn" key information that can be used to thwart well-planned missions to unlawfully cross the border. This familiarity with local customs and practices is vitally important to the more remotely located border agents. Strengthened cooperation could be accomplished in a number of ways, such as using more joint task forces, holding more substantial meetings to share information about ongoing investigations, acquiring more grants or assets to be given to local officials to build trust and solidify relationships, and requiring more sharing of information as a condition of federal grants.

However, the practice of allowing local law enforcement to assist the federal government in immigration regulation is not without controversy. Under INA § 287(g) the Secretary of DHS *may* enter into cooperative written agreements with states and political subdivisions through a Memoranda of Agreement (MOA). MOAs authorize state and local law enforcement officers to perform duties that federal immigration agents typically perform, provided the local officers have received "adequate" training related to federal immigration laws and the states and subdivisions bear the financial burden.[28]

MOAs allow state and local officers to use federal property and to investigate, apprehend, or detain any individuals whom officers reasonably suspect to be unlawfully present.[29] If the agreement permits, officers can transport undocumented immigrants to detention centers.[30] Nearly from inception in 1996, § 287(g) has received considerable attention.[31] Supporters view § 287(g) as a valid way to address the nation's unauthorized immigration problem; over 34,000 individuals have been detained, and forty-one percent[32] of them were placed in removal proceedings since inception.[33]

On the other hand, critics claim that § 287(g) facilitates "legal" racial profiling. In fact, several police departments have denounced § 287(g) for that reason and refuse to exercise the power that it grants.[34] There are numerous concerns over false-positives and potential abuse by local law enforcement because § 287(g) allows for wide-ranging discretion, subject only to the wishes of the state and the Secretary of DHS.[35]

Opponents frequently point to Arizona as a cautionary tale of the dangers of § 287(g) when used by overly zealous local law enforcement officers. Maricopa County, directed by Sheriff Joseph Arpaio, has engaged in many practices that are allegedly unlawful violations of civil rights.[36] As a result, it was stripped of its § 287(g) powers pending a federal investigation regarding the constitutionality of its practices.[37] However, in even more common situations, opponents argue that local officers should avoid § 287(g) because their primary responsibilities may be placed in jeopardy. Some suggest that documented and undocumented immigrants alike may stop cooperating with local officers out of fear of deportation.[38] That is not implausible, as any contact with law enforcement could potentially lead to an individual's status being investigated.[39] Partly as a result of these criticisms, § 287(g) is being phased out, as ICE has decided not to renew any of its agreements with state and local law enforcement agencies operating task forces under this program.[40]

In response to the perceived unfair treatment of undocumented immigrants, and to better assimilate them into local communities, local jurisdictions began to implement measures to create sanctuary communities for undocumented immigrants (discussed earlier). Sanctuary communities are areas within states in which undocumented immigrants are encouraged to communicate with the police and assist in local criminal matters. In return for their cooperation, local officers agree not to report the immigration status of the individual to the federal government discovered during an investigation of a local criminal matter.[41]

Predictably, sanctuary communities arouse passions on both sides. Opponents contend that this concept goes against the "rule of law" by allowing people to unlawfully remain in the country and by discouraging investigation into the status of suspected undocumented immigrants. On one hand, local law enforcement needs information to be able to investigate and solve crimes within their city, but this does not take into account the implications of local law enforcement allowing a known or reasonably suspected undocumented immigrant to remain in the community unlawfully. If local officers never alert the federal government to the presence of an undocumented immigrant, that immigrant arguably is then free to commit other subsequent offenses against the United States or even against the state.

With the need of local law enforcement to protect their communities in mind, the Secure Communities program was initiated. Its main participants are ICE, the FBI, and local law enforcement. Secure Communities was created by DHS, which directs the FBI to send all fingerprints received to ICE, which in turn runs the prints through their immigration databases.[42] The Secure Communities program has received praise because it operates without the need to deputize local law enforcement under § 287(g) powers. Local law enforcement simply shares information with the FBI, which in turn is required by statute to share that information with ICE.[43] This is especially relevant in light of the diminishing role of § 287(g). It is also cost effective because it allows various agencies to share information obtained from existing systems and programs.

The following hypothetical illustrates how the program operates. John Doe is arrested on suspicion of DWI/DUI and, once booked into the local police station, John's prints are taken and run through the FBI database to determine whether he has a record or is wanted for any other offense. Once the FBI receives the prints, the FBI shares the prints and information with ICE, which will begin to run its own search through their immigration databases. Because ICE is charged with the removal of repeat violators, criminal immigrants, and unlawful entrants, if John is discovered within its databases, ICE will take the appropriate action to address the immigrant status and criminal behavior. If it is determined that John is subject to removal, ICE may request local law enforcement to detain him until ICE arrives, but detention cannot exceed forty-eight hours, excluding weekends and holidays.[44] To date, the Secure Communities program, which commenced in 2008, is responsible for over eleven million fingerprint submissions to ICE, approximately 700,000 database matches, and the removal of 142,000 individuals.[45]

Secure Communities is one of many programs employed to curb unauthorized immigration. ICE also created the Border Enforcement Security Task Force (BEST). BEST combines various programs and agencies to identify, disrupt, and dismantle criminal organizations that pose significant threats to border security.[46] BEST teams include personnel from ICE, CBP, the Drug Enforcement Agency, the Bureau of Alcohol, Tobacco, and Firearms (ATF), the U.S. Attorney's Office, and other federal, state, and local law enforcement agencies.[47] BEST personnel also include national law enforcement officials from the countries bordering the United States. For example, along the southern border Mexico's Secretaria de Seguridad Pública participates in BEST efforts. On the northern border, the Canada Border Services Agency and the Royal Canadian Mounted Police are members.[48] To date, there are currently thirty-one BEST locations throughout the United States and Mexico, and many of these locations are along the southwest border. Since its creation, BEST has been responsible for thousands of criminal and administrative arrests, and the detection and confiscation of various drugs, including over 71,744 pounds of cocaine and 770,019 pounds of marijuana.[49] Additionally, BEST has detected over 13,343 weapons, 2.7 million rounds of ammunition, and over $103 million in currency.[50]

Because of the growing lack of cooperation with state and local law enforcement, the Senate has recently proposed doubling the number of border patrol agents. While this is helpful, the U.S. government cannot effectively police the southern border without some assistance from local and state law enforcement because of their knowledge of the community. Consequently, relationships should be developed and strengthened between federal, state, and local officials. While much of what has been proposed is already presently in place, more needs to be done.

Military

The use of the National Guard and regular military soldiers should be used in a support role and in high profile, credible intelligence situations.[51] These service members should not be replacements for the border agents, as their services are largely required elsewhere. The relationship between the National Guard and border protection agencies has existed for decades.[52] However, in 2006 this relationship significantly changed with the launch of Operation Jump Start.[53]

Under the direction of President Bush, Operation Jump Start called for the deployment of National Guard members to assist the CBP in strengthening security efforts, while the CBP worked on integrating over 6,000 new border agents.[54] Over the two years the operation was in effect, the National Guard provided over 29,000 troops, but it did not participate in any law enforcement missions. Instead, the Guard assisted the CBP by providing helicopters and other transportation, building and installing security infrastructure, and improving analysis of border-centered intelligence. The Guard also provided mobile communications and administrative training and support, and operated detection systems.[55] The aid of National Guard troops was invaluable to the CBP, and its continued use in similar capacities could also be beneficial.

In 2009, President Obama launched the Southwest Border Initiative, created to address concerns over spillover violence from Mexico.[56] This initiative called for the enhancement of existing programs and initiatives, including doubling BEST and Violent Criminal Alien teams and tripling intelligence analysts.[57]

With proper and efficient implementation of these programs, the United States should see a decline in unauthorized immigration and spillover violence. However, we recognize the extreme level of violence on the Mexican side of the border, and the need for our president to respond with like force if that violence migrates into the United States. The cartels are waging a war as an armed military force. Using our military against individuals who are citizens of a neighboring country is not ideal, but if necessary, the president must be prepared to deploy the National Guard and the regular military to defend U.S. interests. We suspect and hope that the number of situations requiring the use of the military in a primary role will be relatively small; however, their use should be considered in advance as a contingency. Fortunately, DHS and the many domestic agencies and groups that work along the border should be sufficient to handle routine daily border security efforts.

While we support the use of our military in those rare cases involving terrorism, weapons of mass destruction, or concentrated violence of a military nature, we recognize that using the military for border protection in extreme cases is an option that presents potential problems. First, the military is not trained to handle—as a first priority—the types of situations that civilian authorities such as CBP routinely encounter.[58] The rules of engagement would have to be quite clear and necessarily quite restrictive. As a practical matter, this deficiency in training would create possible problems with the sorts of evidentiary and constitutional issues the civilian authorities are more prepared and better experienced to handle. Furthermore, from a legal perspective, federal legislation potentially impedes the use of the military on our borders. Specifically, the Posse Comitatus Act, which originated in the discord immediately following the American Civil War, limits the use of federal military forces within U.S. borders for domestic law purposes.[59] There are numerous exceptions, but generally the military is prohibited from performing arrests, searches, and seizures, among other activities relevant to border security.[60] The law in this area is unsettled, but recognizing the need for our military elsewhere, the Department of Defense has interpreted such restrictions broadly.[61]

The recent deadlock by Congress allowing the self-inflicted sequester to take effect likely represents another obstacle to the solution of using the military on our borders. Defense bears a substantial amount of the sequester burden, and as such civilian leaders at the Pentagon will most likely be even less willing to voluntarily commit soldiers to traditionally civilian duties, especially with the war on terror ongoing abroad, as well as other hot spots in Iran, Syria, Ukraine, northern Africa, and the Middle East. Nevertheless, the use of the military to secure our borders should remain an option of last resort since the war on terror remains abroad only as long as we can keep it from infiltrating our borders.

The Justice System

Lastly, effective border security will require a boost in legal personnel. As many more undocumented immigrants are discovered, more government attorneys and judges are needed. Congress and the president must find the money to pay for these additional resources. The process to expel an undocumented immigrant requires the use of many legal professionals. Lately, undocumented immigrants are outpacing available beds in detention facilities and creating an impossible situation. This is apparent from the average amount of time it takes for an undocumented immigrant to appear before an immigration judge because of lengthy backlogs. Backlogs in immigration courts are so strained that an undocumented immigrant's notice to appear before an immigration judge is often at least one year beyond the issuance date. It remains a lengthy process even after the individual's initial hearing date, as many seek relief before the courts.[62] Comprehensive immigration reform is needed to help alleviate our backlogged courts, and increased personnel in our justice system may become a more urgent necessity.

Conclusion

Implementing the ideas in this chapter have the potential for dramatically curtailing unauthorized immigration at the floodgates. Preventing the number of undocumented immigrants from continuing to escalate would make the task of addressing the millions currently present within the United States more manageable. Congress must be sensitive to costs when securing our borders, and the suggestions in this chapter offer a number of cost mitigating measures for reform. Through the improvement of existing barriers, continued use of technology, and the implementation of a revised personnel policy, the United States should begin to see a decline in unlawful entries. Any comprehensive bill that lacks a substantial border security component is not likely to pass the Republican-controlled House, nor should it. Many members of Congress are not interested in spending money on reform in this country if the border remains open. The fear is that in 10-15 years, the United States will once again face an immigration problem. For this reason, comprehensive immigration reform must provide for measurable tougher border security. Many of the legislative proposals include triggers based on a secure border, which require evidence that the border has been secured before allowing undocumented immigrants the opportunity to pursue lawful status. As discussed previously, any legislation adopted by Congress will likely have to include realistic procedures to verify border security.

Chapter Seven
Workplace Enforcement

Introduction

The workplace is a major arena for the enforcement of U.S. immigration laws. In an attempt to discourage the hiring of undocumented immigrants, in 1986 Congress added INA § 274A, which imposes fines—and sometimes criminal punishment—on employers who knowingly hire undocumented workers.[1]

Under the authority of INA § 274A and in accordance with its regulations, DHS requires approximately eight million employers to verify and maintain I-9 forms for each employee.[2] DHS enforces immigration laws in the workplace through ICE, its principal investigative arm and the second-largest federal investigative agency.[3]

ICE has become much more aggressive in its enforcement during the Obama Administration, as the following statistics demonstrate:

	2008	2011
Workplace Enforcement Cases Initiated	1,191	3,291[4]
Form I-9 Audits Conducted	503	2,496[5]
Employers Criminally Charged	135	221[6]
Final Orders Issued Against Charged Employers	18	385[7]
Fines Levied Against Strike Employers	$675,209	$10,463,987[8]
Individuals and Business Debarred	0	211[9]

Due to the recent climate of heightened enforcement, employers are increasingly willing to work with ICE in order to avoid punishment for hiring undocumented workers, some of whom use fake immigration documents to obtain a job. Using programs like E-Verify and the IMAGE certification process, ICE is providing employers with resources to avoid hiring undocumented workers by detecting fake immigration documents of prospective or current employees. USCIS processed over seventeen million E-Verify queries in 2011 alone, and over 294,000 employers are enrolled in E-Verify.[10] In 2012 there were more than twenty million queries.[11]

However, programs such as E-Verify, which contain frequent errors, especially as the volume of inquiries increases, are not without criticism. Some allege that programs like E-Verify are an improper use of information by the government and result in a loss of personal privacy. Others accuse such programs of having a discriminatory effect. INA § 274B, discussed in more detail later in this chapter, attempts to prevent discrimination in workplace enforcement, but not without its own controversy.[12]

Programs such as E-Verify receive criticism at least in part because they are a flawed way of solving a massive problem. When an employer terminates an employee who cannot provide adequate documentation of his ability to work lawfully in the United States, that individual does not cease to be an undocumented worker. Unless the individual is detained by ICE and placed in removal proceedings, the only variable that has changed is that he is now out of a job. As workplace enforcement increases, undocumented workers will enter a cycle of unemployment, possibly creating a humanitarian crisis in one of the most developed nations on earth. Furthermore, widespread unemployment within certain industries, like construction and farming, will hurt the U.S. economy.

For this reason, the federal government should consider granting certain qualified undocumented workers in the United States some sort of lawful status. Such an initiative, used in conjunction with programs like E-Verify, would give undocumented workers a chance to obtain lawful status while offering the United States a valuable labor resource. S. 744 allows some of these undocumented workers to obtain temporary lawful status and we support this approach.

Historical Perspective

Enforcement of U.S. immigration laws in the workplace effectively began with the Immigration Reform and Control Act of 1986 (IRCA). Prior to

IRCA penalties for breaking U.S. immigration laws applied only to the undocumented workers themselves. With IRCA Congress attempted to decrease the incentive to unlawfully enter the United States by destroying the job market for undocumented immigrants.[13]

In addition to granting amnesty to certain undocumented seasonal agricultural workers, as well as all undocumented immigrants who resided in the United States since January 1, 1982, or earlier, IRCA also added two new sections to the INA: §§ 274A and 274B.

Section 274A(a) criminalizes hiring or continuing to employ an alien "knowing the alien is an unauthorized alien."[14] The terms "knowingly" and "continue to employ" have been the subject of controversy and their meanings have been defined over time in case law.[15] In *Mester Manufacturing Co. v. INS*, the Ninth Circuit held that "constructive knowledge" is the applicable standard for knowledge, meaning the "deliberate failure to investigate suspicious circumstances imputes knowledge," and such notification imparts constructive knowledge on the employer that one of its employees may be unauthorized.[16]

In the usual case, ICE notifies an employer that it has reason to believe one of its employees is not authorized to work.[17] Furthermore, when ICE notifies an employer of a potentially unauthorized employee, the employer is not guilty of noncompliance for failing to immediately terminate or suspend the employment of the employee in question upon notification.[18] Instead, ICE "must provide an employer with a reasonable amount of time for compliance after the employer acquires knowledge that an employee is unauthorized."[19]

The court provided further guidance in *Collins Foods International, Inc. v. INS*, when it ruled that the failure to compare a document offered for employment to a sample in a government handbook for the purpose of determining authenticity does not constitute a "deliberate failure to investigate suspicious circumstances."[20] An employer does not have constructive knowledge that a potential employee may be unauthorized every time a potential employee offers employment documents.[21]

However, the federal regulations concerning aliens and nationality state that "knowing includes not only actual knowledge but also knowledge which may fairly be inferred through notice of certain facts and circumstances which would lead a person, through the exercise of reasonable care, to know about a certain condition."[22] This standard goes well beyond the standard for constructive knowledge put forth in *Mester Manufacturing* and *Collins Foods*.

To facilitate determination of the status of a potential employee, § 274A also requires all U.S. employers before hiring a potential employee to complete a process designed to verify that he is authorized, regardless of his suspected status.[23] An employer who attempts to complete the verification process in good faith will be excused from any "technical or procedural failure" in the completion of the verification process.[24]

The Employment Eligibility Verification Process

The verification process contains several steps. Before hiring an employee, an employer must verify that the employee has authorization to work in the United States, with certain exceptions.[25] The prospective employee must complete the employee portion of the Employment Eligibility Verification, Form I-9, and present it to his employer along with the documentation confirming the employee's identity and work authorization. The employee can choose from three lists of documents: (A) those establishing both identity and work authorization; (B) those establishing identity only; and (C) those establishing work authorization only.

The employee can establish his work authorization by presenting either one "list A" document or, alternatively, a combination of "list B" and "list C" documents. For example, an employee may provide a U.S. passport, resident alien card, alien registration, or other document designated by the attorney general to establish both his identity and authorization.[26] An employee may also provide a social security card, which establishes authorization, and a driver's license or identification card, which establishes identity.[27] An employer cannot direct an employee to present any specific documents, but instead must show the prospective employee the list of qualifying documents and allow the employee to decide which documents to present.

The employer must examine the documents presented and attest on Form I-9 that the documents "reasonably appear both to be genuine and relate to the individual presenting the document."[28] The employer must "attest, under penalty of perjury and on a form designated or established by the attorney general by regulation, that the individual is not an unauthorized alien."[29] The potential employee must attest on the same form that he is a U.S. citizen or otherwise authorized to work.[30]

The employer must retain all I-9 forms for potential inspection. Noncompliance with a federal request to inspect the employer's I-9 forms can result in sanctions against the employer. An employer who fails to maintain the required records must pay a fine ranging from $100 to $1,000 per employee whose records are missing. Factors determining the fine include: (1) the seriousness of the violation; (2) the employer's history or pattern of similar violations; (3) the size of the business; and (4) whether the employee whose records were not maintained turns out to be an unauthorized alien.

Individuals eligible for employment authorization can obtain an Employment Authorization Document (EAD) to use as proof of their eligibility to work lawfully in the United States. Job applicants can use the EAD for purposes of the I-9 employment verification process. To obtain an EAD, an individual must file with the USCIS an Application for Employment Authorization (Form I-765). Conditional LPRs and LPRs, as well as nonimmigrants authorized for employment with a specific employer under 8 C.F.R. § 274a.12(b), do not need to use Form I-765. The USCIS issues the EADs to the following categories of applicants, among others:

1. Asylees and asylum applicants;
2. Refugees;
3. Certain categories of foreign students seeking employment;
4. Applicants to adjust to permanent residence status;
5. Applicants for temporary protected status;
6. Fiancé(e)s of American citizens;
7. Domestic servants under B-1 category;
8. Family Unity Program participants; and
9. Deferred Action Beneficiaries.[31]

In October 2011 the USCIS began issuing the new, enhanced EAD. The agency is hoping that the state-of-the-art technology incorporated into the new EAD will deter counterfeiting, obstruct tampering, and facilitate quick and accurate authentication. The agency anticipates that more than one million people will receive the new EAD in 2013.[32]

E-Verify System

Information about the employee from Form I-9 serves as the foundation for an E-Verify case. E-Verify is "an Internet-based system that allows an employer, using information reported on an employee's Form I-9. . . to determine the eligibility of that employee to work in the United States."[33] Participation in the program is voluntary for most employers but is mandatory for employers in some states and employers with federal contracts or subcontracts that contain the Federal Acquisition Regulations E-Verify clause.[34] More than 307,000 employers participate in the program, with over seventeen million cases created in the system in fiscal year 2011.[35] In 2012 there were 404,295 employers enrolled, with over twenty million cases in the system.[36]

Although the purpose of both the Form I-9 verification process and E-Verify system is essentially the same—to confirm employment authorization—the two procedures differ in meaningful ways, as summarized in the table below:[37]

Form I-9	E-Verify
Is mandatory	Is voluntary for most businesses
Does not require a social security number	Requires a social security number
Does not require a photo on identity documents	Requires a photo on identity documents
Must be used to re-verify expired employment authorization	May not be used to re-verify expired employment authorization

The employer must create an E-Verify case within three business days after the employee begins working for pay. Employers access E-Verify online and compare an employee's data on Form I-9 "with over 455 million records in the Social Security Administration database and more than 80 million records in the DHS immigration database."[38] The employer usually receives immediate feedback on whether the employee is eligible for work in the United States.

Sometimes, E-Verify's automated search of government records cannot immediately verify employment authorization and a manual search is required.[39] In this case, E-Verify will return a "DHS Verification in Process" response. The employer must check E-Verify until the employee's case is updated. When the employee's case is updated, E-Verify will return either a "Tentative Nonconfirmation" (TNC) response, if the employee information does not match government records, or an "Employment Authorized" response.

To complete the E-Verify process, every case must receive a final case result and then be closed.[40] When E-Verify cannot confirm an employee's employment eligibility after an employee has contacted a Social Security Administration (SSA) field office or DHS during the TNC referral process, the employer receives an "SSA or DHS Final Non-Confirmation" case result. At that point the employer must close the case and may terminate the employee with no civil or criminal liability. However, terminating an employee before the final nonconfirmation could result in the employer's disqualification from participating in the E-Verify program.[41] USCIS monitors employer compliance with E-Verify and investigates employers suspected of noncompliance. If an employer fails to notify DHS of its decision not to terminate an unauthorized employee, the employer may have to pay between $550 and $1,100 as a civil penalty.

E-Verify initially received substantial criticism from employers and attorneys because of its frequent errors and inability to handle a high volume of inquiries. In addition, early E-Verify queries failed to detect incidents of identity theft.[42] However, USCIS is continuously attempting to improve E-Verify in order to address these concerns. For example, it has added a new photo tool to help prevent identity theft. To lower the error rate USCIS launched the E-Verify Self Check service in 2011. Employees can use this free, web-based service to check their own work authorization status against SSA and DHS databases. If a mismatch occurs, the user will receive directions on how to verify and correct the information, for example, by visiting SSA or USCIS field offices and updating their records. To improve the ability of E-Verify to process the high volume of inquiries, USCIS and SSA recently drafted a service-level agreement, under which SSA will establish and maintain the capacity and availability of its system components for E-Verify.

Although not flawless, E-Verify appears to be effective in assisting thousands of employers to comply with immigration regulations. It represents a substantial step toward the creation of a fair and lawful workplace in the United States, but the government should continue to explore ways to make this process more accurate and effective without unnecessary restrictions on hiring.

Other Employment Compliance Programs

As an alternative to E-Verify, employers can check the authenticity of social security numbers (SSNs) through the Social Security Number Verification Service (SSNVS). The SSA created this free online service in 2006. The SSNVS allows employers and payroll services to verify the match between a particular name and an SSN for the purposes of completing a W-2 form. When the SSA cannot verify a match, it notifies the employer with a "no-match" letter. However, the service has a number of limitations, as employers cannot use the SSNVS to verify an employee's U.S. work authorization, to prescreen applicants, or to take punitive measures against an employee whose name does not match.[43]

In an effort to "combat unlawful employment and reduce vulnerabilities that help . . . aliens gain such employment," the federal government has created other programs in addition to E-Verify and SSNVS.[44] Since July 2006 ICE has been implementing the Mutual Agreement between Government and Employers (IMAGE) program, which is designed to educate employers on proper hiring procedures, the detection of fraudulent documents, and antidiscrimination procedures. The IMAGE program is voluntary, but employers must participate in E-Verify before they can enroll in IMAGE.

To become IMAGE-certified, employers must follow a multistep process that requires that they (1) complete the IMAGE application form; (2) enroll in the E-Verify program within sixty days; (3) establish a written hiring and employment-eligibility verification policy, including an internal Form I-9 audit; (4) comply with a Form I-9 inspection; and (5) review and sign an official partnership agreement with ICE. In return for an employer's participation, ICE promises to mitigate the consequences of potential employer violations. Among other things, ICE agrees:

1. To waive potential fines if substantive violations are discovered on fewer than 50 percent of the required I-9 forms;

2. To mitigate fines or issue them at the statutory minimum of $110 per violation in instances where more than 50 percent of the I-9 forms contain substantive violations;

3. Not to conduct another Form I-9 inspection of the company for a two-year period; and

4. To provide information and training before, during, and after inspection.[45]

In light of increased government checks of employee status and sanctions on employers, the participation of employers in programs like IMAGE is growing. As of January 2012 more than one hundred employers had enrolled in IMAGE. Employers are encouraged to attend one of the training forums that ICE and USCIS conduct nationwide twice each month.

Antidiscrimination Provision (§ 274B)

There were major concerns in the deliberations leading up to IRCA that the proposed employer sanctions would lead to discrimination against "foreign-looking" employees.[46] Legislators feared that employers would refuse to hire eligible workers who appeared to be Latino or Asian in order to reduce the risk of inadvertently hiring an undocumented immigrant.[47] Representative Barney Frank proposed that legislation imposing employer sanctions include a set of provisions that expressly prohibited certain forms of employment discrimination and established methods to enforce these provisions.[48] Congress enacted the new antidiscrimination provisions as IRCA § 102, which added § 274B to the INA.[49]

Section 274B makes it unlawful to discriminate against an individual, other than an unauthorized alien, as defined by INA § 274A(h)(3), "with respect to the hiring, or recruitment or referral for a fee, of the individual for employment or the discharging of the individual from employment" because of the individual's national origin or perceived citizenship status.[50] Section 274B also prohibits asking for additional or different employment documents from the ones required under § 274A(b) or refusing to accept employment documents that "on their face reasonably appear to be genuine," and it prohibits the refusal of employment documents "for the purpose or with the intent of discriminating against an individual" based on national origin or perceived immigration status.[51]

Section 274B only applies to "protected individuals," defined as U.S. citizens, LPRs, beneficiaries of IRCA legalization, and refugees and asylees.[52] However, any LPR who failed to apply for naturalization within six months of becoming eligible to do so, or, if later, within six months of the enactment of IRCA in November 1986, or who failed to complete the naturalization process in a timely manner, does not qualify as a protected individual for purposes of § 274B protection.[53]

There are three exceptions to § 274B.[54] The first exempts employers with fewer than four employees.[55] The second prohibits national-origin discrimination claims already covered by 42 U.S.C. § 2000e-2.[56] The third exempts employers who discriminate based on citizenship status because "the law requires citizenship as a condition of employment or as a condition of the employer contracting with federal, state, or local governments."[57]

Section 274B violations are punishable by civil fines that, like sanctions for employer violations, "are graduated to reflect the number of prior offenses."[58] Fines for § 274B violations were once systematically lower than fines for violations of § 274A, but the Immigration Act of 1990 brought § 274B fines in line with § 274A fines.[59]

Section 274B established the Office of Special Counsel for Immigration-Related Unfair Employment Practices (OSC).[60] As part of the Justice Department, the OSC investigates and prosecutes § 274B discrimination claims.[61] The president appoints special counsel and the Senate confirms the appointment for a four-year term.[62]

Does § 1981 Bar Private Alienage Discrimination?

Section 274B has proven to be controversial.[63] At the time of its passage, some, including President Ronald Reagan, disputed the concern that employer sanctions would lead to employment discrimination, arguing that employers would have no need to discriminate because they need only follow the law by completing the necessary employment paperwork and by refraining from hiring anyone who could not provide the necessary valid documents.[64] Opponents of employer sanctions argued that this view overestimated the clarity of proposed employer-sanction laws to employers.[65]

The Reagan administration countered that, even if employer-sanction provisions increased employment discrimination, existing civil-rights laws prohibit discrimination based on national origin, so new legislation prohibiting employment discrimination under the context of employer sanctions for hiring undocumented immigrants would simply create an unnecessary level of bureaucracy.[66] However, because of gaps in existing civil-rights laws, a person subject to discrimination by an employer seeking to avoid employer sanctions arguably may not be protected.[67] For example, Title 7 of the Civil Rights Act of 1964 (Title 7) prohibits employment discrimination based on "race, color, religion, sex, or national origin," but it exempts employers with fewer than fifteen employees and fails to prohibit discrimination in favor of U.S. citizens over LPRs.[68]

Another civil-rights law that may leave victims of employment discrimination based on national origin without legal resource is 42 U.S.C. § 1981.[69] Section 1981 states that "[a]ll persons within the jurisdiction of the United States shall have the same right in every State and Territory to make and enforce contracts . . . as enjoyed by white citizens."[70] Section 1981 is insufficient to prohibit employment discrimination resulting from the fear of employer sanctions because, while it prohibits discrimination based on race, federal courts are split on the issue of "alienage." The Fifth Circuit held in 1989 that § 1981 does not prohibit discrimination based on alienage, but the Second Circuit later disagreed and held that it does.[71] Without § 274B, a protected individual, as defined by § 274A, who was discriminated against based on national origin by an employer in the Fifth Circuit would have no recourse, while one in the Second Circuit would.[72]

"English-only" Employment Cases

In the realm of employment discrimination laws, civil-rights laws generally distinguish "disparate treatment" discrimination from "disparate impact" discrimination.[73] In disparate treatment cases the complainant alleges that the employer intentionally discriminated against an employee based on a protected class, such as race or religion.[74] In disparate impact cases the complainant alleges that an employer's actions or policies had a

substantial disproportionate impact upon members of a particular protected class even though the employer had no discriminatory intent in
taking the actions or creating the policies in question and even though the
actions or policies are not facially discriminatory.[75]

Title 7 protects victims of both types of employment discrimination,
but whether IRCA protects victims of disparate impact discrimination as
well as victims of disparate treatment discrimination has been controversial since IRCA's enactment.[76] When President Reagan signed IRCA into
law, his administration took the position that the legislation did not provide disparate impact protection.[77]

Their first argument was that the language in § 274B parallels the Title
7 language for disparate treatment cases but that it contained no parallel
language for disparate impact cases.[78] The second argument was that
§ 274B does not protect victims of disparate impact discrimination because § 274B requires evidence of intent to discriminate or "a pattern or
practice of discriminatory activity" on the part of the employer. An employer can impose an English-language requirement for employment even
if knowledge and use of the English language is not necessary to perform
the job.[79] The Reagan administration clarified that "unless the plaintiff
presents evidence that the employer has intentionally discriminated on
proscribed grounds, the employer need not offer *any* explanation for his
employee selection procedures."[80]

The occurrence of such English-only employment cases has sharply
increased over the last few years. They are generally found to violate Title
7 when the employer can provide no job-related reason for refusing to
hire non-English speakers.[81] Whether these requirements violate § 274B,
however, is less clear.[82]

Employer Penalties for IRCA Violations

The federal government continues to crack down nationwide on employers who hire and employ undocumented immigrants. In January 2012, for
example, two major Houston-based companies had to pay two million
dollars each to DHS as forfeited funds for employing undocumented
workers.[83] Both companies received numerous "no-match" letters from
the SSA; however, the companies continued to employ the suspect workers, failing to take any corrective measures. The Form I-9 audit of one of

these companies in 2011 revealed that between 2005 and 2009, about 44 percent of the workforce at that company was undocumented. The 2011 audit of the other company revealed that approximately 269 of its 451-person workforce were undocumented immigrants. Additionally, the company managers were falsely attesting on I-9 forms that work authorization documents presented by new hires were "genuine." At the request of the government, both companies terminated their undocumented employees. DHS agreed not to criminally prosecute the two Houston companies in exchange for remedial measures by the companies and future compliance with immigration law in the hiring process. In addition to proper completion and retention of the I-9 forms, the companies had to hire full-time chief compliance officers.

The Houston companies were among thousands of companies that ICE audited or investigated nationwide in 2011.[84] During that time ICE issued 385 final fine notices, totaling more than ten million dollars, to employers across the country. Employer audits and civil penalties are not the only tools ICE uses to combat unlawful employment and protect job opportunities for the lawful domestic workforce. That enforcement strategy also includes extensive criminal investigations. For example, a 2011 ICE criminal investigation resulted in a one-year probation and a forfeiture of $150,000 for one company charged with employing undocumented immigrants.[85]

Monetary penalties for knowingly hiring and continuing to employ undocumented immigrants vary from $375 to $16,000 or more per violation, depending on the circumstances. In determining the size of a fine, "ICE considers five factors (similar to the factors considered for fines for failure to retain I-9 forms): [1] the size of the business, [2] good faith effort to comply, [3] seriousness of violation, [4] whether the violation involved unauthorized workers, and [5] history of previous violations."[86]

In addition to penalizing employers who violate U.S. immigration law, ICE also debars federal contractors. The Federal Acquisition Regulations provide that contractors may be considered for debarment if they "either knowingly hire an unauthorized worker or continue to employ an alien who is or becomes unauthorized."[87] As part of the debarment process, each company's name is entered into the Excluded Parties List System, a "web-based system that identifies parties suspended, debarred, proposed for debarment, or otherwise excluded from receiving federal contracts, certain subcontracts, and certain types of federal financial and non-financial assistance and benefits."[88] Such companies may not compete for new government contracts, and neither ICE nor any other federal agency may award a new contract to a company that is suspended.

Tougher penalties on employers who hire undocumented immigrants, including stiffer fines and jail time for company officials who are repeat offenders, will help deter employers from circumventing the lawful hiring process set forth in the INA. By employing unauthorized workers companies have saved substantial amounts of money on labor, often failing to complete the necessary employment verification and labor certification before they hire a worker; however, this practice inhibits growth in the legitimate labor markets and keeps wages artificially low. Fines alone may not be an effective deterrent for particularly unscrupulous employers, and such employers should continue to be subject to criminal sanctions where appropriate. If the United States is serious about discouraging employers from hiring undocumented immigrants, all the government need do is send a CEO to jail for breaking the law repeatedly. The imposition of fines, sanctions, and possible charges should not hurt legitimate business owners and operators, and such measures, when applied correctly, should help protect American workers.

Recommendations

With the criminalization of knowingly hiring an undocumented worker and the recent increased enforcement of § 274A, the workplace is now an important arena in the enforcement of U.S. immigration laws. Equity requires the prosecution of both employers and employees for violations of the law, but fairness comes at a price.

By requiring employers to hire only documented employees, § 274A arguably makes it more difficult for employers to operate a business. This is why any legislation should mandate safe harbors like E-Verify. In this economy, businesses need all the help and protection that the law can offer; that said, unscrupulous employers who knowingly hire undocumented immigrants arguably damage the economy by paying less than sustainable wages. Conceivably, in the short term § 274A could raise costs for legitimate employers who seek to comply with immigration laws by requiring them to spend time and resources soliciting and examining immigration documents from employees. However, once it becomes the standard to request such information, the procedure will be no more burdensome than the documentation currently required. At the same time, employers who make a good-faith effort at compliance but are deceived by undocumented immigrants should not be penalized.

We must note, however, that in some job sectors willing documented workers may simply be difficult to find because of artificially low wages or other reasons. Americans might have to decide the true overall social cost of maintaining artificially low markets and prices. For example, the overall social cost to pay one dollar for a tomato may actually support an equitable overhaul to the system that results in paying five dollars for the same tomato—but at a considerably lower cost for our society, in that wages are higher and unauthorized immigration is lowered. Agriculture is hardly the only economic sector facing these challenges, and employers and policy makers must be cautious not to discriminate against potential employees because of race or perceived national origin in their attempts to comply with § 274B. Realistically, compliance should be geared toward the larger employers, thereby shielding smaller mom-and-pop businesses with fewer than 10–25 employees from additional employment expenses in an already weak economy.

Conclusion

A smart national dialogue leading to comprehensive immigration policy strengthens national economic policy, promotes commerce, and secures national borders. From many perspectives undocumented immigrants contribute to our nation's economy.[89] For such reasons, maintaining the current system of enforcing § 274A while trying to evict the millions of undocumented immigrants currently in the United States is proving more impractical every day. Wholesale eviction would devastate certain industries. Candidly, we believe that our government is incapable of forcibly removing approximately eleven million people. Further, the positive long-term effects of lawful immigration on the American labor market feasibly includes improved productivity, increased average income for native U.S. citizens, and in a growing economy, an increase of jobs sufficient to ensure that native U.S. citizen employees are not displaced.[90] Consequently, a policy that works with and encourages skilled, hard-working immigrants and employers to comply with immigration laws and regulations will contribute to the strength of our economy.[91]

Realistically, there are millions of undocumented immigrants currently working in the United States, and any immigration policy or reform must address this issue. One way, for example, is to create a program that grants workers who meet certain qualifications (including payment of a fine as an acknowledgment of breaking the law) a limited two-year permit for work eligibility. Understandably, critics of such a plan argue that fairness dictates that an undocumented immigrant who knowingly violated U.S. immigration law should be punished and expelled, but the payment of a penalty refutes the claim of a blanket amnesty.

The point of comprehensive immigration reform is to address the actual, realistic problems at hand, which have, frankly, become too great to address with the simple response that "we are rewarding law breakers with amnesty." Granting eligibility to qualifying undocumented workers would greatly ease the burdens that §§ 274A and 274B currently impose on employers by legitimizing much of the current employee pool. It would also allow ICE to focus its efforts on border enforcement and the search for and removal of remaining undocumented immigrants who do not qualify for eligibility. We do not advocate that those here under a work permit be eligible for permanent status at some point in the future, but neither do we advocate that they not be eligible. We do, however, believe strongly that such individuals should not enjoy the privilege of lawful permanent residency in advance of those who have followed the law to acquire lawful permanent residency.

Chapter Eight

Revising the Visa Process

Introduction

A change to our immigration system should include modifying the non-immigrant visa process. The United States does not have an effective system in place to track the departures of foreign nationals who have previously been admitted. Millions of temporary visitors overstay their visas in an attempt to remain in the United States permanently. Immigration reform should include an effective framework for locating and punishing those who overstay their visas.

The Admission Process—An Overview

Foreign nationals who wish to come to the United States must generally first obtain a visa, with certain exceptions.[1] Depending on the particular status sought, the admission process may involve up to four hurdles for a foreign national.[2] Not every nonimmigrant will need to overcome all four hurdles. Some nonimmigrants, for example, may not need a visa petition and may need only to apply for a particular visa at a U.S. consulate abroad;[3] others may simply seek to enter the United States under the visa-waiver program that allows nationals of certain countries to enter the United States simply by presenting a passport at a port of entry.[4]

The first hurdle generally applies to employers of certain nonimmigrants who must apply for labor certification or file a labor condition application with the Department of Labor.[5] Both the labor certification process and the labor condition application are designed to protect U.S. workers and wage levels.[6] Approval from the Department of Labor is not necessary for the majority of visas issued by the U.S. government, and most visa seekers will not be required to overcome this first hurdle.[7]

The second hurdle, if applicable, involves filing a visa petition with

USCIS.[8] Like the first hurdle, the second hurdle is not always an obstacle to the would-be nonimmigrant. The purpose of the visa petition is to verify the alien beneficiary's eligibility for the status sought.[9] The third hurdle is obtaining a visa to enter the United States.[10] If USCIS approves a visa petition, for example, the beneficiary must then file a visa application at a U.S. consulate abroad.[11] The visa application process involves extensive paperwork and often a personal interview with an immigration officer.[12] Immigration officers have broad discretion in making credibility and eligibility judgments when interviewing a visa applicant.[13] The waiting time for visa approval varies and may depend on the geographic region of the applicant, the number of other applicants from the same region, and the type of visa sought.[14]

The fourth hurdle is admission at the port of entry.[15] Although a visa is usually necessary to gain admission, it is not always sufficient.[16] A CBP officer may reexamine an alien to assure the alien's eligibility for admission.[17] If the officer suspects the alien may be inadmissible based on a particular statutory ground, the officer may order the alien detained for investigation and may ultimately issue an order of expedited removal against the alien.[18]

After successfully clearing the hurdles of admission, the foreign national is allowed to enter the United States. Once admitted, the alien is generally free to travel anywhere in the United States, and no government agency appears to be tasked with tracking the whereabouts of the millions of nonimmigrants who arrive through proper channels. We must do a better job of locating and dealing with visa overstayers.

Types of Visa Programs

As discussed earlier, nonimmigrants seeking employment in the United States must have documentation authorizing them to work. Currently, there is an H-1B visa available for skilled professionals. The H-1B visa is a nonimmigrant visa authorized under INA § 101(a)(15)(H). This visa allows U.S. employers to temporarily employ foreign workers in specialty occupations, which include but are not limited to architecture, engineering, mathematics, medicine and health, fashion models, education, and law. Under the H-1B program skilled professionals are allowed to stay and work in the United States for three years, and sometimes the duration may be extended up to six years and longer.[19] The skilled professional is in an advantageous position for adjustment to LPR status.[20] However, specialty occupant professionals are the only workers eligible to participate in the H-1B program.

While there are similar programs for temporary nonagricultural work for unskilled laborers, they are not as advantageous as the H-1B visa. For example, the H-2B visa allows employers to hire foreign workers to perform temporary nonagricultural services or labor on a one-time seasonal basis.[21] The visa is limited to the dates stated on the visa, not to exceed one year, and in many cases the visa does not allow for multiple reentries.[22] Furthermore, unskilled laborers will have great difficulty adjusting their temporary status to LPR status because temporary workers admitted in the H-2B category are hired to fill a position only for a temporary need. Accordingly, once the visa expires (which typically occurs within months), the immigrant usually has only a ten-day grace period to leave the country with little to no chance for adjustment of status.[23]

We believe the employment-based visa programs for both skilled and unskilled workers should be significantly expanded. This measure will help to reduce the number of undocumented workers employed in the United States. We fully support the provision in S. 744 for increasing the H-1B cap and creating new visas for agricultural and lesser-skilled workers.[24]

To alleviate concerns, at least partly, about further increasing the number of aliens in the United States and the corresponding burdens on the U.S. immigration system, we propose to eliminate the diversity program, briefly discussed in chapter 1. Allowing deserving foreigners to work temporarily in the United States under one of the employment-based categories would be a better policy than allowing just anyone to draw a "lucky admission ticket" to the United States without particular regard to the "lucky ticketholder's" employment skills and education. We no longer have the luxury of making immigration decisions based on the luck of the draw. Instead, as stated earlier, our immigration policy should support the values of family, a strong national security, and a robust economy.

Dealing with Visa Overstays

Currently, the United States has no effective system in place to track the departures of foreign nationals who come with temporary visas.[25] Millions of visitors overstay their visas in an attempt to remain in the United States permanently. As of October 2010, ICE field offices had closed approximately 34,700 overstay investigations from 2004 through 2010,[26] resulting in approximately 8,100 arrests (about 23 percent).[27] To put these numbers in perspective, the total overstay population is estimated at 4–5.5 million.[28] In its April 2011 Government Accountability Office (GAO) report, GAO admitted that DHS lacks a standard mechanism for nonimmigrant aliens who depart the United States through land ports of entry to submit their arrival and departure forms.[29]

We believe that the lack of adequate informational services is one of the reasons for the stunning number of visa overstayers in the United States. Drawing on the experience of the Australian government,[30] the United States might create immigration informational service centers (IISC) in all cities with a population over two hundred thousand. These IISCs would work under the umbrella of USCIS to provide services to people who have overstayed their visas. IISC staff would provide information to alien visitors about their status and their visa or departure options. This prompt and accurate information might help reduce the accrual of unlawful presence, would provide additional information to the government about potential visa overstayers, and would help overstayers to make informed decisions. In addition, the government might create some additional form of temporary bridging visa (borrowing from Australia's immigration system), which would be given to any overstayer while that person is resolving his immigration status.[31] These bridging visas would help reduce the number of persons without lawful status and would toll the accrual of their unlawful presence in the United States.

Of course, people who violate the terms of their stay in this country should not simply be forgiven. Purposeful failure to maintain lawful status should be viewed as a serious violation, and Congress should consider imposing monetary fines and otherwise penalize those who overstay their visas.[32]

Additionally, requiring employers to notify the government (and provide any forwarding information) whenever an alien worker leaves employment might help with tracking noncitizens. Similarly, universities should be required to notify the government whenever an alien student drops out of school or completes the study program in the United States. Still another way of discouraging visa overstays is to increase initial visa fees and offer partial reimbursement upon an alien's successful return to his home country. The government should also consider whether to impose an accelerated hearing system for visa overstayers.

It would be helpful also to have an effective, streamlined process for keeping track of people who are here on visas. A standardized mechanism, discussed below, for submitting and processing arrival-departure forms and the mandatory registration of all foreign nationals upon arrival in the United States are reasonable points to begin the discussion.

Increasing the Effectiveness of I-94 Arrival-Departure Records

Upon arriving to a land border port of entry, CBP issues to non-U.S. citizens an immigration form to complete—either an Arrival-Departure Record (Form I-94) or a Visa Waiver Arrival-Departure Record (Form I-94W). These two forms ask for identification information and the address where the person will stay in the United States. At the port of entry, the CBP officer stamps the completed Form I-94, keeps one half, and detaches the other for the noncitizen. The I-94 sets forth the visitor's nonimmigrant status and the authorized period of stay. The visitor is required to keep the I-94 (a small white or blue card) with his passport and then return the form upon leaving the country. However, not all visitors comply with these simple procedures; some forget to return the forms or lose them, and others never leave the United States.

We believe that greater education of travelers might be helpful. Along with distributing I-94 forms, CBP could also give arriving travelers a one-page instructional pamphlet that would explain the consequences of overstaying a visa or failing to maintain lawful status. These consequences might include possible arrest and removal, and restrictions on future admissibility, including, in extreme situations, a permanent bar on reentry into the United States. The pamphlet should explain the importance of returning the I-94 as evidence of a person's timely departure from the United States and the penalties resulting from failure to comply; the pamphlets should be drafted in different languages so that a visitor from any country can understand it.

CBP should be required to maintain computer databases of the returned I-94 forms, and CBP should also be required to maintain data on persons who have failed to return the I-94 in a timely fashion. These computer databases, in turn, should be linked with databases at all ports of entry—land, air, or sea—so that all arrivals and departures can be recorded. CBP now issues electronic I-94s at air and sea ports, and we think the same strategies can be employed at these ports of entry as well. Although locating an overstayer may not be easy or quick, informing all visitors in advance of the specific consequences of an overstay should help reduce the number of those who decide to violate the terms of their temporary stay.

Registration of Foreign Nationals upon Arrival

Another way to keep track of temporary visitors and to discourage future violations might involve requiring all temporary visitors to register upon their arrival to the United States. The U.S. government is already familiar with such a registration program. In 2002 the Department of Justice created the National Security Entry-Exit Registration System (NSEERS), pursuant to INA §§ 262(a) and 263(a), to provide the federal government with records of the arrival and departure of nonimmigrant aliens from specific countries designated by the attorney general.

Under the NSEERS program male aliens over the age of seventeen from specified countries were subject to special registration, which included fingerprinting and photographing by an immigration officer at the port of entry.[33] Under the regulations the aliens subject to special registration who remained in the United States for more than thirty days had to report any status changes, such as change of address and employment, to DHS by mail or other means.[34] ICE could have also required an alien to report to one of its offices upon a ten-day notice.[35] Those who failed to register during the designated registration period could have been found removable or subject to criminal charges.[36] In 2011 DHS announced the end of the NSEERS registration process and removed the list of countries whose nationals had been subject to NSEERS registration, explaining that the registration process "ha[d] become redundant as [DHS had] strengthened security across the board, while at the same time improving and expanding existing systems to automatically and more effectively capture the same information that was being manually collected via NSEERS."[37]

The essential functions of NSEERS are now performed through the United States Visitor and Immigrant Status Indicator Technology (US-VISIT) program, launched by DHS in January 2004. The purposes of the US-VISIT program include (1) recording the arrival and departure of aliens; (2) verifying the identities of aliens; and (3) authenticating and biometrically comparing travel documents issued to non-U.S. citizens by DHS and the Department of State. Under the US-VISIT requirements, most aliens seeking admission to the United States must provide finger scans and a digital photograph at the port of entry. Currently, all non-U.S. citizens arriving at U.S. ports of entry with nonimmigrant visas are subject to US-VISIT procedures, except for Canadians applying for admission as B-1/B-2 visitors for business or pleasure and those specifically exempted.

We propose to make the US-VISIT program more effective by adding to it some of the features of the former NSEERS program, especially for nationals of certain countries who represent large numbers of visa overstayers. Under our proposed registration program every nonimmigrant—including temporary visitors—would be required to register immediately upon arrival to the United States. A nonimmigrant would fill out and submit a registration form to an appropriate agency, linked to the I-94 Arrival-Departure Record, that monitors arrivals and departures of foreign nationals. The visitor would register the physical address where he is staying and/or working while in the United States. Each time the nonimmigrant changes his address or his place of employment (if applicable), the nonimmigrant would be required to notify DHS of the change within ten days. Certain nonimmigrants and other non-U.S. citizens designated as "special registrants" under 8 C.F.R. § 264.1(f) are already required to notify USCIS of their change of address within ten business days.[38] The registration requirement should be extended to all non-U.S. citizens, regardless of country of origin and gender, but especially to nationals of certain countries. If a visitor fails to timely depart the United States, the agency would alert ICE to locate and apprehend the violator. Even if ICE does not initially locate the violator, he will be identified when he decides to leave the United States or upon his subsequent return to the United States.

The port of entry should maintain a database with information on all foreign visitors who fail to timely depart the United States. By checking the database, an inspector would notice the violation and alert security personnel to detain the departing (or arriving) visitor for further investigation and proceedings.

Registration is a good first step, but the key to an effective policy is in the follow-up. The policy must cover the person who registers initially but then overstays and takes the chance that there will be no follow-up. Some of the ways to follow up might include: (1) a requirement that employers and universities notify the government whenever an alien employee or student leaves employment or drops out of school; (2) federal withholding of a final paycheck from an alien worker's salary until the employer receives proof that the alien has left the United States; (3) withholding a student's degree or credits until the university receives proof that the alien has left the United States before visa expiration (or received evidence of lawful extension of status); (4) a search for the alien at the registered address; and (5) the placement of restrictions on a violator's future ability to receive any kind of visa or other immigration benefit. Of course, our goal is not to chill legitimate travel to the United States, and registration should be as unobtrusive as possible, but we must be explicit that we will not tolerate visa overstayers.

The Visa Security Program

The visa adjudication process is often the first opportunity that the government has to assess whether a potential visitor or immigrant presents a threat to U.S. national security. The Visa Security Program (VSP) is one of several programs that DHS has developed to improve border security and minimize international terrorism risks. The VSP is aimed at interdicting criminals, terrorists, and others who would exploit the visa process to enter the United States. The VSP relies on trained law enforcement agents to examine certain visa applicants in greater depth to assess whether those applicants pose security threats to the United States. ICE agents assigned to Visa Security Units (VSUs) are professional law enforcement agents who focus on selected applicants and their possible connection to terrorism or other criminal organizations. The professionalism and additional training ensure that the added screening mechanism is done in compliance with all state and federal laws and that there is no unlawful racial profiling.

ICE agents do not participate in all visa adjudication procedures; rather, ICE becomes a part of the process following initial screening of an applicant by Department of State consular officers. ICE special agents conduct targeted, in-depth law enforcement–focused reviews of individual visa applications and applicants prior to issuance of a visa, and they recommend refusal or revocation of applications when warranted. ICE now has fourteen high-risk visa adjudication posts in twelve countries. In 2009 ICE agents at these fourteen posts screened 904,620 visa applicants and determined that 301,700 required further review.[39] Following investigation, in collaboration with their DOS colleagues, ICE recommended refusal of over 1,000 applicants.[40]

We support the VSP program and ICE's moving forward to deploy new officers to the highest risk visa adjudicating posts worldwide.

Conclusion

While media portrayals of unauthorized immigration often consist of dramatic scenes of individuals crossing the Rio Grande, digging tunnels, and climbing fences, the truth is that nearly half of unauthorized immigrants enter the United States lawfully as temporary visitors and subsequently overstay their visas. The regulation and enforcement of the terms of nonimmigrant visas are vital to the success of U.S. immigration policy, and this key area should not be overlooked.

The United States should punish those employers who continue to employ visa overstayers, as well as those schools and universities that fail to comply with U.S. immigration laws and regulations. There should also be harsher penalties for visa overstayers themselves, as addressed more fully in chapter 9. In this chapter we have discussed other measures that may educate and thus discourage visa holders from overstaying their terms of admission.

Whatever the combination of "sticks and carrots," more needs to be done with respect to visa overstayers. Even if we build a ten-foot high, concrete, three-thousand-mile-long fence along our southern border, we will continue to have an immigration crisis if we do not discourage overstayers.

Chapter Nine
Amending the INA

Introduction

Any discussion of immigration reform should include an examination of the continued utility of the INA.[1] Passed in 1952, the INA is the principle U.S. statute dealing with immigration law.[2] We propose that simply updating two of the INA's historically important provisions, §§ 245(i) and 249, amending §§ 212(a)(9)(B) and (C), and adding a new ground of inadmissibility in § 212(a)(6) would go a very long way toward sensible long-term immigration reform. We also believe that the definition of an "aggravated felony" for immigration purposes has grown too broad, and we propose that Congress more narrowly define it in the INA.

Using Existing Provisions of the INA as Part of Comprehensive Legislation

We appreciate the reluctance of certain members of Congress to vote for a comprehensive bill that revamps our entire immigration system. One need only consider the problems associated with revamping our entire health-care framework through the Affordable Care Act. It is much easier to ask members to make necessary amendments to existing law. While we believe a comprehensive bill is the right approach, if necessary, we support separate bills that amend the INA. These changes we propose to the INA are better for the country than the status quo.

Congress has relied on the INA for over sixty years to regulate immigration, and the INA has in many ways proven to be an effective set of laws.[3] However, the INA is inconsistent in certain areas. Further, unless one practices in the area of immigration and uses the INA daily, certain provisions can appear confusing. Like many laws passed by Congress, the

INA could stand some editing for clarity. We would caution, however, against scrapping the INA entirely in favor of a new regulatory framework. A bill focused solely on our current problems may have little relevance ten or twenty years from now. Current efforts to achieve immigration reform should keep future immigration flow in mind. Amending provisions in the INA to achieve reform leaves in place a permanent set of laws that will guide immigration to the United States for years to come.

Immigration reform should, at a minimum, focus on eliminating permanent, nonwaivable bars for certain minor offenses, increasing the quotas for select family-based and nonimmigrant employment-based categories, reviving past successful provisions of the INA, such as §§ 245(i) and 249, while creating new grounds to inadmissibility that may be waived with discretion and payment of penalty fees. The reality is that there are approximately 11.5 million people unlawfully present in the United States[4] who have largely been drawn here by our insatiable economy and our long-standing tradition of allowing immigration to the United States. These factors cannot be overlooked by members of either side when considering long-term reform.

Update of INA § 245(i)

When immigrating to the United States through a family-based petition, an alien may acquire lawful permanent residency at either a U.S. consulate abroad[5] or within the United States through a procedure known as "adjustment of status" under INA § 245.[6] In fiscal year 2012 adjustment of status accounted for roughly 53 percent of all lawful immigration.[7] An alien who seeks to adjust his status in the United States, and thereby acquire LPR status, must be able to successfully clear the grounds of inadmissibility.[8]

INA § 212(a)(6)(A)(i), which makes entry without inspection and admission or parole a ground of inadmissibility, precludes adjustment of status in the United States because, with such ground of inadmissibility attached to the alien, the alien cannot successfully overcome the grounds of inadmissibility.[9] Moreover, under INA § 245(a), in order to adjust status in the United States, an alien must have been inspected and admitted[10] or paroled[11] into the United States.[12] The alien also may not be disqualified under INA § 245(c).[13]

In 1994 Congress enacted legislation that largely took the bite out of these restrictions by adding § 245(i) to the INA.[14] This new section of the INA "implicitly waived"[15] the requirement that one be "inspected and admitted or paroled" into the United States, and it made further exemptions to the § 245(c) disqualifications.[16] The § 245(i) provision was passed, in part, to raise revenue for the government and to ease the burden on U.S. consulates abroad.[17] To qualify for § 245(i) adjustment, however, the alien was required to remit a payment of $1,000 at the time of filing the application to adjust status.[18]

The original § 245(i) was scheduled to sunset on September 30, 1997, but was extended until November 26, 1997, by a series of continuing congressional resolutions.[19] Eventually, however, § 245(i) expired.[20] Nevertheless, due to its tremendous success, in 1997 Congress extended § 245(i) and added new requirements.[21] In addition to the remittance of $1,000, the alien must have been the beneficiary of a visa petition[22] or application for labor certification[23] filed on or before January 14, 1998.[24] This cutoff date, in effect, became the new sunset provision.[25]

Since § 245(i) continued to enjoy great success, Congress once again extended it in 2000 and moved the cutoff date to April 30, 2001; it also added a physical presence requirement[26] for those applicants seeking to adjust status under the new cutoff date.[27] Congress has since failed to extend INA § 245(i), and there are increasingly fewer people who can take advantage of it.[28]

Many immigration law experts view INA § 245(i) as highly efficient and successful.[29] The provision clearly eases the caseload on the already overburdened U.S. consulates abroad and, in turn, saves U.S. government resources and unnecessary expenses while increasing greater revenue for the government. The provision also eases the burden on the alien and the alien's family by avoiding a costly and unnecessary trip abroad, in addition to keeping U.S. dollars and wage-earners here in the United States. Surely our economy is better served with the § 245(i) provision than it is without it. Moreover, if an alien is substantively eligible for LPR status, it does not make much sense to force him to go through the unnecessary, burdensome, and expensive step of consular processing. Our proposed amended § 245(i) can be found in appendix 3 at the end of this book.

Update of INA § 249 ("Registry")

As an act of administrative discretion, a record of lawful admission for permanent residence may be granted to an alien if such alien (1) has not previously been admitted for permanent residence, (2) is not inadmissible under the more serious grounds of inadmissibility,[30] (3) entered the United States prior to January 1, 1972, (4) has resided continuously in the United States since such entry, (5) is a person of good moral character, (6) is not ineligible for U.S. citizenship, and (7) is not deportable under INA § 237(a)(4)(B).[31]

While the registry provision has been part of U.S. immigration law since 1929[32] and has been updated periodically by Congress,[33] recent failure to update this provision has nearly rendered this long-standing policy of U.S. immigration law obsolete.[34] To be awarded LPR status under the registry provision, an alien must have entered the United States before a certain cutoff date.[35] The current cutoff date, as amended, is January 1, 1972.[36]

Because Registry has long proven to be a fair and efficient rule of U.S. immigration law,[37] Congress should update the entry requirement[38] and further require that eligibility be determined by a fixed period of time, rather than by a certain cutoff date.[39] Congress should also impose heavy monetary fines and stringent conditions subsequent on those aliens seeking to obtain a benefit under this section.[40] Further, the alien should be required to demonstrate basic citizenship skills, such as a minimal understanding of ordinary English and a knowledge and understanding of U.S. history and government.[41] Our proposed amended § 249 can be found in appendix 4 at the end of this book; here we propose a fixed period of at least twenty-five years, along with heavy monetary fines and stringent conditions subsequent.

We note that by simply updating the registry provision, Congress could partly answer recent calls for passage of the DREAM Act.[42] One version of the DREAM Act, if passed, would provide immigration relief and LPR status to aliens who are between twelve and thirty-five at the time the law is enacted, who arrived in the United States before age sixteen, and who have resided continuously in the United States for at least five years since their arrival.[43] Under the DREAM Act if one were to consider, for example, a thirty-four-year-old alien who entered the United States at age fourteen, one might safely assume that alien must demonstrate he has resided continuously in the United States since age fourteen.[44] In effect, the alien would have to show continuous residence for the past twenty years.[45] Updating the registry provision, however, would also provide relief as long as the alien can demonstrate the requisite period of continuous residence and other requirements.[46] Nevertheless, we should be mindful that Registry would not fully provide relief to millions of undocumented youth in this country, as many youth have not yet even reached age twenty-five. This example merely demonstrates how immigration reform might overlap in areas.

In making this recommendation, we are sensitive to the valid concerns that updating the registry provision may actually encourage some undocumented immigrants to come to the United States. For this reason any updating of the registry provision should be made hand-in-hand with tougher border security measures, tougher employment sanctions, and heavy monetary fines and stringent conditions subsequent imposed on those aliens seeking to obtain a benefit under this section.

It may seem counterintuitive that while we are doing more to discourage unauthorized immigration, we simultaneously provide a pathway to lawful status for those who, in the future, will have managed to live and work undetected for a period of years. We do so because we understand the realities of immigration and the difficulties of legislative action. The truth is that, despite what Congress does to discourage unauthorized immigration, there will be some who continue to come to this country unlawfully, and a subset of those will continue to live and work undetected. Hopefully, because of the measures discussed, that number will be relatively small going forward. Rather than depending on further congressional action in the future to deal with these new undocumented immigrants, the better course may be to deal with it now once and for all by simply updating § 249. We make this recommendation because we believe Congress will undoubtedly be preoccupied with other major issues and reluctant to tackle immigration reform again in the near future until there is another immigration crisis.

Amendments to INA §§ 212(a)(6) and (9)(B) and Repeal of INA § 212(a)(9)(C)

Under INA § 212(a)(6)(A)(i) an alien who has entered the United States without inspection and admission or parole is inadmissible.[47] The law considers that alien to be continuously seeking admission every moment he is unlawfully present, and he remains inadmissible until he makes a proper entry through inspection and admission or parole.[48]

Under INA § 212(a)(9)(B), an alien who has been unlawfully present for a period of more than 180 days, but less than one year, and then departs the United States, is inadmissible for three years.[49] Moreover, an alien who has been unlawfully present for one year or more and then departs the United States is inadmissible for ten years.[50] The INA allows for a waiver of § 212(a)(9)(B) inadmissibility in § 212(a)(9)(B)(v).[51] An alien who is the spouse or son or daughter of a U.S. citizen or an LPR may be granted a waiver if refusal would result in extreme hardship to the intending immigrant's citizen or LPR spouse or parent.[52]

Under INA § 212(a)(9)(C), an alien who has been unlawfully present in the United States for an aggregate period of more than one year or has been previously ordered removed, and who then enters or attempts to enter without inspection and admission or parole, is inadmissible.[53] This ground of inadmissibility will not apply if the alien is seeking admission more than ten years after having triggered the ground and is granted consent to reapply for admission.[54] The § 212(a)(9)(C) ground of inadmissibility is largely meant to punish recidivist behavior, i.e., those repeat violators of the immigration laws.[55] With these few basic provisions of inadmissibility in mind,[56] we now turn to a discussion of our recommended amendments to INA §§ 212(a)(6) and (9)(B) and the repeal of INA § 212(a)(9)(C).

Amendment to INA § 212(a)(6)

Presently, there is no ground of inadmissibility for the alien who enters the United States unlawfully and remains for 180 days or less prior to departure[57] nor is there a ground of inadmissibility for the alien who enters lawfully and subsequently overstays for 180 days or less prior to departure.[58] In effect, these aliens get a free pass for their unlawful behavior.[59]

Moreover, an immediate relative alien[60] who enters the United States lawfully and subsequently overstays (regardless of duration) or otherwise violates the terms of admission can nevertheless adjust his status in the United States under § 245(a) despite being subject to removal under § 237(a)(1)(C)(i).[61] We propose a new ground of inadmissibility that imposes a civil monetary fine, with limited exceptions, to address these immigration violators.

Our proposed new ground of inadmissibility, INA § 212(a)(6)(H), can be found in appendix 5 at the end of this book. Under this new ground of inadmissibility, our proposed § 212(a)(6)(H) "Civil Monetary Fine," any alien present or previously present in the United States unlawfully shall be inadmissible until such alien remits to the government a fine of $1,000. We specifically note that the proposed ground of inadmissibility is not limited to just those who enter unlawfully but would also attach to those who enter lawfully with a nonimmigrant visa and then overstay or otherwise violate the conditions of their stay.[62] Remittance of the $1,000 fine would not confer any lawful status to an alien; rather, the fine would be required as part of such alien's application for adjustment to LPR status or for an immigrant or nonimmigrant visa. In other words, an alien subject to § 212(a)(6)(H) would still have to otherwise qualify for adjustment of status under §§ 245(a) or (i) or for an immigrant or nonimmigrant visa. We believe that remittance of the fine will serve not only as a punishment to violators but also as a deterrence to further violations.

Amendment to INA § 212(a)(9)(B) and Repeal of INA § 212(a)(9)(C)

We believe that the permanent ground of inadmissibility found in INA § 212(a)(9)(C) is overly harsh and contributes to unauthorized immigration. Under the government's interpretation of § 212(a)(9)(C), an infant brought unlawfully into the United States on as few as two occasions is permanently inadmissible.[63] This sort of extreme position is reason without compassion and needlessly breaks up families. Moreover, the government holds the view that INA § 212(a)(9)(C) trumps § 245(i), thereby decreasing the use of the latter.[64] We believe that § 212(a)(9)(C) should no longer be an impediment to lawful immigration. Consequently, we propose that § 212(a)(9)(B) be modified and altered to absorb some of the provisions of § 212(a)(9)(C) and that Congress strike § 212(a)(9)(C) altogether.[65] Our proposed amended §§ 212(a)(9)(B) and (C) can be found in appendix 6.

Stateside Waiver

The waiver authorized at INA § 212(a)(9)(B)(v) requires most aliens to return to their home country in order to enter the United States lawfully.[66] This is because a ground of inadmissibility attaches to an immigrant who has entered the United States unlawfully without inspection and admission or parole.[67] In particular, the alien must leave the United States, file a visa application with the embassy or consulate in the alien's home country—and seek a waiver—and then wait in the home country for approval before lawful admittance can occur.[68] While some view this requirement as a formality to lawful admission, others see it as another unnecessary hurdle for aliens seeking lawful permanent residency in the United States.[69] Part of the opposition comes from the fact that returning to the country of origin and seeking a waiver abroad can take months or even years, which creates a serious burden on immigrants with families lawfully present in the United States.

We applaud the recent passage of the stateside waiver regulation, which allows "certain immediate relatives of U.S. citizens who are physically present in the United States to request provisional unlawful presence waivers prior to departing from the United States for consular processing of their visa applications."[70] The purpose of the regulation is to reduce the length of time that U.S. citizens are separated from their foreign national immediate relatives who pursue consular processing abroad.[71] In addition, we believe that the new regulation makes consular processing more efficient for both the U.S. government and most waiver applicants.[72]

Amend the Definition of "Aggravated Felony"

The 1996 immigration reforms expanded the definition of "conviction" to include an extensive list of offenses that trigger removal.[73] Under the INA simple misdemeanors can be classified as aggravated felonies,[74] and the categories of offenses that subject a noncitizen to deportation do not always correspond with the criminal codes in various states.[75] For example, two convictions for turnstile jumping can subject an LPR to deportation.[76] Considering the extreme consequences for such minor offenses, a separate criminal code arguably exists for immigration purposes, one that labels misdemeanor convictions as "aggravated felonies."[77] An immigrant convicted of an aggravated felony is automatically deportable and ineligible for most relief (such as cancellation of removal or asylum).[78]

The recent Supreme Court case of *Carachuri-Rosendo v. Holder* illustrates the onerous effects of expanding the definition of "aggravated felony." In this case, the government argued that an LPR who had received "only a 10-day sentence for his Texas misdemeanor simple possession offense" was an "aggravated felon" for purposes of the immigration laws.[79] According to the government, the mere possibility of the defendant receiving a two-year sentence in a federal trial based on the fact of his prior simple possession offense labeled the alien as one "convicted of an aggravated felony," making him ineligible for any relief from deportation. [80] The Court rejected this argument as an "unorthodox" interpretation of offenses that qualify as aggravated felonies.[81] Although Congress "has the power to give words unorthodox meanings," the meaning of the statutory language should still comply with plain English.[82] The Court resolved a conflict among federal courts of appeal regarding whether subsequent simple possession offenses are aggravated felonies.[83] The fact that there was such a conflict indicates that the INA definition of "aggravated felony" is inconsistent with the common understanding of the term and needs reform.

Presumably, this disparate treatment of noncitizen offenders is designed to discourage and further punish bad behavior. In reality, the unorthodox definition of "aggravated felony" in the INA produces highly unfair and inconsistent results. Hopefully, we all agree that our government should be consistent in the administration of our immigration laws. Congress should amend the INA definition to conform to the common understanding of the term, as reflected in federal and state criminal codes. For example, Congress could add to the current definition of "aggravated felony" a requirement that such a conviction must be a felony conviction, for which a convicted noncitizen might serve a sentence of at least one year.[84] This requirement will prevent treatment of misdemeanor convictions as aggravated felonies under the INA and ensure that only noncitizens who face a sentence of one year or more for a felony conviction suffer the harsh consequences attached to an aggravated felony conviction.[85]

Invisible Fence

Although it is important to discourage violations of our laws, fines and other similar penalties are somewhat limited as deterrents. Many immigrants are either unaware of or not bothered by such sanctions. Some who are seeking a better life, convinced that the opportunities America affords are worth the risk, are likely to be undeterred by these sorts of measures. In light of the limited deterrent effect, it is important to recognize that one purpose of reform is to allow a measure of relief in extreme cases for the most sympathetic and deserving undocumented immigrants.

Nevertheless, tougher penalties and comprehensive reform of the INA will help to create a "virtual border," or an "invisible fence" to complement the existing physical barriers that we already have in place. If intending immigrants know that we seriously enforce our immigration laws, and that there are consequences to immigration violations, then this knowledge itself becomes a barrier to surreptitious entries and visa overstays. If, on the other hand, intending immigrants believe that we will not seriously enforce our immigration laws, the result will be a continued strain on border and interior enforcement.[86] This virtual border will supplement the current physical borders and lessen the need for additional structures. As stated, the solution does not lie solely with additional physical barriers. Simply amending the INA could go a long way toward accomplishing the goal of securing our borders. The United States is a beacon of hope, and there will always be people in other countries who want to migrate here. If necessary, some of these people will come unlawfully. It is difficult to anticipate future burdens on our immigration policy, but sensible amendments to the INA will help better prepare us to face these burdens.

Conclusion

As we contemplate major revisions to address our current immigration challenges, we should also be forward thinking and anticipate future challenges. These simple amendments to the INA could potentially provide other forms of immigration relief to hundreds of thousands of people unlawfully present in the United States. This, in turn, would bring people who qualify out of the shadows, giving them lawful status and providing further security for our country in a post-9/11 world. These simple amendments also address the very real humanitarian crisis within the United States and the pressing need for immigration reform.

Given the current political climate, it is unlikely that Congress will pass a comprehensive immigration bill. Consequently, we will continue to have undocumented immigrants living and working in the United States. Over time, those numbers will grow, and we will once again need Congress to do what it has already shown itself to be incapable of doing—passing comprehensive legislation. Although we prefer that the amendments to the INA proposed in this chapter be included in a comprehensive bill, we would welcome these amendments in any legislation. We strongly support these changes to the INA that should allow our government to better deal with current and future immigration challenges administratively.

Chapter Ten
Dealing with the Children of Unauthorized Immigrants beyond High School

Introduction

The reasons that immigrants come to America are as varied as their countries of origin. Many immigrants bring with them strong work ethics, skills, hope, and often, their children. Many children enter on temporary visas that expire or with their parents without inspection. Regardless of how they enter, these undocumented children have no control over their original and resulting immigrant status in this country—and more importantly they are often powerless as to their own futures.[1] These children are the focus of this chapter.

The Dilemma

There are an estimated eleven million undocumented immigrants present in the United States[2] and an estimated one million undocumented minors.[3] These children are faced with a dilemma: primed to thrive after receiving a K–12 education,[4] they are stopped short of fulfilling their potential. Undocumented students are ineligible to work, to serve in the military, or to qualify for in-state college tuition in most states.[5] There are an estimated sixty-five thousand undocumented students graduating from American high schools every year who find themselves in difficult situations because of their unlawful status.[6] We do not believe that young children should be burdened by the sins of their parents. Sound immigration reform should seriously consider a comprehensive solution that would allow these children to achieve lawful status, providing them with an opportunity to achieve their goals of becoming productive members of American society.

Deferred Action for Childhood Arrivals (DACA)

On June 15, 2012, President Barack Obama signed an executive order providing "deferred action" to many immigrants brought to the United States as children who meet certain specific requirements.[7] Specifically, individuals are eligible for deferred action if they:

- Came to the United States before their 16th birthday;
- Were under age 31 and had no valid immigration status on June 15, 2012;
- Have continuously resided in the United States between June 15, 2007, and the present;
- Are currently in school, graduated from high school, obtained a GED, or were honorably discharged from the Armed Forces;
- Have not been convicted of a felony, a "significant" misdemeanor, or three or more other misdemeanors, and do not otherwise pose a threat to national security or public safety.[8]

The program involves prosecutorial discretion with regards to deferring removal actions against an individual.[9] USCIS is tasked with reviewing each request for a determination of whether deferred action should be granted. If deferred, the individual will not be removed from the United States "for a two year period, subject to renewal, and may also receive employment authorization."[10] Importantly, the deferred-action process does not place an individual on a track to LPR status.

While many saw the order as a win for immigrant rights, the law did little as a long-term solution. In fact, DACA found considerable opposition following its signing.[11] On August 15, 2012, Arizona Governor Jan Brewer signed her own executive order, instructing state agencies that President Obama's order did not grant lawful status and that DACA immigrants in Arizona should not be granted driver's licenses or other state-funded benefits and services.[12] Governors from other states followed Governor Brewer's actions.[13] Furthermore, the U.S. Department of Health and Human Services, Centers for Medicare & Medicaid Services issued a letter to state health and Medicaid directors, echoing the notion that individuals who receive deferred action remain ineligible for certain state-funded benefits and services.[14]

We should also point out that deferred action, in essence, is merely a form of prosecutorial discretion. The government takes the position that it will defer taking action against an individual for now. In other words, the government chooses not to apply the immigration laws to remove an individual. Congress has granted this discretion to the executive branch for a number of reasons—limited resources, humanitarian factors, government interest, etc. The danger with taking this sort of executive action on a large scale is that it severely undermines the laws we have in place to regulate immigration, thereby undermining Congressional authority. Another danger, when taken on a scale as large as DACA, is that the rule of law is threatened and outside pressures, whether innocent or not, immediately begin to test and strain the existing legal framework. President Obama's order creating DACA has encouraged a mass influx of undocumented immigrant children at our southern border. This not only dramatically increases costs and burdens to the American taxpayers, it also handicaps our border agents and jeopardizes our national security.

Additionally, while DACA proposes to help the children of immigrants, the fact remains that it is simply an executive order subject to revocation by the next president or by a subsequent Congressional statute. What would occur in the future if the order were revoked? Admittedly, revocation would be rare, as history has shown that presidents tend to leave executive orders on controversial political topics alone. Nevertheless, revocation could leave millions of DACA-registered immigrants subject to immediate removal. A permanent legislative solution is the better course to take. If our previous proposals fail to adequately address the undocumented youth in this country, we propose a program similar to the DREAM Act—but with sufficient differences to warrant serious consideration for passage into law.

Identifying the Participants

In order to facilitate a successful program to benefit undocumented youth, we must identify them, establish bright-line eligibility requirements, and enforce strong penalties for violation of the program.

The identification of these young people is paramount. Generally, these children have been raised in the shadows, their parents attempting to avoid detection, apprehension, and detention. The key to success will be establishing a program to entice undocumented youth to come forward, enroll, and begin taking affirmative steps toward lawful residency. Another benefit is enhanced security through mass registration. The government must be prepared for the massive number of people who may come forward. Reports from government agencies showed small numbers trickling in after DACA was signed, with many people awaiting the outcome of the presidential election. With President Obama's re-election, the agencies handling DACA applicants have been inundated and are facing personnel and budget shortages.[15] This situation calls for organization and streamlining of the process so as not to overwhelm governmental resources and add to further immigration chaos.

Some parameters will need to be established. For example, Congress might decide that in order to be eligible, young undocumented immigrants need to have been present for at least five years prior to passage of the proposed legislation and to have entered into this country before age fourteen or fifteen perhaps. The program should be open to all undocumented individuals who satisfy the eligibility requirements, and Congress might decide that in order to be eligible applicants may not yet have reached a particular age, maybe as low as twenty-one or as high as twenty-five (or whatever age Congress deems most appropriate). We believe that Congress should impose an age limit that reflects a clear expression of legislation aimed for the benefit of children. While some may consider this sort of approach to be unduly harsh, especially when considering that many young people have simply aged-out by becoming young adults, we take the position that a line must be drawn somewhere, and that line is best drawn at an appropriate age of accountability.

At some point, a person's continued unlawful presence in this country is no longer "innocent," and the child who becomes a young adult and who continues to disregard U.S. immigration laws is arguably no longer innocent. For purposes of illustration, a well-known immigrant advocate and Pulitzer Prize winning journalist, who is also unlawfully present in the United States, has challenged us to "define American" as part of his advocacy campaign on behalf of undocumented immigrants.[16] We do not believe that this advocate remains innocent in his continued violations of our immigration laws.

This advocate has had job offers and employment with leading publications in the United States such as the *San Francisco Chronicle*, the *Phila-*

delphia Daily News, the *Washington Post*, and the *Huffington Post*.[17] With a job offer from any one of these news agencies, he could seek a temporary employment-based visa. It is true that he would be required to leave the United States, and, upon departure, he would be subject to a ten-year period of inadmissibility.[18] This advocate, however, could seek a waiver of inadmissibility under INA § 212(d)(3), and the BIA has set a pretty low standard to be used when adjudicating these waivers.

As set forth in *Matter of Hranka*, the determining criteria when seeking a 212(d)(3) waiver are: (1) the risk of harm to society if the applicant is admitted; (2) the seriousness of the applicant's prior immigration or criminal law violations; and (3) the reasons for wishing to enter the United States.[19] Most people would probably agree that individuals such as this advocate pose little risk of harm to society, that his prior immigration violations resulted largely in part from having been brought here as a child, and that his reasons for wishing to enter the United States are legitimate (and that the United States is arguably better served by adding a journalist of his caliber and background). Rather than seek a waiver, this immigrant advocate, instead, appears to be asking us to embrace a definition of the term "American" that he endorses so that he is neither inconvenienced nor put at risk by having to travel abroad and seek a waiver of a violation that is only counted against him because he chose to violate our immigration laws as an adult.[20] Respectfully, individuals such as this educated professional are no longer innocent in their continual violation of our immigration laws. The recommendations set out in this chapter with respect to undocumented children are not intended to apply to such individuals. To do so would be inconsistent with American values of fairness, accountability, and respect for the rule of law.

The Proposed Plan

Eligible youths should be afforded the opportunity to acquire a temporary status that operates on a graduated scale. Undocumented students still receiving a K–12 education would be afforded temporary status and allowed to establish residency within their domicile state for the purposes of college tuition and would later be eligible for enlistment in the military under our proposal (so long as they otherwise qualify for military service). Other similarly situated undocumented youth not enrolled in school would be given temporary status upon enrollment in a K–12 institution leading to a high school diploma or General Educational Development (GED) program. Upon high school graduation or completion of an approved GED program, the temporary status would unlock doors that could eventually lead to U.S. nationality (as discussed previously). The student should first be required to pursue a bachelor's degree, vocational or technical school training, or enlist in the military. Those young people who have not yet aged-out, and who have already obtained a high school diploma or GED, would also be required to pursue a bachelor's degree, vocational or technical school training, or enlist in the military.

It is impossible to present a situation that would result in guaranteed successful attainment of lawful status. There will be those undocumented people who simply do not complete the process and who will find themselves in violation of the plan. For the success of the program, appropriate measures must be taken against those individuals who violate the program. Those found in violation of the program should be fined, stripped of their lawful status, and subject to removal. Included with this caveat, of course, are the INA § 237 grounds of removal for criminal and other offenses.

Education

Undocumented students may continue under conditional temporary lawful status if they pursue accredited higher education. Students should be allowed to pursue any area of approved study. Maintenance of temporary status would require successful completion of a full-time course load, as defined by the school. The temporary lawful status would be lost if at any point the student dropped out or failed to enroll for a new semester (absent exceptional circumstances). Once his education was successfully completed, however, the student, now a graduate, would be eligible to apply for U.S. nationality.

Obviously, this proposal is not without its flaws or opposition. The question of education for undocumented students has been hotly debated for years. As discussed earlier, in 1982 the Supreme Court decided that each state is required to educate all children within its borders from K–12.[21] That decision was based in part on the reasoning that at least some of the undocumented students will eventually acquire lawful status and an educated person is more likely to be a productive person, contribute to society, and not be a burden on welfare programs.

This reasoning is still true today; what has changed is the standard associated with the idea of an "educated person." According to the National Center for Educational Statistics, the average salary for a graduate of a high school education or the equivalent in the 1980s was in the range of $40,000. This level of compensation for a high school graduate allowed for self-sufficiency; however, this figure and its reasoning need to be revisited. In the current trend the average income for a high school graduate in 2009 was $32,000, compared to the average income of $51,000 for the holder of a bachelor's degree. This discrepancy points out the difficulty posed to the high school graduate who does not attend a college or university. Couple this hardship with the lack of work authorization in the United States, and undocumented students face a bleak future.

Continued education poses an opportunity to address both issues facing undocumented students without massive change or overhauling the immigration system. Currently the biggest hurdle for undocumented students to enter a university is the financial burden. Many discover that they do not meet the residency requirements to qualify for in-state tuition, which can multiply the cost of attending a college or university by three or four times. To combat this issue, there is a trend among the states that addresses the in-state residency requirements. Beginning with Texas in 2001, and followed shortly by California, thirteen states have created legislation that allows undocumented students to meet residency requirements, changing the qualifications from requiring "legal presence" to requiring successful (in-state) high school completion.[22] In contrast, only five states have specifically barred undocumented students from receiving in-state tuition by requiring that applicants be lawfully present in the United States to qualify. The one hybrid state is Oklahoma, which reverted back to not allowing in-state tuition for undocumented students but did leave a provision that allows Oklahoma State University to admit undocumented students if they meet certain criteria.[23]

Not to be discounted are the opponents who believe that tax dollars and educational incentives should be spent on poor and deserving U.S. citizens rather than undocumented immigrants. Many times, however, these students are indistinguishable from their American counterparts.

They are all but American citizens with the exception of lawful status. Some incredibly bright students have worked their way through the American educational system, and the system itself suffers if the best and the brightest are kept from completing and realizing their goals. American citizens should have the first opportunity at proposed funding, but undocumented students should also have access, with their funding tied to specific restrictions and requirements. In the end, with a better educated immigrant community, we all stand to benefit.

Military Service

Continued conditional lawful status should also be granted to those who choose military service. This status is conditioned on successful assimilation into the military and satisfactory completion of one's duties and responsibilities within the military. As with the educational path, the conditional lawful status would be lost if at any point the service member was discharged before completion of his term of service. Essentially, these soldiers would be required, like all soldiers, to follow their orders and meet the missions and objectives of the military. After completing four years of service, or honorable discharge by the military, the previously undocumented youth would then be eligible to apply for U.S. nationality.

There are few better ways of showing one's patriotism and love for this great country than through military service. Currently, one of the basic requirements for enlistment in the military, and rightfully so, is citizenship or lawful status within our country.[24] The type of proposed program we present here offers a rare "win-win-win" situation. Military recruitment receives a much needed boost since it could take advantage of an untapped market full of valuable human resources already present in the United States. Undocumented students are afforded the significant opportunity to earn lawful status on their own merits and service. Finally, the United States can seek to ameliorate a perpetual lower class of people relegated to the shadows of this country. No approach, however, is without concern. Some have voiced reservations about a form of dilution within the military ranks, or the appearance of outsourcing military forces, and the actual ability to facilitate such a program. Although valid concerns, they are short-lived when we examine the history and current practices of the military as it pertains to noncitizen members.

The presence of immigrants within our military has deep historical roots.[25] Statistics show that foreign-born residents have served in our military since the Revolutionary War.[26] Noncitizens provide a significant number of the service-men and -women in our military today, with about thirty-five thousand noncitizens serving.[27] Our military is representative of the American population,[28] a mixture of all races, religions, creeds, sexual orientations, and even some countries.[29] The military not only identifies with its diversity but recognizes diversity as a future necessity; it recruits to satisfy its diversity needs.[30] Allowing the military access to the approximately sixty-five thousand undocumented students who graduate from high school each year would not only assist the military in its diversity objectives but would also help with recruiting in general.[31]

While striving for a "melting pot" military, the appearance of an "outsourced" military force remains a potential issue. According to a 2010 Department of Defense report, the military is comprised of 3,697,646 members.[32] As previously stated, approximately thirty-five thousand currently serving members are noncitizens. The proposed undocumented students who would be eligible to enlist in the military would certainly raise the number of foreign-born service members. For illustrative purposes, assume that 100 percent of the undocumented students in a given year opted for the path provided by the military. The influx of new recruits would bring the total immigrant military population to one hundred thousand— or 2.7 percent of the current military force. This is still a far cry from having a military force largely composed of "outsourced" noncitizens.[33]

Proposing that the military be part of a program to implement a legalization program may appear to be dumping a social issue into the military machine; however, the military has previously established programs that expedite the immigration process available to noncitizens who are currently serving.[34] The assistance does not stop at the service member either, as there are also assistance programs for situations in which a soldier marries an alien who then requires lawful status to enter the country. The military has a program designed to assist in the immigration process for these spouses and new family members.[35] This familiarity with the immigration process makes the military a logical choice for undocumented youth seeking lawful status. The infrastructure of the program is already present since the military currently assists both service members and their families to obtain lawful status and naturalization. The only roadblock to the undocumented student today is the lack of lawful status in order to apply to the military.[36] A policy that furthers temporary lawful status upon graduation or obtaining a GED would allow undocumented youth to enlist in the military and utilize the options available to immigrants already serving in our military.

Most of the discussion thus far has considered how we should help the undocumented youth, but why should we want to help them, aside from having a better-educated immigrant community? Frankly, the military enlistment and recruitment numbers have dwindled considerably over the years as many Americans would rather serve their country in alternate ways. The need for a strong and formidable military presence is necessary to maintain our role as a superpower. By opening up this previously untapped channel to allow the military to approach the undocumented sector, the American people, the undocumented youth, and the military all gain a huge benefit. Undocumented youth carry strong ties to the United States, the country they consider home. They are essential in the areas of diversity, as well as linguistics, and their presence is an asset in our military's expanded global presence.[37] After four years of service, or upon honorable discharge, the individual would have earned the right to apply for U.S. nationality.

Conclusion

For many of the children brought here unlawfully by their parents, America is the only home they have ever known. Their language, values, and culture are as American as any child born in this country. Our sense of fairness tells us that children should not be punished for the wrongs of their parents. We agree with many of the proposals to provide a pathway to lawful status for qualified children. We have young, aspiring, hardworking people who would like to be a part of our society. Largely, they want to go to school, serve in the military, and pursue the American dream. By providing a path for worthy undocumented young people, we are able to aid our military and further educate our present populace. Accomplishments in both areas would lead to the infusion of new life into our economy, which is a benefit to all Americans.

We appreciate the concern some may have that by legalizing these children we are rewarding the unlawful actions of their parents. We believe, on balance, that some type of legalization for these children is the fairest approach. We would, however, support measures to deny these children, should they ever become naturalized, the right to petition for legalization of their parents who violated our immigration laws, and we would point out that pursuant to BIA precedent decisions a U.S. national cannot file an immigrant petition for a parent. (See previous discussion on U.S. nationality in chapter 5.)

We do not advocate that these children should be given a pathway to citizenship, but neither do we argue that they should not be afforded that opportunity. However, we are reminded that individuals who are educated or who sacrifice by serving in our military are precisely the type of people all of us should want as fellow citizens. If we do not address the issue of their immigration status now, we will certainly have to address it in the future.

Chapter Eleven
Mexico's Impact

Introduction

Given the current state of our economy, it is no secret that many Americans are looking for a solution to combat the nation's influx of undocumented immigrants. Americans are looking for ways to preserve jobs and limit the use of taxpayer dollars. Unauthorized immigration is a hindrance to these goals. Proposed solutions to the immigration problem have ranged from two extremes: the mass legalization of the millions already present within the United States[1] or their mass removal.[2] Imagine the social and economic costs that either one of these extremes would have on our already troubled economy. The most successful solution lies somewhere between these extremes.

Improved immigration policies and collaboration with Mexico's government are certainly needed, and the United States should, if possible, focus on how to better assist Mexico in improving its social conditions. Given that the United States is currently dealing with its own economic challenges, we appreciate the political realities of advocating for more direct economic assistance. On the other hand, since most undocumented immigrants travel to the United States in hopes of finding better economic and social conditions, it follows that any solution to our immigration problem will require attention to Mexico's economic problems and to a lesser degree conditions in Central American countries.

It is certainly not our responsibility to "fix" Mexico's troubles; however, unauthorized immigration is a huge American problem, and the only way to fix a problem of this magnitude is to discover and deal with the root issues. After all, Mexico has little incentive to stop its poor and improverished populations—potential wards of the state—from migrating to the

United States. Addressing these issues will require the United States to analyze the role that we may have played, if any, in Mexico's current economic and social state. Have U.S. policies directly or indirectly harmed Mexico's economy? What steps can we take to foster growth in Mexico's economy? Have U.S. gun policies led to an increase in Mexican crime? Has U.S. demand for drugs led to Mexico's current social turmoil? Perhaps most important, how can the United States help address these issues while fully respecting Mexican sovereignty? The remainder of this chapter will address these controversial questions and propose possible solutions.

But first, it is important to note that Mexico's problems are deeply rooted and, in our opinion, require fundamental institutional changes that will take time. Addressing issues of this magnitude requires long-term solutions and long-term commitment. While this may be unappealing to confront, the reality may well be much worse and much more difficult to reverse if we fail to accomplish lasting reform. The United States must demonstrate patience and resolve on this issue for the sake of both countries. The American people may resist the changes necessary, but America's leaders must commit to long-term thinking and explain why our efforts with Mexico are good for America. Additionally, our political leadership will have to be tactful when dealing with Mexico. Our southern neighbor is a sovereign nation and rightfully proud of its heritage and nationality. Blatant demands for institutional reform by outsiders will most certainly fall on deaf ears. We must keep in mind that some of Mexico's problems are, unfortunately, to some degree our problems, and likewise what is in Mexico's best economic interest is also usually in America's best interest.

NAFTA

NAFTA was formed in 1994 with great aspirations. The treaty's goal was to benefit the economies of the United States, Canada, and Mexico by eliminating trade barriers and encouraging investment between the countries. NAFTA has succeeded in some respects, but the overall impact on the Mexican economy has been less than desirable. It has been over twenty years since the treaty was signed, and Mexico still has the lowest economic growth of the three countries.[3]

It is arguable that the treaty has caused more harm than good within

Mexico. Prior to NAFTA Mexico experienced a higher employment rate and the average Mexican citizen was able to support his family and make an honest living. After NAFTA many businesses and investors fled the Mexican economy and exploited the new trade and investment opportunities that NAFTA permitted. Due to lack of investment within the Mexican economy, there were fewer jobs available and the ones remaining supplied lower wages. As a result, Mexico had fewer jobs and too many workers vying for those positions.

There are differing theories as to the role that NAFTA played in the decline of Mexico's economy. Another possible factor is the peso crisis of the mid-1990s. NAFTA certainly was not the cause of the peso crisis; however, NAFTA did nothing to alleviate the strains that Mexico was experiencing.[4] Poor Mexican citizens have been harmed the most, particularly those lacking formal training or education. These citizens have found it difficult to find jobs that would allow them to take care of their families. The free trade that NAFTA allowed resulted in the decrease of agricultural prices.[5] In certain areas post-NAFTA agricultural prices fell below farmers' production costs.[6]

All of these factors likely contributed to the dangerous challenges present in Mexico. This new economic situation, according to many experts, has made Mexico a breeding ground for drug lords and other organized crime leaders. Due to the living conditions and the lack of safe jobs, many Mexican citizens fled the country in hopes of finding a better life. Nearly twenty years after NAFTA, the United States has an imperfect immigration problem. Assuming that any of the theories regarding NAFTA are true, there is not much the United States can immediately do. There is no quick fix to Mexico's economic problems, and given the fact that our country is in the middle of its own economic problems, we are unlikely to have the solutions or resources to assist Mexico in any meaningful way. The United States must address its own challenges before attempting to provide meaningful assistance to another country.

The Role of the United States

By helping to address the job and safety issues facing poor and middle-class Mexican citizens, the United States would decrease the number of undocumented immigrants crossing our southern border. Families would be able to reunite within their own countries and not have to seek safety and better job opportunities in the United States. However, the question of how to address these issues remains. Drug-related violence in Mexico is an enormous problem for both countries.

Most undocumented immigrants who come to the United States from Mexico seek job opportunities in hopes of a brighter future for themselves and their children. Nevertheless, the tendency of drug-related violence to exacerbate and perpetuate poor economic conditions cannot be discounted. Nevertheless, the inverse is almost certainly also true, that is, poor economic conditions tend to cause increased vulnerability to drug-related violence. It may be impossible to isolate one condition as the cause of the other. It is therefore apparent that our countries must work together to improve Mexico's economic situation as a goal in and of itself. The resulting conclusion is that to address Mexico's impact on America's immigration problem, the efforts of the United States should be deployed on two fronts: the war on drugs and the Mexican domestic economy.

The Mexican domestic economy suffered unanticipated losses as a result of NAFTA, particularly in the agricultural sector.[7] Consequently, Mexico's economy is largely dependent on the United States.[8] The United States receives the vast majority of Mexico's exports. The Mexican agricultural sector needs help from the United States as a starting point in the effort to aid the Mexican economy. Although Mexico's agricultural sector has enjoyed a recent resurgence and the Mexican economy is growing,[9] many believe that further assistance is needed. One way to do this is through immigration reform that legalizes at least a portion of those currently in the United States unlawfully. This might allow such persons to get better jobs in the United States and enable them to send more money to their families in Mexico.[10] Another area that offers potential for Mexican economic growth is the energy sector.[11] Foreign investment in Mexico's potentially robust energy sector could provide the boost that Mexico needs to continue its recent economic growth. Such solutions in the energy sector are largely beyond the reach of American policy, but we should consider any possible investment in Mexico's economy as an investment in our own future.

Crime

Initially, we propose that we focus on creating and improving programs that address the criminal activities that plague Mexico and spill over into the United States. In particular, we should develop additional programs that target the cartels, illegal guns, and drugs. It is no secret that the driving forces behind practically all violence, whether at the border or within Mexico, are drugs and guns. We must improve our partnership with Mexican authorities to help deter crime. It is in our own self-interest to help when we can. The United States should start by further collaborating with the Mexican government to create a database that would allow for the identification, detection, and punishment of various criminals.

The United States currently assists Mexico in its fight against Mexican crime by providing access to American resources, assets, training, and intelligence techniques. We should continue to provide any information and resources that would help the Mexican government in its efforts to take back its country, while continuing to respect Mexican sovereignty. Our goal should simply be to help Mexico by continuing to work with the Mexican government and by educating officials on how to carry out better crime detection and enforcement operations.

The United States should be open to sharing all basic information that may be helpful in detecting and deterring the criminal activity abundant in Mexico, provided this sharing does not harm our national security. If officials tasked with national security fear that sharing will leave our country exposed, then the United States and Mexico should jointly create new methods for crime detection tailored for Mexico. Currently, U.S. intelligence analysts are working to eliminate cartel violence along the southern border, and U.S. liaison officers are working with Mexican law enforcement to investigate and prevent crime and to plan operations.[12]

These current collaborations with the Mexican government have been beneficial, but for order to be restored to Mexico and for the undocumented immigrants to return to Mexico, there must be a long-term, collaborative relationship between our countries. One of the largest obstacles to restoring order to Mexico is finding a way to deal with corrupt Mexican officials who shirk their duty to protect Mexico's citizens and businesses. The United States has had, and unfortunately will contiune to have, its own share of public corruption. Nevertheless, the situation in Mexico is even more serious. As long as Mexican officials capitulate to threats of violence and remain susceptible to bribery, the Mexican government will remain in a battle of control with the drug lords. Fortunately, Mexico has begun steps to reform its correctional and judicial systems. The United States has supported Mexico by helping them develop new training, detection, and enforcement programs to help uncover dishonest officials who have fallen victim to the intense pressures of the drug lords. These officials need to be separated from their offices because they pose a security risk to all who are involved in the removal of the drug lords.

Currently, the United States and Mexico have joined forces to combat organized crime and related violence through the Merida Initiative.[13] The Merida Initiative, which has been in existence since 2008, has four main objectives: (1) the disruption of organized criminal groups, (2) strengthening institutions, (3) building a twenty-first-century border, and (4) building strong and resilient communities.[14] In addition to reform support, the United States has also provided helicopters and a variety of inspection equipment.[15] This partnership between the United States and Mexico has strengthened the relationship between the two countries.

Illegal Guns

Guns have always been a large component of the violence and terror that is rampant within Mexico. Again, this is another area where Mexico believes that the United States shares some responsibility. Mexicans see American gun laws as effectively arming traffickers, while the Second Amendment to our Constitution, which provides for the right of U.S. citizens to bear arms, is widely treasured by many Americans. Any attempt to pass legislation in the United States pertaining to guns is met with intense scrutiny and resistance. Debate on the gun control issue has been building in the United States as a result of the terrible tragedies of the last several years. That debate is now raging after the massacre of twenty-six people, including twenty children, in Newtown, Connecticut. President Obama responded by issuing twenty-three executive orders aimed at curbing gun violence in America.[16] The response, in turn, has been passionate from supporters and detractors alike, and the issue still dominates news reporting today. This subject matter is more controversial now than ever, but gun violence is an issue that we cannot ignore in considering Mexico's impact on our immigration problems.

Each year thousands of guns are trafficked illegally across our southern border from the United States into Mexico. Today, a background check is required only for those transactions involving a federally licensed firearms dealer. If the seller is not a federally licensed dealer, then no background check is required in connection with a gun sale. Many of the guns trafficked into Mexico are purchased at U.S. gun shows along the southern border. At these gun shows an individual can purchase a weapon from a private seller without undergoing a background check. This enables criminals to purchase weapons and traffic them into Mexico. Furthermore, some criminals are using "straw purchasers" to acquire weapons for them from federally licensed dealers.

It is estimated that only 60 percent of firearms transactions in the United States involve a background check.[17] While we fully support individual rights to bear arms under the Second Amendment, we believe in responsible gun ownership, and we support increasing the number of background checks for businesses and individuals who sell firearms at gun shows and over the Internet. We do not favor requiring background checks for private sales or gifts between relatives. The National Rifle Association once supported expanded background checks, and its members should get behind it again.

Improved technology makes background checks more efficient and less burdensome, even for sales at one-day gun shows. We already require background checks on a majority of firearms transactions, so increasing the number of eligible transactions that would qualify for background checks would almost certainly not conflict with the Second Amendment. Our recommendation is based on the assumption that our databases are complete and accurate. The federal government should provide additional inducements to states to supply accurate and timely information to the national database relating to individuals who have a criminal record, a history of domestic violence, or a mental illness. Our recommendation is also based on the assumption that the data collected for background checks will be secured and not used for any other purpose in violation of our privacy rights. Congress should conduct vigorous oversight, and there should be robust and frequent review by the general counsel and the inspector general of the responsible federal agencies over how collected data is being used.

In addition to expanding the number of background checks, we support new laws that criminalize trafficking in guns and knowing participation in "straw purchases." There is no defendable Second Amendment right that allows American citizens to surreptitiously purchase a weapon for someone who is unable to purchase one legally on his own. Likewise, we find no Second Amendment support for the right to engage in trade with the cartels and arm them with weapons. We believe these are common-sense constitutional regulations that will help Mexican authorities address gun violence and stabilize communities in Mexico and along our border, all consistent with the Second Amendment.

Supporters of gun rights believe that any attempt to regulate gun shows is an intrusion on their constitutional rights under the Second Amendment. We respectfully disagree. To the contrary, we believe these requirements fit comfortably within the guidance from the U.S. Supreme Court. However, we acknowledge that these proposals raise serious policy considerations that deserve honest and rational discussion.

There are a variety of programs used by ICE and other agencies to discover and confiscate illegal weapons and ammunition.[18] The United States could assist Mexico by helping to create a Mexican version of the firearms tracing system of ATF, which could be used to detect and flag weapons and other illegal accessories when they are used to perpetrate various criminal acts. This system should be electronic (eTrace), easy to access and operate, and available to all thirty-one Mexican states and nine U.S. consulates housed in Mexico. The system should be created in both English and Spanish so as to provide information efficiently, regardless of which nation's agencies are using it. Avoiding time delays related to translation will reduce the number of missed opportunities.[19]

In 2006 ATF initiated Project Gunrunner. The purpose of this highly anticipated strategic program was to deny the Mexican drug cartels access to the tools of their trade, that is, guns and ammunition.[20] Since its inception the program has received mixed reviews. The first few years of the program were positive as the investigations produced favorable results, including the seizure of more than ten thousand guns and one million rounds of ammunition that were prevented from crossing into Mexico. During the same timeframe the program helped to uncover numerous U.S. organizations that were supplying weapons and ammunition to the drug cartels. Furthermore, the program led to recommendations to prosecute more than 2,500 defendants.[21] The program appeared to be quite successful.

Recently, however, Project Gunrunner has become a source of great controversy. In October 2009 the public learned of Operation Fast and Furious, a classified program involving a highly controversial and dangerous practice called "gun-walking." Gun-walking was a strategy that allowed illegal weapons to "walk away" into the hands of suspects in the hopes of tracking the weapons and ultimately uncovering criminal networks.[22] Allowing contraband to move is often a method used by law enforcement to uncover additional accomplices in a criminal enterprise. Officials believed that gun-walking would enable them to follow weapons from straw-purchasers to the Mexican cartels; however, these beliefs were tragically misplaced as two firearms connected to the program were found near the scene where a border agent was killed.[23] Certain Republican members of Congress disagree with the Obama administration's claim that the American people have been provided a full account of the events surrounding Operation Fast and Furious. However, what is not in dispute is the reality that addressing gun issues on both sides of the border will be helpful in curbing violence, reducing unauthorized immigration, and improving the relationship between Mexico and the United States.

Drug Demand

The U.S. demand for drugs is another factor that contributes to social problems in Mexico. The drug trade in Mexico is as large as its gun trade, if not larger. The drug kingpins have an apparently unlimited access to drugs and are in need of buyers; for decades U.S. consumers have been more than willing to purchase. The source of our own national drug problem has been well documented. We will dedicate only a few paragraphs to exploring the relationship between it and immigration.

The U.S. "war on drugs" began in the 1970s when President Richard Nixon declared drugs to be the number one enemy of the United States.[24]

The goal of this war was to eradicate the use of illegal drugs within the United States, a feat that may be impossible to accomplish. To date, the war on drugs has not achieved the success that either President Nixon or his successors hoped for; in fact, it appears to be worse than ever.

The typical American drug user is more than likely an individual who is seeking a cheap way to meet an addiction without regard to the origin of the drug. Mexican dealers often offer cheaper prices than the American user can get anywhere else. This added demand and willingness to pay for large amounts of cheap drugs has led to an increase in the number of drug lords, traffickers, and related violence. The situation is best summarized by simple economic analysis: as more Americans demand drugs, the number of suppliers will increase, and when too many suppliers are in the market, the price will likely be lower than what the drug kingpins desire. Thus, violence erupts as drug lords and rival gangs kill one another for control.

Assuming it is possible, the question is whether reducing the American demand for drugs would diminish the violence that plagues Mexico. Although the answer is unclear, it is likely that the Mexican dealers would simply revise their methods and areas of operation, finding buyers in other countries. Furthermore, the leaders of the cartels are businessmen first. If the cost of doing business in the drug trade becomes prohibitive, they will likely move to another product. Unfortunately, it is likely that there will continue to be some sort of violence within Mexico. Nevertheless, the U.S. goal remains simply to reduce the American demand for drugs, which is contributing to the current problems of violence and corruption within Mexico. In efforts to curb the American demand, the United States should focus more on the rehabilitation, education, and prosecution of addicts.

Over the years the popular drugs of choice may have changed, but in general there has not been a substantial decrease in substance abuse. In the beginning the war on drugs focused on tougher penalties and increased prosecutions of Americans arrested for possession. There was widespread disparity among the available penalties, based on the type of drug that the defendant was charged with using or possessing. For example, the penalties for crack cocaine were more severe than the penalties for powder cocaine.[25] This created controversy and sparked much debate about whether the legislation was targeting certain minority groups who were more likely to abuse crack cocaine rather than powder cocaine due to its lower price.[26]

In 2010 the Obama administration took the first steps in attempting to correct the disparity in penalties assigned to different types of cocaine by signing the Fair Sentencing Act (FSA). The FSA eliminated the mandatory minimum sentence for crack cocaine possession and increased fines for major drug traffickers.[27] Over the years the war on drugs has become notorious for its perceived failures. There are many who believe that the war was lost long ago and that its continued existence is a waste of U.S. resources. [28]

Proposals to address the U.S. drug problem have included a shift away from law enforcement, more focus on the related health-care issues, and the mass legalization of certain types of drugs, namely, marijuana. Washington and Colorado have legalized recreational marijuana use. The U.S. attorney general recently called for the need for federal prosecutors to exercise discretion when prosecuting minor drug cases involving first-time offenders. Supporters of marijuana legalization claim that black markets and drug violence will decline as a result of legalization because most Americans are "recreational" drug users.[29] Additionally, the legalization, regulation, and taxation of marijuana could have profound positive implications for the United States.[30] Most obviously, the U.S. demand for Mexican drugs would likely decline because the American marijuana purchaser would no longer need Mexican dealers, and federal and state coffers would benefit from added tax revenues.

The implications of any type of drug legalization are beyond the scope of this book, but we believe that there are effective methods of combating drug use that do not involve legalization. As stated earlier, the initial focus of the war on drugs was law enforcement; today the focus also includes education, treatment, and rehabilitation.[31] We agree that the United States cannot prosecute its way out of the drug war.

The American addict facing a first-time drug charge for recreational use should be allowed to attend some type of rehabilitation program, depending on the nature and severity of the drug charge. In conjunction with this rehabilitation program, the addict should be educated on the dangers of drugs and the effects of continued abuse. If these steps repeatedly fail, it may be necessary and appropriate to prosecute and incarcerate the addict as an additional measure to keep the addict off drugs and to protect the public by keeping the addict off the streets.

Faced with the immensity of America's drug problems, drug courts are being used more frequently. According to the National Institute of Justice (NIJ), drug courts are specialized court programs that target defendants who have addiction and dependency problems.[32] Drug courts vary by jurisdiction, but all share the common goal of reducing future arrests and other criminal activity, reducing substance abuse, and rehabilitating program participants.[33] Currently, there are over 2,500 drug courts located within the United States and its territories.[34]

Drug courts vary, as each court is tailored to address the specific needs of participants. For example, there are courts that cater to adults, juveniles, veterans, families, and tribes. Defendants who meet eligibility requirements, which are determined by each jurisdiction, are able to enter the drug courts rather than face possible incarceration.[35] The basic drug-court model requires intensive drug treatment, frequent meetings with the judge regarding the participant's obligations and performance assessment, frequent and random drug testing, and rewards and sanctions, as needed.[36]

Upon successful completion of the program, defendants may receive lesser penalties, have charges reduced or dropped, or any other alternative the judge deems appropriate under the circumstances.[37] Research is still being conducted to determine the overall success of drug courts. However, available research suggests that a drug court's impact on recidivism is the greatest when there are frequent interactions between the judge and the defendant.[38] The United States should invest in the expansion of the drug courts and the various associated programs that educate and attempt to rehabilitate addicts. The war on drugs is not likely to end soon, but through continued efforts it may be possible to reduce the American demand for drugs, which in turn could lead to a reduction in Mexican drug violence and lessen unlawful immigration.

Conclusion

This chapter has explored various alternatives to the current U.S. approach to helping Mexico address its social problems, as well as the vital partnerships that Mexico and the United States should maintain. We acknowledge that, to a degree, one source of our undocumented immigration problem is Central America. Poverty and violence help to motivate Central Americans to migrate northward. We need to better encourage Mexico to enforce its own southern borders.

One point that cannot be overstated is that Mexico is a sovereign country; although much of what happens in Mexico influences the United States, changes must begin from within and under the leadership of Mexican officials. Drug and organized-crime violence weakens the Mexican economy, resulting in increased unauthorized immigration and spillover violence. That said, our main focus must continue to be the current economic and social problems of the United States. However, if there are areas in which U.S. training, knowledge, or resources would be mutually beneficial, the United States should continue to provide help. In no way are we suggesting that the United States should interfere in Mexico's affairs. On the contrary, the United States should continue to remain respectful of Mexico's sovereignty; however, there is no reason why the two countries cannot work better together for their mutual interests.

Epilogue

In summary, we support greater border security and workplace enforcement. We believe that the INA should be updated and simplified and that our visa process must be substantially revised in order to better address current and future immigration pressures, as well as to attract the necessary skilled and unskilled workers. Of the estimated eleven million undocumented immigrants presently in the United States, we support placing those who are eligible and without a criminal record into temporary lawful status after they pay a fine and back taxes. We do not oppose their becoming eligible for permanent lawful status if they learn English and American civics and pay taxes—provided that those who followed the law are not disadvantaged. We also support providing relief to young people brought here unlawfully by their parents.

We understand that Americans feel passionately about these issues. However, if we are to achieve meaningful reform, then we have to tone down the harsh rhetoric. Our friends on the left should understand and accept that not all state legislation requirements or qualifications are anti-immigrant or government imposed and that as a sovereign nation of laws we should not grant citizenship carte blanche to all those here unlawfully, without regard to circumstances. To do so may be at cross purposes with our goal of protecting our national security and promoting our economy. Our friends on the right should remember that most undocumented immigrants come to America for a better life for themselves and their families, much like our ancestors, and that most are hardworking and otherwise law-abiding.

The Republican Party has hurt itself among Hispanics because of the harsh way that some Republicans have spoken about immigration reform. We believe Republicans can be true to their principles of rule of law, border security, and tougher workplace enforcement (principles that we and many Americans endorse, including most Hispanic Americans) and still be respectful and compassionate in the debate over these immigrant families. The Democratic party has hurt itself by projecting the image of a party that pays lip service to the rule of law and does not care about those immigrants who have followed the law and are waiting patiently to come to America.[1] Additionally, President Obama has failed to deliver on his promise of immigration reform and has governed over a historic number of deportations that have angered many Hispanic families.[2] Achieving the appropriate tone requires patience and leadership. It will be difficult, but to fail here puts the economy and our national security at risk.

We believe that America is great because of its diversity. Lawful migration brings about diverse ideas, culture, and customs. We are both products of Texas, a border state that is uniquely diverse. We understand the beauty and strength of lawful migration. But we are also a nation of laws. For too long, our immigration laws have been ignored. To ignore the law with impunity breeds further disrespect for the law. That is not the America we know.

Besides being a "numbers game," there are substantial consequences related to having millions of undocumented immigrants living within the United States, and the possible negative consequences of allowing a pervasive undocumented community are many. Some of the more tangible issues include fostering disrespect for the rule of law, an economy that is floundering or stagnant, and the potential for security breaches by terrorists.

There is no magic answer, and there are no sure-shot quick fixes. However, with this book we hope to have proposed ways with which to ease, if not permanently address, some of the larger-scale problems associated with a sizeable undocumented immigrant population. Our recommendations go beyond the automatic rubber stamping of the label "illegal" and the granting of full-scale reprieves. While what we have proposed may appear daunting and to some degree costly, neglecting to take bold action will ultimately lead to an even larger crisis in the near future.

As we have explored, reducing the number of undocumented immigrants will require considerably more than just waving a wand and changing "unlawful" to "lawful." That said, valid pathways to some type of lawful status must be created for those who qualify. Essentially, what we have proposed is not groundbreaking. The basic concepts have already largely been drafted, debated, and put in place in the INA, and we believe that a large part of the answer to dealing with the millions unlawfully present is to focus on the INA itself. Even if we do nothing else, by amending the INA in a few critical ways, we will take a significant step toward tackling many of our current immigration problems.

We also believe that certain provisions in recent legislative proposals discussed in this book have considerable merit. The right changes to our current immigration laws will help address our many immigration challenges. The default reaction to any sensible legislative proposal should be careful circumspection—not blind obstinacy.

We remain hopeful that our federal leadership will step up to the challenge and pass meaningful reform through a comprehensive plan. That hope is fueled by an unshakeable belief in the human spirit's tendency to act with courage and compassion. It is, after all, what helps to make us uniquely American.

Appendix 1: Nonimmigrant Visas

A Visa

The A-1 visa is designated for ambassadors, public ministers, career diplomats, or consular officers who have been accredited by a foreign government that is recognized by the United States.[1] The A-2 visa is for other officials or employees who do not fall into the definition of the A-1 visa but have been accredited by a foreign government recognized by the United States.[2] The A-3 visa is specified for attendants, servants, personal employees, and the immediate family members of such persons.[3] This preference of nonimmigrant visas accounts for about one-half of a percent of all nonimmigrant visas annually.[4]

B Visa

B visas are separated into two different types, B-1 for temporary visitors for business purposes and B-2 for temporary pleasure purposes, although the visa application is the same.[5] The B-1 visa allows for temporary business that does not include any form of labor, either skilled or unskilled.[6] The B-2 visa allows for temporary pleasure. Both B-visa classifications prohibit the holder from engaging in any form of work, paid or voluntary.[7] Likewise, B-visa holders may not enroll in any educational institution.[8] This preference category accounts for nearly 42 percent of all nonimmigrant visas issued annually.[9]

C Visa

C visas are reserved for aliens in transit through the United States.[10] There are three designations of visas for aliens passing in transit, non-diplomats in transit through the United States (C-1), aliens in transit to and from the United Nations headquarters district in New York City (C-2), and alien diplomats in transit through the United States (C-3).[11] This preference accounts for almost 1 percent of all nonimmigrant visas annually.[12]

D Visa

D visas are reserved for alien crewmen.[13] The D-1 visa is reserved for crewmen aboard a vessel or aircraft that does not have its home port or operating base in the United States where the alien intends to depart from the United States on the same vessel or aircraft or similar means of transportation.[14] The D-2 is designated for alien crewmen in the same situation as D-1 holders except that the vessel that brings the alien is permitted to have a home port or an operating base in the United States.[15] Additionally, the vessel must land in either Guam or the Mariana Islands and intend to depart after a temporary stay, with the alien crewman leaving on the same vessel.[16]

E Visa

E visa designation is reserved for aliens, and their spouses and children, who are nationals of a country with which the United States has a treaty of commerce or navigation, and who are entering to carry on some form of business.[17] The E-1 visa is reserved for aliens carrying on substantial trade, whether in services or technology, between the United States and the state of which the alien is a national.[18] The E-2 visa is reserved for aliens entering to develop or direct the operations of a company of which the alien has or is investing a substantial amount of capital.[19] The E-3 is reserved for nationals of the Commonwealth of Australia who enter to perform services in a specialty occupation and whose employer has filed a labor attestation.[20] This nonimmigrant preference accounts for a little over one-half percent of all nonimmigrant admissions annually.[21]

F Visa

F visas are reserved for aliens, and their spouses and minor children, who seek to enter temporarily to pursue a course of study.[22] F-visa classification contains three designations: F-1 designation is reserved for aliens who are bona fide students qualified to pursue a course of study at any established academic institution or accredited language training program.[23] F-2 designation is specifically reserved for the spouse and minor children of an F-1 visa holder, if they are accompanying or following to join such alien.[24] F-3 designation is reserved for nationals of Canada and Mexico who fall under the F-1 classification. The distinction between F-1 and F-3 is that the course of study for the Canadian or Mexican national can be a part-time or full-time course, and the national must commute to the institution of study from his country of nationality.[25] F visa preference accounts for about three percent of nonimmigrant annual admissions.[26]

G Visa

The G preference visa is designated for representatives of foreign governments who have principal residence representative status in the United States, and their immediate family, staff, and employees.[27] G-1 preference is given to principal resident representatives of a foreign government recognized by the United States, and the government representative is entitled to privileges and immunities under the International Organizations Immunities Act.[28] This preference applies to accredited resident members of the staff of the G-1 holder as well as the holder's immediate family.[29] G-2 visas are for other accredited representatives who are not principal resident representatives of a foreign government mentioned in G-1 status, as well as their immediate family members.[30] The G-3 preference is reserved for accredited alien representatives, and their immediate family members, who qualify under the G-1 or G-2 categories, but their foreign government either is not recognized by the United States or is not covered under the International Organizations Immunities Act.[31] G-4 is reserved for officers and employees of organizations covered under the Immunities Act and members of their immediate family.[32] The last category, G-5, is reserved for attendants, servants, and personal employees of any of the four previous categories and their immediate family members.[33] This preference category accounts for one-third of a percent of all nonimmigrant visas annually.[34]

H Visa

The H visa preference is reserved for aliens entering to perform short-term labor or service or receive training from an employer that has petitioned for such alien.[35] For each classification, except for H-1C (registered nurses participating in the Nursing Relief for Disadvantaged Areas),[36] an employer must file Form I-129, Petition for Nonimmigrant Worker, and a Labor Condition Application before the alien may apply for a visa.[37] If the occupation that the alien seeks requires a state or local license, the license must be obtained before approval of the petition.[38] This classification accounts for about 2 percent of nonimmigrant admissions annually.[39]

H-1B classification is reserved for aliens coming temporarily to the United States to perform services in a specialty occupation.[40] This includes fashion models of distinguished merit and ability.[41] The authorized period of time that an alien granted an H-1B visa can stay may not exceed six years.[42] There is a numerical cap on the number of aliens who may be granted this visa status—sixty-five thousand for each fiscal year.[43] This preference category alone accounts for almost 52 percent of all temporary worker (H) visas.[44]

H-1B1 visas are reserved for aliens subject to the United States–Chile Free Trade Agreement and the United States–Singapore Free Trade Agreement.[45]

H-2A visas are reserved for aliens coming to perform agricultural labor or service of a temporary or seasonal nature.[46] The provisions for admission of an H-2A temporary worker are found in INA § 218. The numerical cap on this visa is set at sixty-six thousand per fiscal year.[47] Similar to the H-1B visa, the numerical limitation applies only to the principal alien petitioner and not spouses or children.[48] This category accounts for 22 percent of all H visas and about one-half percent of all nonimmigrant visas annually.

H-2B visas are reserved for aliens coming to the United States to perform temporary nonagricultural labor or service.[49] As in other temporary employment-based categories, the granting of this visa to an alien is dependent on the potential employer's demonstration that there are no U.S. citizens available to perform the labor and that the wages that the alien will earn will not adversely affect the wages and working conditions of U.S. workers.[50] The annual cap on workers receiving this visa is set currently at sixty-six thousand.[51] This category of H visa accounts for about one tenth of a percent of all nonimmigrant admissions.[52]

H-3 visas are reserved for trainees who are coming to participate in a training program that is not designed to lead to employment in the United States.[53] This category accounts for one-tenth of a percent of all nonimmigrant visas.[54]

H-4 visas are reserved for the spouses and unmarried minor children of H-visa recipients.[55] This category accounts for about one-third of a percent of nonimmigrant admissions annually and 16 percent of all H-visa admissions annually.[56]

I Visa

I visas are reserved for bona fide representatives[57] of the foreign press, radio, film, or other foreign information media who are entering the United States for the sole purpose of engaging in their form of work.[58] Additionally, the alien must be a citizen of a foreign country that has reciprocity with the United States.[59] The spouse and minor children of such alien are also allowed to enter under the I visa.[60] The issuance of this visa accounts for about one-tenth of a percent of total nonimmigrant admissions annually.[61]

J Visa

The J visa is reserved for alien exchange visitors classified as student, scholars, or trainees who will be participating in a program approved by the State Department.[62] Aliens entering to receive graduate medical education are subject to additional restrictions under this visa provision.[63]

K Visa

K visas are reserved for fiancé(e)s of U.S. citizens who are entering the United States to follow through with marriage to the citizen within ninety days of their admission (K-1)[64] or an alien who has already married a U.S. citizen petitioner and is entering to await the approval of an immediate relative petition (K-3).[65] The minor children of both a K-1 and K-3 visa recipient are allowed to enter whether they are coming with the alien parent or follow to join later.[66]

L Visa

The L visa is reserved for intracompany transferees.[67] In order to qualify for this visa, the alien seeking admission must have at least one year of continuous employment with the entity or one of its subsidiaries for which it will receive the transfer to the United States.[68] Additionally, the alien must be assuming a managerial or executive role, or a position that requires specialized knowledge possessed by the alien.[69] The L-1 visa is for the principal beneficiary of the petition, and the L-2 visa is for the spouse and minor children of the principal beneficiary alien.[70] This visa category accounts for about one and one-half percent of all nonimmigrant admissions annually.[71]

M Visa

M visas are reserved for aliens entering to participate in a full course of study at a vocational school that has agreed to accept the alien.[72] The alien's spouse and minor children may also enter if following or joining the primary visa beneficiary; they are granted M-2 status.[73] Additionally, M-3 status is granted to nationals of Canada or Mexico who meet the requirements of the M-1 visa except that the alien commutes to and from the school and the country of nationality.[74] This visa category accounts for less than one-half of a percent of all nonimmigrant admissions.[75]

N Visa

The N visa is further separated into two additional visas, the N-8 and the N-9. The N-8 is reserved for the parents of aliens who are granted special immigrant status.[76] Thus, when a nonimmigrant in G-4 status receives special immigrant status, and the alien is under the age of 21, the parents of such alien may receive the N-8 visa.[77] N-9 status is reserved for the children of a parent who has been granted special immigrant status.[78]

O Visa

O visas are reserved for aliens with extraordinary abilities in the fields of science, art, education, business, athletics, and the motion picture and television industries.[79] The extraordinary ability must be demonstrated by national or international acclaim or, in reference to the motion picture or television industries, by a record of demonstrated extraordinary achievement.[80] Further, individuals who are accompanying and assisting the alien with extraordinary abilities may receive an O-2 visa if they possess critical skills and experience above those of a general nature, are integral to the performance of the work of the principal alien, and intend to return to their country of nationality.[81] The spouse and children of O-1 and O-2 visa holders may also be admitted on an O-3 visa.[82] This category accounts for about one-fifth of a percent of annual nonimmigrant admissions.[83]

P Visa

P visas are reserved for athletes and entertainers who have a residence in their country of nationality that they have no intention of abandoning and who have had an employer or sponsor petition with the Service for their temporary employment.[84] The spouse and children of such aliens may also be admitted.[85] P-visa recipients account for about one-fifth of 1 percent of nonimmigrant admissions annually.[86]

Q Visa

The Q visa is reserved for aliens who are coming to the United States to participate in an international cultural exchange program.[87] The traditional visa will be the Q-1 category.[88] The Q-2 and Q-3 visas were previously reserved for aliens coming to participate in the Irish peace process cultural and training program and their dependents.[89]

R Visa

The R visa is reserved for religious workers and their spouses and children.[90] A religious worker is a person who has been a member of a religious organization for at least the past two years and is coming to perform work as either a minister, a professional within the religious organization, or another form of religious vocational work.[91] The religion must have a bona fide nonprofit organization in the United States; the alien will be admitted for a time not to exceed five years.[92] This category accounts for about one-half of 1 percent of annual nonimmigrant admissions.[93]

S Visa

The S visa is reserved for aliens who are witnesses or informants regarding criminal organizations or terrorist organizations or operations and may include family members.[94] The S visa classifications are S-5, S-6, and S-7.[95]

S-5 classification is reserved for informants or witnesses of criminal organizations or enterprises; it is limited to two hundred admissions annually.[96] The S-6 classification is for an alien in possession of critical reliable information regarding a terrorist organization or operation[97] and is limited to fifty admissions annually.[98] The S-7 classification is reserved for family members, including parents, spouses, and children (both married and unmarried) of the principal S-visa beneficiary.[99]

T Visa

T visas are reserved for victims of severe forms of trafficking[100] and certain family members accompanying or following to join.[101]

U Visa

The U visa is reserved for aliens who meet four requirements:[102] (1) the alien has suffered substantial mental or physical abuse caused by certain criminal activity,[103] (2) the alien possesses information regarding the criminal activity that caused the mental or physical abuse;[104] (3) the alien has been, is currently, or is likely to be helpful to the investigation or prosecution of the criminal activity that caused the mental or physical abuse;[105] and (4) the criminal activity that occurred was in violation of the laws of the United States or occurred in the United States.[106] If the alien meets the requirements for a U visa, the spouse, children, and in certain cases, the unmarried siblings of the U visa beneficiary may accompany or follow to join.[107]

V Visa

The V visa is reserved for the spouse and children[108] of lawful permanent residents.[109] An alien may benefit from this visa if he meets the requirements of INA § 101(a)(15)(V)(i) and (ii).[110] According to the Department of State, this visa has not been issued in several years, and the department does not foresee V visas being issued in the future.[111] According to the last available records this visa category accounted for less than one tenth of a percent of nonimmigrant admissions.[112]

TN and TD Visas

The TN visa is reserved for citizens of Mexico and Canada who are entering to participate in business at a professional level.[113] The TD visa is reserved for the dependents[114] of the TN visa recipient.[115] This visa category accounts for about one third of one percent of nonimmigrant admissions annually.[116]

NATO Visas

NATO visas are classified as NATO-1 through NATO-7 and are reserved for certain NATO employees and their immediate families.[117] This limited category accounts for just over one-half of a percent of annual nonimmigrant admissions.[118]

Visa Waiver Program

The Visa Waiver Program, created in 1986,[119] allows aliens from certain countries[120] to bypass the valid visa requirement.[121] Generally, aliens holding a visa issued through this program are designated as WT (waiver tourist) or WB (waiver business) visa holders.[122] Recipients of WT and WB visas account for about 45 percent of all nonimmigrant visas issued annually.[123]

Appendix 2: Relevant Sections of Law Pertaining to U.S. Nationality

INA Section 341:

(b) A person who claims to be a national, but not a citizen, of the United States may apply to the Secretary of State for a certificate of non-citizen national status ... [u]pon ... proof to the satisfaction of the Secretary of State that the applicant is a national, but not a citizen, of the United States.

INA Section 101(a)(22):

The term "national of the United States" means (A) a citizen of the United States, or (B) a person who, though not a citizen of the United States, owes permanent allegiance to the United States.

INA Section 101(a)(29):

The term "outlying possessions of the United States" means American Samoa and Swains Island.

INA Section 101(a)(36):

The term "State" includes the District of Columbia, Puerto Rico, Guam, and the Virgin Islands of the United States.

INA Section 308:

Unless otherwise provided in section 301 of this title, the following shall be nationals, but not citizens of the United States at birth:

(1) A person born in an outlying possession of the United States on or after the date of formal acquisition of such possession;

(2) A person born outside the United States and its outlying possessions

of parents both of whom are nationals, but not citizens, of the United States, and have had a residence in the United States, or one of its outlying possessions prior to the birth of such person;

(3) A person of unknown parentage found in an outlying possession of the United States while under the age of five years, until shown, prior to attaining the age of twenty-one years, not to have been born in such outlying possessions; and

(4) A person born outside the United States and its outlying possessions of parents one of whom is an alien, and the other a national, but not a citizen, of the United States who, prior to the birth of such person, was physically present in the United States or its outlying possessions for a period or periods totaling not less than seven years in any continuous period of ten years—

(A) during which the national parent was not outside the United States or its outlying possessions for a continuous period of more than one year, and

(B) at least five years of which were after attaining the age of fourteen years.

The proviso of section 301(g) shall apply to the national parent under this paragraph in the same manner as it applies to the citizen parent under that section.

INA Section 325:

A person not a citizen who owes permanent allegiance to the United States, and who is otherwise qualified, may, if he becomes a resident of any State, be naturalized upon compliance with the applicable requirements of this title, except that in applications for naturalization filed under the provisions of this section residence and physical presence within the United States within the meaning of this title shall include residence and physical presence within any of the outlying possessions of the United States.

Section 302 of Public Law 94-241:

Any person who becomes a citizen of the United States solely by virtue of the provisions in Section 301 [applying to those born in or residing in the Northern Mariana Islands] may within six months after the effective date of that Section or within six months after reaching the age of 18 years, whichever date is later, become a national but not a citizen of the United States by making a declaration under oath before any court established by the Constitution or laws of the United States or any other court of record in the Commonwealth in the form as follows: "I _____ being duly sworn, hereby declare my intention to be a national but not a citizen of the United States."

Appendix 3: Proposed Amended INA § 245(i)

Sec. 245

(i) (1) Notwithstanding the provisions of subsections (a) and (c) of this section, an alien physically present in the United States—

(A) who—

(i) entered the United States without inspection; or

(ii) is within one of the classes enumerated in subsection (c) of this section;

(B) who is the beneficiary (including a spouse or child of the principal alien, if eligible to receive a visa under section 203(d)) of—

(i) a petition for classification under section 204 ~~that was~~ filed with the Attorney General ~~on or before April 30, 2001~~; or

(ii) an application for a labor certification under section 212(a)(5)(A) ~~that was~~ filed pursuant to the regulations of the Secretary of Labor ~~on or before such date; and~~

(C) ~~who, in the case of a beneficiary of a petition for classification, or an application for labor certification, described in subparagraph (B) that was filed after January 14, 1998, is physically present in the United States on the date of the enactment of the LIFE Act Amendments of 2000;~~ may apply to the Attorney General for the adjustment of his or her status to that of an alien lawfully admitted for permanent residence. The Attorney General may accept such application only if the alien remits with such application a sum equaling $1,000 as of the date of receipt of the application, but such sum shall not be required from a child under the age of seventeen, or an alien who is the spouse or unmarried child of an individual who obtained temporary or permanent resident status under section 210 or 245A of the Immigration and Nationality Act or section 202 of the Immigration Reform and Control Act of 1986 at any date, who—

(i) as of May 5, 1988, was the unmarried child or spouse of the individual who obtained temporary or permanent resident status under section 210 or 245A of the Immigration and Nationality Act or section 202 of the Immigration Reform and Control Act of 1986;

(ii) entered the United States before May 5, 1988, resided in the United States on May 5, 1988, and is not a lawful permanent resident; and

(iii) applied for benefits under section 301(a) of the Immigration Act of 1990. The sum specified herein shall be in addition to the fee normally required for the processing of an application under this section; and

(2) Upon receipt of such an application and the sum hereby required, the Attorney General may adjust the status of the alien to that of an alien lawfully admitted for permanent residence if —

(A) the alien is eligible to receive an immigrant visa and is admissible to the United States for permanent residence; and

(B) an immigrant visa is immediately available to the alien at the time the application is filed.

(3) (A) The portion of each application fee (not to exceed $200) that the Attorney General determines is required to process an application under this section and is remitted to the Attorney General pursuant to paragraphs (1) and (2) of this subsection shall be disposed of by the Attorney General as provided in subsections (m), (n), and (o) of section 286.

(B) Any remaining portion of such fees remitted under such paragraphs shall be deposited by the Attorney General into the Breached Bond/Detention established under section 286(r), except that in the case of fees attributable to applications for a beneficiary with respect to whom a petition for classification, or an application for labor certification, described in paragraph (1)(B) was filed after January 14, 1998, one-half of such remaining portion shall be deposited by the Attorney General into the Immigration Examinations Fee Account established under section 286(m).

(4) Remittance of the sum equaling $1,000 described herein shall not act to waive the ground of inadmissibility found at section 212(a)(6)(H),[1] but an alien may also remit the civil monetary fine pursuant to section 212(a)(6)(H) at the time of filing the application described herein.

APPENDIX 4: PROPOSED AMENDED INA
§ 249

Sec. 249

A record of lawful admission for permanent residence may, in the discretion of the Attorney General and under such regulations as he may prescribe, be made in the case of any alien, as of the date of the approval of his application or, if entry occurred prior to July 1, 1924, as of the date of such entry, if no such record is otherwise available and such alien shall satisfy the Attorney General that he is not inadmissible under section 212(a)(3)(E) or under section 212(a) insofar as it relates to terrorist activities,[1] criminals, procurers and other immoral persons, subversives, violators of the narcotic laws or smugglers of aliens, and he establishes that he—

(a) entered the United States ~~prior to January 1, 1972~~ at least twenty-five years prior to the filing of his application;

(b) has had his residence in the United States continuously since such entry;

(c) is a person of good moral character;

(d) is not ineligible to citizenship and is not deportable under section 237(a)(4)(B); and

(e) demonstrates basic citizenship skills.

(1) In general.—The alien must demonstrate that he either—

(A) meets the requirements of section 312(a) (relating to minimal understanding of ordinary English and a knowledge and understanding of the history and government of the United States), or

(B) is satisfactorily pursuing a course of study (recognized by the Attorney General) to achieve such an understanding of English and such a knowledge and understanding of the history and government of the United States.

(2) Exception for elderly or developmentally disabled individuals.—The Attorney General may, in his discretion, waive all or part of the requirements of paragraph (1) in the case of an alien who is 65 years of age or older or who is developmentally disabled.

(3) Relation to naturalization examination.—In accordance with regulations as prescribed by the Attorney General, an alien who has demonstrated under paragraph (1)(A) that the alien meets the requirements of section 312(a) may be considered to have satisfied the requirements of that section for purposes of becoming naturalized as a citizen of the United States under title III.

(f) Monetary Fine.—The Attorney General may accept such application along with application fees only if the alien remits with such application and application fees a sum equaling $1,000 as of the date of receipt of the application and application fees.

(g) Application Fees.—

(1) Fee Schedule.—The Attorney General shall provide for a schedule of fees to be charged for the filing of applications under this section.

(2) Use of fees.—The Attorney General shall deposit payments received under this paragraph in a separate account and amounts in such account shall be available, without fiscal year limitation, to cover administrative and other expenses incurred in connection with the review of applications filed under this section.

(h) In general.—

(1) Conditional basis for status.—Notwithstanding any other provision of this Act, an alien shall be considered, at the time of obtaining the record of lawful admission for permanent residence under this section, to have obtained such status on a conditional basis subject to the provisions herein.

(2) Notice of requirements.—

(A) At time of obtaining record of lawful admission for permanent residence.—At the time an alien obtains permanent resident status on a conditional basis under this section, the Attorney General shall provide for notice to such alien respecting the provisions of this section and the requirements of subsection (j)(1) to have the conditional basis of such status removed.

(B) At time of required petition.—In addition, the Attorney General shall attempt to provide notice to such alien at or about the beginning of the 90-day period described in subsection (k)(2)(A), of the requirements of subsections (j)(1)(B).

(C) Effect of failure to provide notice.—The failure of the Attorney General to provide a notice under this paragraph shall not affect the enforcement of the provisions of this section with respect to such alien.

(i) Termination of Status if Finding that Alien failed to meet requirements herein.—

(1) In general.—In the case of an alien with permanent resident status on a conditional basis under this section, if the Attorney General determines at any time before or after the fourth anniversary of the alien's obtaining the record of lawful admission for permanent residence that the alien has failed to meet the requirements of subsection (j)(1); the Attorney General shall so notify the parties involved and, subject to paragraph (2), shall terminate the permanent resident status of the alien involved as of the date of the determination.

(2) Hearing in removal proceeding.—Any alien whose permanent resident status is terminated under paragraph (1) may request a review of such determination in a proceeding to remove the alien. In such proceeding, the burden of proof shall be on the Attorney General to establish, by a preponderance of the evidence, that the alien failed to meet the requirements of subsection (j)(1).

(j) Requirements of Additional Monetary Fines and Timely Petition for Removal of Condition.—

(1) In general.—In order for the conditional basis established under subsection (h) to be removed—

(A) the alien must remit annually to the Attorney General a

sum equaling $1,000 for the four years immediately following the date on which the alien obtained the record of lawful admission for permanent residence on a conditional basis, and

(B) submit to the Attorney General, during the period described in subsection (k)(2)(A), a petition which requests the removal of such conditional basis and which states, under penalty of perjury, that the alien has met the requirements described in subsection (j)(1)(A).

(2) Termination of permanent resident status for failure to timely remit monetary fines or to file petition.—

(A) In general.—In the case of an alien with permanent resident status on a conditional basis under this section, if—

(i) unless there is good cause shown, the alien fails to timely remit the monetary fines described in paragraph (1)(A), the Attorney General shall terminate the permanent resident status of the alien as of the date the Attorney General knows or has reason to believe that the alien has failed to meet the requirements of paragraph (1)(A), or

(ii) unless there is good cause shown, no petition is filed with respect to the alien in accordance with the provisions of paragraph (1)(B), the Attorney General shall terminate the permanent resident status of the alien as of the fourth anniversary of the alien's lawful admission for permanent residence.

(B) Hearing in removal proceeding.—In any removal proceeding with respect to an alien whose permanent resident status is terminated under subparagraph (A), the burden of proof shall be on the alien to establish compliance with the requirements of paragraphs (1)(A) and/or (1)(B).

(3) Determination after petition to remove conditions.—

(A) In general.—If—

   (i) a petition is filed in accordance with the provisions of paragraph (1)(B),

   (ii) the Attorney General shall make a determination as to whether the alien has met the requirements described in paragraph (1)(A).

  (B) Removal of conditional basis if favorable determination.—If the Attorney General determines that the alien has met the requirements described in paragraph (1)(A), the Attorney General shall so notify the parties involved and shall remove the conditional basis of the parties effective as of the fourth anniversary of the alien's obtaining record of lawful admission for permanent residence.

  (C) Termination if adverse determination.—If the Attorney General determines that the alien has not met the requirements described in paragraph (1)(A), the Attorney General shall so notify the parties involved and, subject to subparagraph (D), shall terminate the permanent resident status of the alien as of the date of the determination.

  (D) Hearing in removal proceeding.—Any alien whose permanent resident status is terminated under subparagraph (C) may request a review of such determination in a proceeding to remove the alien. In such proceeding, the burden of proof shall be on the alien to establish compliance with the requirements described in paragraph (1)(A).

(k) Details of Petition to Remove Conditions.—

 (1) Contents of petition.—Each petition under subsection (j)(1)(B) shall contain, at a minimum, the following facts and information:

  (A) Evidence that the alien has met the requirements of subsection (j)(1)(A).

  (B) A police or other law enforcement clearance letter from each jurisdiction in which the alien has resided during the four-year conditional residency period.

 (2) Period for filing petition to remove conditions.—

  (A) 90-day period before fourth anniversary.—Except as provided in subparagraph (B), the petition under subsection (j)(1)(B) must be filed during the 90-day period before the fourth anniversary of the alien's obtaining the record of lawful admission for permanent residence on a conditional basis.

(B) Late petitions for good cause.—Such a petition may be considered, but only if the alien establishes to the satisfaction of the Attorney General good cause and extenuating circumstances for failure to file the petition during the period described in subparagraph (A).

(C) Filing of petitions during removal.—In the case of an alien who is the subject of removal hearings as a result of failure to file a petition on a timely basis in accordance with subparagraph (A), the Attorney General may stay such removal proceedings against an alien pending the filing of the petition under subparagraph (B).

(l) Payment of Monetary Fines.—

(A) Except as provided in subparagraph (B), the alien shall remit payment under subsection (j)(1)(A) during each year of the four years following the date on which the alien obtained the record of lawful admission for permanent residence on a conditional basis, each payment due during the 90-day period before the anniversary of the alien's obtaining the record of lawful admission for permanent residence on a conditional basis, but payment for the fourth year may be remitted before or at the time of filing the petition described in subsection (j)(1)(B).

(B) Late remittance of payment for good cause shown.—Such remittance may be considered timely, but only if the alien establishes to the satisfaction of the Attorney General good cause and extenuating circumstances for failure to remit the monetary fine during the period described in subparagraph (A).

(C) Remittance of payment.—The alien shall remit payment under subsection (j)(1)(A) to the Attorney General, and the Attorney General shall establish a fund to provide for academic scholarships and job training for U.S. citizens.

(m) Treatment of Period for Purposes of Naturalization.—For purposes of title III, in the case of an alien who is in the United States as a lawful permanent resident on a conditional basis under this section, the alien shall be considered to have been admitted as an alien lawfully admitted for permanent residence and to be in the United States as an alien lawfully admitted to the United States for permanent residence.

APPENDIX 5:
PROPOSED INA § 212(a)(6)(H)

(6) Illegal entrants and immigration violators.—

. . .

    (H) Civil Monetary Fine.—

        (i) Any alien described in subparagraph (A)(i), or who has ever been an alien described in subparagraph (A)(i), shall be inadmissible until the alien remits to the Attorney General a sum equaling $1,000. Remittance of the civil monetary fine described herein shall not act to waive subparagraph (A)(i) or any other ground of inadmissibility, but such fine may be remitted when an alien files an application for the adjustment of his or her status to that of an alien lawfully admitted for permanent residence pursuant to section 245(a) or (i), or when an alien files an application for an immigrant or nonimmigrant visa.

            (I) Exception for certain battered women and children.—Clause (i) shall not apply to an alien who demonstrates the requirements of subparagraph (A)(ii) for every specific period of presence in the United States without having been admitted or paroled, and for every specific arrival in the United States at any time or place other than as designated by the Attorney General.

        (ii) Any alien described in section 237(a)(1)(C)(i), or who has ever been an alien described in section 237(a)(1)(C)(i), shall be inadmissible until the alien remits to the Attorney General a sum equaling $1,000. Remittance of the civil monetary fine described herein shall not act to waive any other ground of inadmissibility, but such fine may be remitted when an alien files an application for the adjustment of his or her status to that of an alien lawfully admitted for permanent residence pursuant to section 245(a) or (i), or when an alien files an application for an immigrant or nonimmigrant visa.

> (I) Exception for certain special immigrants.— Clause (ii) shall not apply to an alien described in section 101(a)(27)(H), (I), (J), or (K).
>
> (II) Exception for failure to continuously maintain lawful status.—Clause (ii) shall not apply to an alien who through no fault of his own or for technical reasons has failed to continuously maintain a lawful status since entry into the United States.

(iii) The fine described herein shall not be charged to an alien who has previously been admitted as a lawful permanent resident, unless such alien subsequently seeks admission as a lawful permanent resident alien and has since his previous admission as a lawful permanent resident alien been an alien described in subparagraph (A)(i) or an alien described in section 237(a)(1)(C)(i).

Appendix 6: Proposed Amended INA § 212(a)(9)(B) and Deletion of INA § 212(a)(9)(C)

(9) Aliens previously removed.—

. . .

    (B) Aliens unlawfully present.—

        (i) In general.—Any alien (other than an alien lawfully admitted for permanent residence) who—

            (I) ~~was unlawfully present in the United States for a period of more than 180 days but less than 1 year, voluntarily departed the United States (whether or not pursuant to section 244(e)) prior to the commencement of proceedings under section 235(b)(1) or section 240, and again seeks admission within 3 years of the date of such alien's departure~~ or removal, or

            (II) ~~has been unlawfully present in the United States for one year or more, and who again seeks admission within 10 years of the date of such alien's departure or removal from the United States, is inadmissible.~~

            (I) has been unlawfully present in the United States for an aggregate period of more than 1 year, or

            (II) has been ordered removed under section 235(b)(1), section 240, or any other provision of law, and who enters or attempts to reenter the United States without being admitted is inadmissible.

(ii) Construction of unlawful presence.—For purposes of this paragraph, an alien is deemed to be unlawfully present in the United States if the alien is present in the United States after the expiration of the period of stay authorized by the Attorney General or is present in the United States without being admitted or paroled.

(iii) Exceptions.—

(I) Minors.—No period of time in which an alien is under 18 years of age shall be taken into account in determining the period of unlawful presence in the United States under clause (i)(I).

(II) Asylees.—No period of time in which an alien has a bona fide application for asylum pending under section 208 shall be taken into account in determining the period of unlawful presence in the United States under clause (i)(I) unless the alien during such period was employed without authorization in the United States.

(III) Family unity.—No period of time in which the alien is a beneficiary of family unity protection pursuant to section 301 of the Immigration Act of 1990 shall be taken into account in determining the period of unlawful presence in the United States under clause (i)(I).

(IV) Battered women and children.—Clause (i)(I) shall not apply to an alien who would be described in paragraph (6)(A)(ii) if "violation of the terms of the alien's nonimmigrant visa" were substituted for "unlawful entry into the United States" in subclause (III) of that paragraph.

(V) Victims of a severe form of trafficking in persons.—Clause (i)(I) shall not apply to an alien who demonstrates that the severe form of trafficking (as that term is defined in section 103 of the Trafficking Victims Protection Act of 2000 (22 U.S.C. 7102)) was at least one central reason for the alien's unlawful presence in the United States.

(iv) Tolling for good cause.—In the case of an alien who—

(I) has been lawfully admitted or paroled into the United States,

(II) has filed a nonfrivolous application for a change or extension of status before the date of expiration of the period of stay authorized by the Attorney General, and

(III) has not been employed without authorization in the United States before or during the pendency of such application, the calculation of the period of time specified in clause (i)(I) shall be tolled during the pendency of such application, but not to exceed 120 days.

(v) Waiver.—The Attorney General has sole discretion to waive clause (i)(I) in the case of an immigrant who is the spouse or son or daughter of a United States citizen or of an alien lawfully admitted for permanent residence, if it is established to the satisfaction of the Attorney General that the refusal of admission to such immigrant alien would result in extreme hardship to the citizen or lawfully resident spouse or parent of such alien. No court shall have jurisdiction to review a decision or action by the Attorney General regarding a waiver under this clause.

(vi) Exception.—Clause (i)(II) shall not apply to an alien seeking admission more than 10 years after the date of the alien's last departure from the United States if, prior to the alien's reembarkation at a place outside the United States or attempt to be readmitted from a foreign contiguous territory, the Attorney General has consented to the alien's reapplying for admission.

(vii) Waiver.—The Attorney General may waive the application of clause (i) in the case of an alien who is a VAWA self-petitioner if there is a connection between—

(I) the alien's having been battered or subjected to extreme cruelty; and

(II) the alien's removal; departure from the United States; reentry or reentries into the United States; or attempted reentry into the United States.

(C) Aliens unlawfully present after previous immigration violations.—

(i) In general.—Any alien who—

(I) has been unlawfully present in the United States for an aggregate period of more than 1 year, or

(II) has been ordered removed under section 235(b)(1), section 240, or any other provision of law, and who enters or attempts to reenter the United States without being admitted is inadmissible.

(ii) EXCEPTION.—Clause (i) shall not apply to an alien seeking admission more than 10 years after the date of the alien's last departure from the United States if, prior to the alien's reembarkation at a place outside the United States or attempt to be readmitted from a foreign contiguous territory, the Attorney General has consented to the alien's reapplying for admission. The Attorney General in the Attorney General's discretion may waive the provisions of section 212(a)(9)(C)(i) in the case of an alien to whom the Attorney General has granted classification under clause (iii), (iv), or (v) of section 204(a)(1)(A), or classification under clause (ii), (iii), or (iv) of section 204(a)(1)(B), in any case in which there is a connection between—

(1) the alien's having been battered or subjected to extreme cruelty; and

(2) the alien's—

(A) removal;

(B) departure from the United States;

(C) reentry or reentries into the United States; or

(D) attempted reentry into the United States.

Notes

Foreword

1. Dan Walter, "Legislature's Session Ends on Note of Mistrust," *Orange County Register* (Sept. 18, 2013), Local 11.
2. Letters to the Editor, *Orange County Register* (Sept. 17, 2013), Local 15.
3. Akhil Reed Amar, *America's Unwritten Constitution: The Precedents and Principles We Live By* (New York: Basic Books, 2012), 56.
4. Ibid., 454.

Preface

1. Office of Immigration Statistics, *2011 Yearbook of Immigration Statistics,* U.S. Dep't of Homeland Security (September 2012), http://www.dhs.gov/sites/default/files/publications/immigration-statistics/yearbook/2011/ois_yb_2011.pdf.
2. Ibid.; Office of Immigration Statistics, *2010 Yearbook of Immigration Statistics,* U.S. Dep't of Homeland Security (August 2011), http://www.dhs.gov/xlibrary/assets/statistics/yearbook/2010/ois_yb_2010.pdf.
3. Ibid.
4. Ibid.
5. Ibid.
6. *See generally* Julian Aguilar, "ICE Removes Record Number of Immigrants in FY 2011," *Texas Tribune* (Oct. 19, 2011), http://www.texastribune.org/2011/10/19/ice-removes-record-number-immigrants-fy-2011/; *see also* United States Immigration & Customs Enforcement, *Removal Statistics,* U.S. Immigration & Customs Enforcement, http://www.ice.gov/news/releases/1110/111018washingtondc.htm.
7. United States Immigration & Customs Enforcement, *Removal Statistics,* U.S.

Immigration & Customs Enforcement, https://www.ice.gov/news/releases/1212/121221washingtondc2.htm.

8. United States Immigration & Customs Enforcement, *Removal Statistics,* U.S. Immigration & Customs Enforcement, https://www.ice.gov/news/releases/1312/131219washingtondc.htm.

9. We want to stress that, while we support certain measures of relief for many of those who are unlawfully present, we strongly believe that tough enforcement of our immigration laws cannot be ignored. We believe that we can, and we should, combine tough enforcement with some remedial measures to develop an effective comprehensive plan for immigration reform.

Chapter One

1. An alien means any person not a citizen or national of the United States. Immigration & Nationality Act (INA) § 101(a)(3), codified at 8 U.S.C. § 1101(a)(3) (West, Westlaw through P.L. 113-22).

2. A temporary category generally (but not always) requires that the alien not have immigrant intent, and admission is for a specific purpose and ordinarily for a fixed duration of time. INA §§ 101(a)(15); 214 (a), (b), & (h); *accord Matter of Hosseinpour,* 15 I. & N. Dec. 191, 192 (BIA 1975) ("a desire to remain in this country permanently in accordance with the law, should the opportunity to do so present itself, is not necessarily inconsistent with lawful nonimmigrant status").

3. A lawful immigrant is one who has been "lawfully admitted for permanent residence." *See,* e.g., INA § 101(a)(20). Documentary proof of such status is most often a small, plastic card identified as Form I-551, also known as a "green card." Generally, after five years of lawful permanent residence and demonstration of good moral character, an alien may seek U.S. citizenship through naturalization. *See,* e.g., INA § 316.

4. Although U.S. immigration law is often much more complex (for example, humanitarian parole under INA § 212(d)(5) is probably neither a temporary nor a permanent category), this simple view of temporary and permanent categories will suffice for the purposes of this book.

5. By definition, any alien present in the United States who does not fit into a nonimmigrant category is an immigrant. *See,* e.g., INA § 101(a)(15). Consequently, aliens unlawfully present are also categorized as immigrants.

6. Nonimmigrants were first recognized by U.S. law in 1819. *See*, e.g., Office of Immigration Statistics, *2003 Yearbook of Immigration Statistics*, U.S. Dep't of Homeland Security (Sept. 2004), http://www.dhs.gov/xlibrary/assets/statistics/yearbook/2003/2003Yearbook.pdf.

7. Immigration and Nationality Act, Pub. L. No. 82-414, 66 Stat. 163 (1952) (as amended).

8. INA §§ 101(a)(15)(A)-(V). A few nonimmigrant categories, e.g., TN and NATO visas, are created by treaty law and thus not found in INA § 101(a)(15). *See*, e.g., INA § 214(e)(2); Aliens & Nationality, 8 C.F.R. §§ 214.2(s), 214.6.

9. In this book, we have chosen to use the generic "he," rather than the more cumbersome "he/she."

10. INA § 214(b).

11. "The term . . . 'admission' . . . mean[s] the lawful entry of an alien into the United States after inspection and authorization by an immigration officer." INA § 101(a)(13)(A).

12. Office of Immigration Statistics, *2012 Yearbook of Immigration Statistics,* United States Dep't of Homeland Security, Table 25, https://www.dhs.gov/yearbook-immigration-statistics-2012-nonimmigrant-admissions.

13. Ibid., Table 6, https://www.dhs.gov/yearbook-immigration-statistics-2012-legal-permanent-residents.

14. *See*, e.g., Comprehensive Immigration Reform Act of 2006, S. 2611, 109th Cong. (2006); Border Security, Economic Opportunity, & Immigration Modernization Act, S. 744, 113th Cong. (2013).

15. Congress has been charged with the task of regulating immigration. *See*, e.g., U.S. Const. art. I, § 8, cls. 3, 4, & 11; § 9, cl. 1. *See also*, e.g., *Chae Chan Ping v. United States* (The Chinese Exclusion Case), 130 U.S. 581 (1889) (recognizing Congressional regulation of immigration).

16. It is not enough that the alien seeking admission into the United States is a good person. He or she must be able to fit into one of the categories designated by Congress.

17. *See* INA §§ 212(a)(1)–(10). The grounds of inadmissibility include, but are not limited to, such grounds as criminal grounds, health-related grounds, terrorism grounds, public-charge grounds, illegal entry and immigration violation grounds. The INA offers some waiver provisions that enable some aliens to overcome certain grounds of inadmissibility. *See*, e.g., the various waiver provisions found throughout INA § 212.

18. INA § 201(a)(1).

19. INA § 201(a)(2).

20. INA § 201(a)(3). Diversity immigrants are aliens from foreign states or regions of the world from which the United States has recently received low percentages of immigration. *See*, e.g., INA § 203(c).

21. The miscellaneous other category includes, but is not limited to, aliens granted relief from removal (e.g., INA § 240A), refugees (e.g., INA § 207), registry (INA § 249), etc. The highly specialized "other" immigrant subcategories will not be discussed in this book at any great length. For present purposes it is enough to say that Congress has granted immigration relief through other provisions of the INA to certain aliens not fitting into one of the three categories at INA § 201(a).

22. INA §§ 201(b)(2); 203(a)–(c).

23. INA §§ 201(a)–(e); 203(a)–(c). The quota limits the number of immigrant visas that may be issued in any fiscal year.

24. INA § 201(c)(1)(A).

25. JNA § 201(c)(1)(B).

26. INA § 201(d).

27. INA § 201(e). The Nicaraguan Adjustment and Central American Relief Act [NACARA], Pub. L. No. 105-100, 111 Stat. 2160, 2193 (1997), allows for a deduction of five thousand visas from the diversity-based category. *See*, e.g., INA § 203(d).

28. For example, the form of relief known as "cancellation of removal," which is included in the "miscellaneous other" category and leads to lawful permanent residency, is limited to only four thousand per year. INA § 240A(e)(1).

29. The per-country limits are only applicable to the family-based, employment-based, and diversity-based categories.

30. INA § 202.

31. INA §§ 202(b)–(c).

32. INA § 202(a)(2). Employment-based immigrants may be exempted from these per-country levels under certain specified conditions pursuant to § 104 of the American Competitiveness in the Twenty-First Century Act, Pub. L. No. 106-313, 114 Sta. 1251 (2000).

33. For a good illustration of this effect, see the State Department Visa Bulletin, issued monthly, that lists waiting times for aliens charged to individual foreign states. In effect, a person charged to Mexico may have a longer waiting time than someone charged to France, for example.

34. INA § 1153(c)(1)(E)(v).

35. INA § 203(d) allows spouses and children to accompany, or follow to join, aliens immigrating to the United States in a preference category (within the broader family-based, employment-based, and diversity-based categories). There is no provision in the INA that allows spouses or children to accompany, or follow to join, immediate relative aliens.

36. Office of Immigration Statistics, *2012 Yearbook of Immigration Statistics,* United States Dep't of Homeland Security, Tables 6 & 7, https://www.dhs.gov/yearbook-immigration-statistics-2012-legal-permanent-residents.

37. *See,* e.g., Immigration Policy Center, American Immigration Council, Focusing on the Solutions—Family Immigration: Repairing our Broken Immigration System, Jan. 15, 2010.

38. INA §§ 202(b)(2); 203(a). These provisions describe the aliens for whom immigrant petitions may be filed.

39. A child is generally defined as unmarried and under the age of twenty-one. *See,* e.g., INA § 101(b)(1). *See also* INA § 203(h); Child Status Protection Act (CSPA), Pub. L. No. 107-208, 116 Stat. 927 (2002). The CSPA lays out elaborate rules that serve to protect some children from aging-out during the immigration process.

40. The term "spouse" referred only to a person of the opposite sex under the Defense of Marriage Act (DOMA), Pub. L. No. 104-199, § 3, 110 Stat. 2419 (1996). In addition, an earlier Ninth Circuit decision held that the term "spouse" referred only to a person of the opposite sex under the INA. *Adams v. Howerton,* 673 F.2d 1036 (9th Cir. 1982), *cert. denied,* 458 U.S. 1111 (1982). The U.S. Supreme Court recently struck down § 3 of DOMA as unconstitutional. *United States v. Windsor,* 570 U.S. (2013). Following the *Windsor* decision, the BIA ruled that DOMA no longer precludes recognition of same-sex spouses (if the marriage is valid under the laws of the jurisdiction where it was celebrated). *Matter of Zeleniak,* 26 I & N Dec. 158 (BIA 2013).

41. A parent is generally defined by way of reference to the definition of "child." *See,* e.g., INA § 101(b)(2).

42. INA § 201(b)(2)(A)(i).

43. Ibid.; INA § 204(a)(1)(A)(i).

44. Ibid. Because the required age is twenty-one, the effect is that a child (who, by definition, is under twenty-one) cannot file an immigrant petition for a parent. Accordingly, the idea of an "anchor baby" is severely flawed.

45. INA § 201(b)(2)(B).

46. INA § 201(b).

47. INA §§ 201(a); 203(a).

48. INA §§ 203(a)(1)–(4).

49. Ibid.; INA §§ 204(a)(1)(A)(i); 204(a)(1)(B)(i)(I).

50. INA §§ 203(a)(1)–(4).

51. INA §§ 204(a)(1)(A)(i); 204(a)(1)(B)(i)(I).

52. INA § 203(a)(1). A "child" is an unmarried person under twenty-one. A "son" or a "daughter," therefore, is either married or is twenty-one years or older, whether married or not. *See*, e.g., INA § 101(b)(1).

53. INA § 203(a)(1).

54. INA § 203(a)(2).

55. INA § 203(a)(2)(A).

56. INA § 203(a)(2)(B).

57. INA § 203(a)(2).

58. Ibid.

59. INA § 203(a)(3).

60. *See*, e.g., INA § 101(b)(1).

61. INA § 203(a)(3).

62. INA § 203(a)(4).

63. Ibid.

64. Ibid.

65. The second and third employment-based categories require a labor certification from the Department of Labor. The labor certification is a certification from the Secretary of Labor that there are not sufficient able, willing, and qualified workers already in the United States at (1) the time an alien seeks employment-based admission and (2) the place where the intending alien will perform labor pursuant to that admission. *See*, e.g., INA § 212(a)(5). There is, however, a national-interest waiver in some instances. *See*, e.g., INA § 203(b)(2)(B).

66. *See,* e.g., Immigration Policy Center, American Immigration Council, Focusing on the Solutions—Family Immigration: Repairing our Broken Immigration System, Jan. 15, 2010.

67. *Compare* INA §§ 203(b)(1)–(4) with INA § 203(b)(5).

68. *2012 Yearbook, supra* note 36.

69. *See*, e.g., INA § 201(b).

70. INA §§ 201(a)(2) & (d).

71. INA §§ 203(b)(1)–(5).

72. Ibid.; 8 C.F.R. §§ 204.5 & 204.6.

73. INA §§ 203(b)(1)–(5).

74. 8 C.F.R. § 204.5(h)(2). Under the INA, "[e]xtraordinary ability means a level of expertise indicating that the individual is one of that small percentage who have risen to the very top of the field of endeavor." Ibid.

75. Generally, a U.S. employer desiring and intending to employ an alien must file a petition on behalf of the alien. *See*, e.g., INA § 204(a)(1)(F); 8 C.F.R. § 204.5(c). However, aliens who fit into the first prong of the employment-based first preference category may file a self-petition. Ibid. Moreover, certain special immigrant aliens who fit into the employment-based fourth preference category may also file a self-petition. Ibid.; *see also* INA § 101(a)(27)(C).

76. INA §§ 203(b)(1)(A)–(C).

77. INA § 203(b)(1).

78. INA § 203(b)(2). Extraordinary ability is an ability that is something higher than exceptional ability. *Compare, e.g.,* 8 C.F.R. § 204.5(h)(2) with § 204.5(k)(2). For the employment-based second preference category, the exceptional ability must be demonstrated in the sciences, arts, or business.

79. INA § 203(b)(2)(A).

80. INA § 203(b)(3).

81. INA § 203(b)(3)(A).

82. INA § 203(b)(3)(B).

83. INA § 203(b)(4). Special immigrants described in INA § 101(a)(27) include, but are not limited to, employees of the U.S. government abroad, certain medical school graduates or medical practitioners, and certain immigrant juveniles.

84. INA § 203(b)(4).

85. Ibid.

86. INA § 203(b)(5).

87. INA § 203(b)(5)(A).

88. Ibid.

89. *See,* e.g., Immigration Policy Center, American Immigration Council, Focusing on the Solutions—Family Immigration: Repairing our Broken Immigration System, Jan. 15, 2010.

90. *See,* e.g., INA § 203(c)(1).

91. *2012 Yearbook, supra* note 36.

92. Ibid.

93. The regulations for diversity immigrants are found at 22 C.F.R. § 42.33.

94. *See generally* Office of Immigration Statistics, *2012 Yearbook of Immigration Statistics,* United States Dep't of Homeland Security, https://www.dhs.gov/yearbook-immigration-statistics-2012-legal-permanent-residents.

95. INA §§ 207; 208; 209.

96. INA § 249.

97. Exceptional and extremely unusual hardship is a high threshold that few aliens will be able to demonstrate. *See,* e.g., *Matter of Recinas*, 23 I. & N. 467 (BIA 2002).

98. INA § 240A.

99. *2012 Yearbook, supra* note 36.

100. For an excellent review of many of the "miscellaneous other" provisions, *see* Joseph A. Vail, *Essentials of Removal and Relief, Representing Individuals in Immigration Proceedings* (American Immigration Lawyers Association) (2006).

101. INA § 101(a)(15)(B).

102. *See generally*, e.g., INA § 101(a)(15).

103. *See*, e.g., INA §§ 101(a)(15), 201–04.

104. *See*, e.g., INA § 212(a). Also, note that certain forms of relief will expect certain aliens from the § 212(a) grounds of inadmissibility.

105. There are other provisions in U.S. law that address inadmissibility (e.g., INA §§ 211; 212(e), (f), (j), (m), & (n); 214(k)(3); 222(g); 306; & Enhanced Border Security & Visa Entry Reform Act of 2002, Pub. L. No. 107-173, 116 Stat. 543 (2002)), but INA § 212(a) is the principle provision used to exclude aliens from the United States).

106. While the spousal petition may or may not be approved (which only speaks to the validity of the marriage), the alien described in this example will be inadmissible under the terrorist-related ground of INA § 212(a)(3)(B).

107. Other grounds of inadmissibility include, but are not limited to, failure to present documentation showing vaccination against vaccine-preventable diseases (INA § 212(a)(1)(A)(ii)), likely to become a public charge (§ 212(a)(4)(A)), ineligible for U.S. citizenship (§ 212(a)(8)(A)), previously unlawfully present (§ 212(a)(9)(B)), practicing polygamists (§ 212(a)(10)(A)).

108. To be sure, intending nonimmigrants are also subject to the INA § 212(a) grounds of inadmissibility. Moreover, an alien already accorded lawful permanent resident status may be subject to § 212(a) grounds of inadmissibility

as well. *See*, e.g., § 101(a)(13). The INA also contains grounds of deportability, found principally at INA § 237, that allow for the deportation, or expulsion, of aliens who have previously been admitted in any status.

109. *Lok v. INS*, 548 F.2d 37 (2d Cir. 1977).

Chapter Two

1. However, on June 15, 2012, President Obama signed into law the Deferred Action for Childhood Arrivals, which gave certain immigrants who came to the United States as children the option to request deferred action of removal for two years, along with work authorization.

2. On carrying the Latino vote, *see generally* Julia Preston and Fernando Santos, "A Record Latino Turnout, Solidly Backing Obama," *New York Times* (Jul. 31, 2008), http://www.nytimes.com/2012/11/08/us/politics/with-record-turnout-latinos-solidly-back-obama-and-wield-influence.html?_r=0.

3. "Obama Promises Immigration Reform if Re-Elected, According to Iowa Paper," *Fox News Latino* (Oct. 24, 2012), http://latino.foxnews.com/latino/politics/2012/10/24/obama-promises-immigration-reform-if-re-elected-according-to-iowa-paper/.

4. While the Immigration Act of 1990 and the Illegal Immigration Reform and Immigrant Responsibility Act of 1996 were certainly important pieces of legislation, we do not include them here as comprehensive because the former focused mainly on expanding numerical limits and the latter primarily focused on punitive-type measures. Other immigration legislation since the late 1980s similarly lacks the comprehensive impact that is currently being debated.

5. In this book, in order to avoid any potentially pejorative terms, we will refer to the unlawful entry of aliens into the United States and the unlawful overstaying of visas as "unauthorized immigration." We note that the term "alien" is offensive to some, but we have chosen to use this term in some places because it is defined specifically in the INA and, consequently, is helpful in discussing U.S. immigration law.

6. Similarly, we will refer to those who have entered unlawfully as well as those who have overstayed visas as "undocumented immigrants."

7. Kris W. Kobach, "Reinforcing the Rule of Law: What States Can and Should Do to Reduce Illegal Immigration," 22 Geo. Immigr. L. J. 459 (2008).

8. Kevin R. Johnson and Bernard Trujillo, "Immigration Reform, National

Security after September 11, & the Future of North American Integration," 91 *Minn. L. Rev.* 1370 (2007).

9. *See* American Immigration Council, *The DREAM Act,* Immigration Policy Center, http://www.immigrationpolicy.org/issues/DREAM-Act. *See also* infra chap. 9 note 42.

10. DACA does not lead to LPR status and, consequently, does not lead to U.S. citizenship. We also think it important to note that we believe that President Obama was properly acting in the discretionary authority delegated to him by Congress when he signed DACA into law. How far that authorization extends (e.g., granting DACA benefits to family members of DACA beneficiaries) is a question of law, and we express no opinion in this regard. We would, however, caution against executive action in lieu of comprenhsive immigration reform.

11. "Immigration Bills," Govtrack.us, http://www.govtrack.us/congress/bills/subjects/immigration/6206#sort=-introduced_date.

12. Ibid.

13. Ibid.

14. Another proposal, promoted by the Vernon K. Krieble Foundation, calls for issuing a "red card" that would allow noncitizen workers to enter the United States temporarily to work. *See*, e.g., http://redcardsolution.com/. We believe this proposal has a number of serious flaws. For example, the argument put forth by supporters of the red card—that the United States does not provide enough work visas—fails to consider the protection of the American work force and prevailing wages. We also believe that allowing employment agencies abroad to issue the red card, which the proposal advocates, would not be sound policy. We do not believe that the federal government would be able to adequately monitor employment agencies throughout the world, and fraud and exploitation would become an immediate problem. We have other objections to the proposal, but we need not here express each of our objections.

15. For example, Congressman Ted Poe has been characterized as one of these hardliners. Elizabeth Llorente, "Senior GOP Congressman Ted Poe, Once An Immigration Hardliner, Softens Stance," *Fox News Latino* (Apr. 11, 2013), http://latino.foxnews.com/latino/politics/2013/04/11/senior-gop-congressman-ted-poe-once-immigration-hardliner-softens-stance/.

16. *See* Border Security, Economic Opportunity, and Immigration Modernization Act, S. 744, 113th Cong. (2013).

17. *See*, e.g., Ashley Parker and Jonathan Martin, "Senate, 68–32, Passes Overhaul for Immigration," *New York Times* (Jun. 27, 2013).

18. Immigration Modernization Act, *supra* note 16.

19. Ibid.

20. Ibid.

21. Ibid.

22. Ibid.

23. Ibid.

24. Ibid.

25. E-Verify is an Internet-based system that allows businesses to attempt to determine the eligibility of their employees to work in the United States. *See generally* U.S. Citizenship & Immigration Services, *E-Verify,* U.S. Citizenship & Immigration Services (last updated Aug. 15, 2013), http://www.uscis.gov/portal/site/uscis/menuitem.eb1d4c2a3e5b9ac89243c6a7543f6d1a/?vgnextoid=75bce2e261405110VgnVCM1000004718190aRCRD&vgnextchannel=75bce2e261405110VgnVCM1000004718190aRCRD.

26. J.D. Tuccille, "E-Verify Makes Working for a Living a Privilege Granted by the Government," Reason.com (May 9, 2013), http://reason.com/blog/2013/05/09/e-verify-makes-working-for-a-living-a-pr.

27. *See generally*, Bob Corker, U.S. Senator for Tennessee, "Highlights of the Hoeven-Corker Amendment to the Immigration Bill," News Room (Jun. 22, 2013), http://www.corker.senate.gov/public/index.cfm/news?ID=9b091a42-f7e4-4751-a361-731db54d835d.

28. Immigration Modernization Act, *supra* note 16.

29. Ibid.

30. Ibid.

31. Ibid.

32. Ibid. (This means, at a minimum, the use of enhanced methods of technology for full surveillance of the southern border.)

33. Ibid.

34. Ibid.

35. Ibid.

36. Ibid.

37. Ibid.

38. Ibid.

39. *See* Seung Min Kim, "Immigration Bill: John McCain Says 'Border Surge'

Isn't Certain," *Politico* (Jul. 30, 2013), http://www.politico.com/story/2013/07/immigration-border-surge-john-mccain-94927.html.

40. Immigration Modernization Act, *supra* note 16.

41. Ibid.

42. Ibid.

43. Ibid.

44. Ibid.

45. Ibid.

46. Ibid.

47. Ibid.

48. Ibid. We believe this should be tied to a specific reduction in the number of unlawful entries, not the unclear "substantially complete" standard above, and if there is a significant reduction in the number of apprehensions, it would be logical to conclude that the border is more secure.

49. Immigration Modernization Act, *supra* note 16.

50. Ibid.

51. Ibid.

52. *See*, e.g., Alberto R. Gonzales, "We Must Do Better On Immigration Reform," *The Hill* (Jul. 10, 2013), http://thehill.com/opinion/op-ed/310307-we-must-do-better-on-immigration-reform.

53. Ibid.

54. Immigration Modernization Act, *supra* note 16.

55. Ibid. Siblings, however, would be allowed to file petitions for an additional eighteen months after enactment of the bill.

56. Immigration Modernization Act, *supra* note 16.

57. Ibid.

58. The V visa is a temporary nonimmigrant visa available to spouses and minor children of U.S. lawful permanent residents who have been waiting for at least three years to immigrate to the United States. *See, e.g.,* INA § 101(a)(15)(V).

59. Immigration Modernization Act, *supra* note 16.

60. Ibid.

61. Ibid.

62. Ibid.

63. Ibid.

64. Ibid.

65. Ibid.

66. Ibid.

67. Ibid.

68. Ibid.

69. Ibid.

70. Ibid.

71. Ibid.

72. Ibid.

73. Ibid.

74. Ibid.; *see also* Harold L. Sirkin, "To Fix Immigration, Improve U.S. Education and Link Visas to Employer Needs," *Business Week* (Dec. 2, 2013), http://www .businessweek.com/articles/2013-12-02/to-fix-immigration-improve-u-dot-s-dot-education-and-link-visas-to-employer-needs.

75. Immigration Modernization Act, *supra* note 16.

76. Ibid.

77. Ibid.

78. Ibid.

79. Ibid.

80. Ibid.

81. Ibid.

82. Ibid.

83. Ibid.

84. Ibid.

85. Ibid.

86. Ibid.

87. Ibid.

88. Ibid.

89. Ibid. Regarding any discussion of increased numbers of temporary workers, we should not overlook the humanity of the workers and those with whom they come in contact. These workers are, after all, people, and people tend to establish roots (with families often being in the mix). We must be sure that our immigration laws are capable of embracing this reality compassionately and fairly. *See generally* "Man hat Arbeitskräfte gerufen, und es kommen Menschen" [We sought workers, and human beings came], Max Frisch, Überfremdung I, in *Schweiz als Heimat*, at 219 (1990).

90. American Immigration Council, *A Guide to H.R. 15: The Border Security, Economic Opportunity, and Immigration Modernization Act,* Immigration Pol-

icy Center (Oct. 10, 2013), http://www.immigrationpolicy.org/special-reports/guide-hr-15-border-security-economic-opportunity-and-immigration-modernization-act.

91. Ibid.

92. Ibid.

93. *See*, e.g., "The Issue: Supporters Want Immigration Reform back in the Limelight," *United Press International* (Oct. 20, 2013), http://latino.foxnews.com/latino/politics/2013/06/30/immigration-bill-will-not-offer-pathway-to-citizenship-gop-leader-says/.

94. Ezra Klein, "READ: President Obama's Immigration Proposal," *Washington Post* (Jan. 29, 2013), http://www.washingtonpost.com/blogs/wonkblog/wp/2013/01/29/read-president-obamas-immigration-proposal/.

95. *See*, e.g., ibid.

96. Robert Costa, "A Gang of Six Plots a Revolt," *National Review Online* (Apr. 15, 2013), http://www.nationalreview.com/articles/345548/gang-six-plots-revolt-robert-costa.

Chapter Three

1. Michael Hoefer, Nancy Rytina, and Christopher Campbell, "Immigration Population Residing in the United States: January 2006," Office of Immigration Statistics (Aug. 2007), http://www.dhs.gov/xlibrary/assets/statistics/publications/ill_pe_2006.pdf.

2. "Modes of Entry for the Unauthorized Migrant Population," Pew Historic Center (May 22, 2006), http://pewhispanic.org/files/factsheets/19.pdf; "A Nation of Immigrants: A Portrait of the 40 Million, Including 11 Million Unauthorized," Pew Research.

3. Julia Preston, "Decline Seen in Numbers of People Here Illegally," *New York Times* (Jul. 31, 2008), http://www.nytimes.com/2008/07/31/us/31immig.html?_r=1&partner=rssnyt; *but see* Judson Berger, "Feds See Surge in Children Crossing US–Mexico Border amid Concerns over Immigration Policy, *Fox News* (Dec. 23, 2013), http://www.foxnews.com/politics/2013/12/23/feds-see-surge-in-children-crossing-us-border-amid-concerns-over-immigration/.

4. Ibid.

5. USCIS Strategic plan, 2008–2012, U.S. Citizenship and Immigration Services (December 2007), available at http://www.uscis.gov/sites/default/files/USCIS/

About%20Us/Budget,%20Planning%20and%20Performance/USCIS_
Strategic_Plan_2008-2012.pdf.

6. Ibid.

7. Ibid.

8. Ibid.

9. *See*, e.g., "16,000 Current Insurance Industry Jobs Open in Nation, But
Aging Workforce Poses Future Risk," *PR Newswire* (Mar. 4, 2013), http://www.
prnewswire.com/news-releases/16000-current-insurance-industry-jobs-open-
in-nation-but-aging-workforce-poses-future-risk-195104221.html.

10. United States Census Bureau, *U.S. & World Population Clock,* U.S. Department of Commerce (Jun. 28, 2013), http://www.census.gov/popclock/.

11. Jeremy Pelofsky and Vicki Allen, "Number of Illegal Immigrants in U.S.
is Stable: DHS," *Reuters* (Mar. 24, 2012), http://www.reuters.com/arti-
cle/2012/03/24/us-usa-immigration-idUSBRE82N09I20120324.

12. Office of the Inspector General, *Follow-Up Report on INS Efforts to Improve
the Control of Nonimmigrant Overstays: Report No. I-2002-006,* U.S. Department of Justice (Apr. 2002), http://www.justice.gov/oig/reports/INS/e0206/
intro.htm#bac. Rey Koslowski, "Real Challenges for Virtual Borders: The
Implementation of US-VISIT," Migration Policy Institute (Jun. 2005), www.
migrationpolicy.org/pubs/Koslowski_Report.pdf. *Overstay Tracking: A Key
Component of Homeland Security and a Layered Defense*, U.S. Government
Accountability Office (May 2004), http://www.gao.gov/new.items/d0482.pdf.

13. Gordon H. Hanson, "The Economics and Policy of Illegal Immigration in the
United States," Migration Policy Institute (Dec. 2009), http://www.immigra-
tionresearch-info.org/report/migration-policy-institute/economics-and-poli-
cy-illegal-immigration-united-states.

14. Julia Preston, "Defeat Worries Employers Who Rely on Immigrants," *New
York Times* (Jun. 29, 2007), http://www.nytimes.com/2007/06/29/washington/
29react.html?_r=0.

15. Hope Yen, "Number of Illegal Immigrants in US Steady at 11.2M," *CNS
News* (Feb. 1, 2011), http://cnsnews.com/news/article/number-illegal-immi-
grants-us-steady-112m.

16. Ibid.

17. Pelofsky and Allen, *supra* note 11.

18. Ibid.

19. Ibid.

20. "Employment-Based Immigration to the United States: A Fact Sheet," American Immigration Council (Mar. 29, 2011), http://www.immigrationpolicy.org/just-facts/employment-based-immigration-united-states-fact-sheet.

21. "Employment-Based Immigration Visas," U.S. Department of State, Bureau of Consular Affairs, http://travel.state.gov/visa/immigrants/types/types_1323.html#petition.

22. "Hiring Foreign Workers," U.S. Department of Labor (last updated Jan. 15, 2013), http://www.foreignlaborcert.doleta.gov/hiring.cfm.

23. "Employment-Based Immigration Visas," U.S. Department of State, Bureau of Consular Affairs, http://travel.state.gov/visa/immigrants/types/types_1323.html#petition.

24. *See generally* ibid.

25. For many, an employment visa is not an option because they either do not qualify or they cannot find an employer willing to sponsor them. They might not qualify because (1) they lack skills, or (2) they are inadmissible under the INA. In many instances, employers are not pressed to sponsor immigrants because they have unlawful aliens on the payroll already.

26. Pew Hispanic Center Analysis, "Working Under the Radar," *New York Times*, http://4.bp.blogspot.com/_1V7wnZxPqok/RlkGAuBee6I/AAAAAAAAElc/4JS08cyXV7Y/s400/illegal+graph.gif.

27. "The Dark Side of Illegal Immigration: Facts, Figures & Statistics on Illegal Immigration," U.S. Illegal Aliens, http://www.usillegalaliens.com/impacts_of_illegal_immigration_jobs.html. Some argue that these are jobs that many Americans do not want, and that the employers are willing to hire American workers, but many times they hire undocumented workers because they cannot find American workers.

28. Karin Brulliard, "Study: Immigrants Pay Tax Share," *Washington Post* (Jun. 5, 2006), http://www.washingtonpost.com/wp-dyn/content/article/2006/06/04/AR2006060400965.html.

29. Robert Justich and Betty Ng, "The Underground Labor Force Is Rising to the Surface," *Bear Stearns* (Jan. 3, 2005), http://www.illegalaliens.us/images/Bear%20Stearns%20Study.pdf.

30. Ibid.

31. Mike Burns et al., "10 Myths Conservative Media Will Use Against Immigration Reform," Media Matters for America (Feb. 1, 2013), http://mediamatters

.org/research/2013/02/01/10-myths-conservative-media-will-use-against-im/192494.

32. Elizabeth Llorente, "Immigration Summit: Are Undocumented Workers Really Taking 'American' Jobs?," *Fox News Latino* (Jun. 12, 2012), http://latino.foxnews.com/latino/politics/ 2012/06/12/immigration-summit-are-un-doc-workers-really-taking-american-jobs/.

33. "The Impact of Unauthorized Immigrants on the Budgets of State and Local Governments," Congressional Budget Office (Dec. 2007), p. 6, http://www.cbo.gov/sites/ default/files/cbofiles/ftpdocs/87xx/doc8711/12-6-immigration.pdf.

34. Justich and Ng, *supra* note 29.

35. Kris W. Kobach, "Reinforcing the Rule of Law: What States Can and Should Do to Reduce Illegal Immigration," 22 Geo. Immigr. L. J. 459 (2008).

36. Ibid.

37. Ibid.

38. This is not a complete loss because a certain number of these undocumented immigrants eventually become U.S. citizens who contribute beneficially to our society. *See*, e.g., *Plyler v. Doe*, 457 U.S. 202 (1982).

39. Kobach, *supra* note 35.

40. Robert McNatt and Frank Benassi, "Econ 101 on Illegal Immigrants," *Bloomberg Business Week Market & Finance* (Apr. 6, 2006), http://www.businessweek.com/investor/content/apr2006/ pi20060407_072803.htm.

41. Justich and Ng, *supra* note 29.

42. Ibid.

43. *Plyler,* 457 U.S. 202.

44. Ibid.

45. Ed Rubenstein, "The Burden of Plyler v. Doe," *The Social Contract* (Summer 2010), http://www.thesocialcontract.com/artman2/publish/tsc_20_4/tsc_20_4_rubenstein_plyer_doe_printer.shtml.

46. "Arizona Bilingual Programs Must Discontinue by Fall," *Heartland* (Mar. 1, 2001), http://news.heartland.org/newspaper-article/2001/03/01/arizona-bilin-gual-programs-must-discontinue-fall.

47. Mary Carol Combs et al., "Bilingualism for the Children: Implementing a Dual Language Program in an English Only State" (July 2004), http://uacoe.arizona.edu/serp404-504/Bilingualism%20for%20the%20Children.pdf.

48. "Health Care for Undocumented Immigrants Cost $1.1B in 2000, Study Finds," *Medical News Today* (Nov. 17, 2006), http://www.medicalnewstoday.

com/releases/ 56809.php; "Informing Currently Public Policy Debate & Topics on the Public Agenda," Rand Corp., http://www.rand.org/research_areas.html.

49. Richard Wolf, "Rising Health Care Costs Put Focus on Illegal Immigrants," *USA Today* (Jan. 22, 2008), http://www.usatoday.com/news/washington/2008-01-21-immigrant-healthcare_ N. html.

50. 42 U.S.C.A. § 1395dd (West, Westlaw current through Pub. L. 112-238).

51. James R. Edwards, Jr., "The Medicaid Costs of Legalizing Illegal Aliens," Center for Immigration Studies (July 2010), http://cis.org/medicaid-costs. Next Gen. Md., http://www.nextgenmd.org/archives/456.

52. Ibid.

53. Ibid.

54. "Illegal Aliens: Extent of Welfare Benefits Received on Behalf of U.S. Citizen Children," U.S. Gen. Accounting Office (Nov. 1997), http://www.gao.gov/archive/1998/he98030.pdf.

55. Ibid.

56. Ibid.

57. See *1996 Welfare Amendments,* U.S. Social Security Administration (last updated Nov. 14, 2012), http://www.ssa.gov/history/tally1996.html.

58. Ibid.

59. *See*, e.g., Wisconsin Dep't of Justice, http://www.doj.state.wi.us/absolutenm/templates/template_ share.aspx?articleid=883&zoneid=5.

60. Kobach, *supra* note 35.

61. Ibid.

62. Ibid.

63. Ibid.

64. Larry Copeland, "One in Seven Drivers Have No Insurance," *USA Today* (Sept. 12, 2011), http://usatoday30.usatoday.com/news/nation/story/2011-09-11/uninsured-drivers/50363390/1.

65. Julia Preston and Robert Gebeloff, "Some Unlicensed Drivers Risk More Than a Fine," *New York Times* (Dec. 9, 2010), http://www.nytimes.com/2010/12/10/us/10license.html?pagewanted=al)l.

66. *See*, e.g., Andrea Billups, "States Buck Public Opinion, Offer Driver's Licenses to Illegals," *Newsmax* (Jan. 10, 2014), http://www.newsmax.com/Newsfront/illegals-drivers-licenses-states/2014/01/10/id/546325/.

Chapter Four

1. *See*, e.g., Michael A. Olivas, "Immigration-Related State and Local Ordinances: Preemption, Prejudice, and the Proper Role for Enforcement," 2007 *U. Chi. Legal F.* 27 (2007) (citing Maria Pabon Lopez, "Reflections on Educating Latino and Latina Undocumented Children: Beyond Plyler v. Doe," 35 Seton Hall L. Rev. 1373, 1375 (2005) (arguing despite *Plyler* decision, Latino undocumented students remain hostages of political argument over immigration)).

2. *See*, e.g., *Arizona v. United States*, 132 S. Ct. 2492 (2012).

3. U.S. Const. amend. X.

4. *United States v. Sprague*, 282 U.S. 716, 733 (1931).

5. Ibid.

6. *Fry v. United States*, 421 U.S. 542, 547 n.7 (1975).

7. Lymari Morales, "Americans' Immigration Concerns Linger: Nearly Two-thirds Are Dissatisfied with the Current Level of Immigration, *Gallup Politics* (Jan. 17, 2012), http://www.gallup.com/poll/152072/americans-immigration-concerns-linger.aspx.

8. Isabel Lyman, "The Cost of Educating the Children of Illegal Aliens: Exorbitant," *New American* (May 11, 2010), http://www.thenewamerican.com/usnews/constitution/item/7731-the-cost-of-educating-the-children-of-illegal-aliens-exorbitant.

9. *See* brief discussion of *Plyler* in chapter 3.

10. Olivas, *supra* note 1.

11. Ibid.

12. Ibid.

13. Ibid.

14. Ibid.

15. Mary Carol Combs et al., "Bilingualism for the Children: Implementing a Dual Language in an English Only State," *Educational Policy Journal* 19, no. 5: 701–28.

16. Evaon Wong-Kim et al., "Breast Health Issues of Undocumented Women in California and Texas," *Journal of Cancer Education* (Jun. 2009), http://link.springer.com/article/10.1007%2FBF03182318.

17. Richard Wolf, "Rising Health Care Costs Put Focus on Illegal Immigrants," *USA Today* (Jan. 22, 2008), http://www.usatoday.com/news/washington/2008-01-21-immigrant-healthcare N.htm.

18. Olivas, *supra* note 1.

19. Ibid. (citing "2006 State Legislation Relating to Immigration: Enacted, Vetoed, & Pending Gubernatorial Action," National Conference of State Legislatures (Jun. 7, 2006), http://www.ncsl.org/issues-research/immig/2006-state-legislation-related-to-immigration-ena.aspx).

20. "2007 Enacted State Legislation Related to Immigrants & Immigration," National Conference of State Legislators (revised Jan. 31, 2008) http://www.ncsl.org/Portals/1/documents/immig/2007Immigrationfinal.pdf.

21. Ibid. *See also* Julia Preston, "In Reversal, Courts Uphold Local Immigration Laws," *New York Times* (Feb. 10, 2008).

22. Kobach, *supra* chap. 3, note 35.

23. Olivas, *supra* note 1.

24. Calvin L. Lewis, David Strange, and Michael Blake Downey, "Why Arizona Senate Bill 1070 is Constitutional and Not Preempted by Federal Law," 89 *U. Det. Mercy L. Rev*. 283, 290 (2012).

25. Ibid.

26. Illegal Immigration Reform and Immigrant Responsibility Act (IIRIRA), Pub. L, 104-208, 110 Stat. 3009–546 (1996); 8 U.S.C.A. § 1357(g) (2006).

27. 8 U.S.C.A. § 1357(g), INA § 287(g) (2006); *see also* Nicholas D. Michaud, "From 287(G) to SB 1070: The Decline of the Federal Immigration Partnership and the Rise of State-level Immigration Enforcement," 52 *Ariz. L. Rev*. 1083, 1085 (2010) (defining the law as "codified legislation that created what is now known as the 287(g) program").

28. *See* Michaud, *supra* note 27, at 1085.

29. Kobach, *supra* chap. 3, note 35.

30. Ibid.

31. *Arizona v. United States,* 567 U.S. ___, 132 S. Ct. 2492 (2012).

32. Lewis, Strange, and Blake Downey, *supra* note 24, at 290.

33. Support Our Law Enforcement & Safe Neighborhoods Act, S. 1070, 49th Leg., 2d Sess. §2B (Az. 2010) (amended by H.R. 2162, 49th Leg., 2d Sess. (Az. 2010)).

34. Ibid.

35. Ibid.

36. Ibid.

37. Ibid.

38. Ibid.

39. Ibid.

40. Jonathan J. Cooper and Paul Davenport, "Immigration Advocacy Groups to Challenge Arizona Law," *Washington Post* (Apr. 25, 2010), http://www.washingtonpost.com/wp-dyn/content/article/2010/04/24/AR2010042402200.html.

41. Ibid.

42. Jonathan J. Cooper, "Ariz. Immigration Law Target of Protest," MSNBC (Apr. 26, 2010), http://www.msnbc.msn.com/id/36768649/.

43. Cooper and Davenport, *supra* note 40.

44. Ibid.

45. Lewis, Strange, and Blake Downey, *supra* note 24, at 290.

46. Ibid., at 290–91.

47. Ibid.; Jeanne J. Grimmett, "State & Local Economic Sanctions: Constitutional Issues," Congressional Research Service (Jun. 27, 2012), at 8, http://www.fas.org/sgp/crs/homesec/R42719.pdf (*citing, e.g., Crosby v. Nat'l Foreign Trade Council*, 530 U.S. 363, 373 (2000)); *English v. Gen. Elec. Co.,* 496 U.S. 72, 78–79 (1990); *Silkwood v. Kerr-McGee Corp.,* 464 U.S. 238, 248–49 (1984); *Pac. Gas & Elec. Co. v. State Energy Res. Conservation & Dev. Comm'n,* 461 U.S. 190, 203–4 (1983).

48. Lewis, Strange, and Blake Downey, *supra* note 24, at 291–92.

49. *DeCanas v. Bica*, 424 U.S. 351, 354 (1976).

50. Ibid., 355.

51. *See* Michaud, *supra* note 27, at 1090–91.

52. *DeCanas*, 424 U.S. at 354; *see also* Michaud, *supra* note 27, at 1088.

53. David A. Patten, "Arizona-Style Rebellions Over Immigration Spread," *Newsmax* (May 5, 2010), http://www. Newsmax.com/PrintTemplate.aspx?nodeid=357991.

54. "Immigration Plan Draws Fire, Praise," KOCO (Apr. 29, 2010), http://www.fire-education.com/WhatsNew/immigration-plan-draws-fire-praise-koco-oklahoma-city.html.

55. Ibid.

56. Nicholas Riccardi, "On Immigration, Momentum Shifts Away from Arizona," *Los Angeles Times* (Mar. 6, 2011), http://articles.latimes.com/2011/mar/06/nation/la-na-illegal-immigration-20110306.

57. Ibid.

58. Ibid.

59. Ibid.

60. Betty Beard and Megan Neighbor, "National Council of La Raza Calls Off Boycott," *Arizona Republic* (Sept. 9, 2011), http://www.azcentral.com/arizonarepublic/local/articles/20110909arizona-boycott-called-off-la-raza.html.

61. Ethan Sacks, "Battle over Arizona's SB 1070: Oklahoma Eyes Similar Immigration Law; City Councils Eye Boycotts," *N.Y. Daily News* (Apr. 30, 2010), http://www.nydailynews.com/news/national/battle-arizona-sb-1070-oklahoma-eyes-similar-immigration-law-city-councils-eye-boycotts-article-1.169948; *see also* Associated Press, "Seattle City Council Approves Arizona Boycott," *Seattle Times* (May 17, 2010), http://seattletimes.nwsource.com/html/nationworld/2011890438_apusarizonaboycottseattle.html.

62. Elliot Spagat, "Other Border States Shun Arizona's Immigration Law," MSNBC (May 13, 2010), http://www.msnbc.com/id/37116159.

63. Ibid.

64. Ibid.

65. Ibid.

66. Ibid.

67. Ibid.

68. Ibid.

69. Ibid.

70. Ibid.

71. Ibid.

72. Gary Reich and Jay Barth, "Immigration Restriction in the States: Contesting the Boundaries of Federalism?," *Publius* (Jun. 1, 2012), http://publius.oxford-journals.org/content/early/2012/06/01/publius.pjs025.full.pdf+html.

73. Beard and Neighbor, *supra* note 60.

74. Reich and Barth, *supra* note 72.

75. *See* Richard Fausset, "Alabama Enacts Anti-Illegal Immigration Law Described as Nation's Strictest," *Los Angeles Times* (June 10, 2011), http://articles.latimes.com/2011/jun/10/nation/la-na-alabama-immigration-20110610.

76. *See* ibid.

77. *See* ibid.

78. *See* ibid.

79. *See* ibid.

80. *See* ibid.

81. *See* ibid.

82. Lewis, Strange, and Downey, *supra* note 24.

83. *See* Ryan Terrance Chin, "Moving Toward Subfederal Involvement in Federal Immigration Law," 58 *UCLA L. Rev.* 1859, 1906 (2011).

84. *See* Christina M. Rodriguez, "The Significance of the Local in Immigration Regulation," 106 *Mich. L. Rev.* 567, 572 (2008).

85. Lewis, Strange, and Downey, *supra* note 24.

86. Chin, *supra* note 83.

87. Jonathan J. Cooper, "Ariz. Immigration Law Target of Protest," MSNBC (Apr. 26, 2010), http://www.msnbc.msn.com/id/36768649/.

88. *See* Chin, *supra* note 83.

89. Lewis, Strange, and Downey, *supra* note 24.

90. *See* Keith Cunningham-Parmeter, "Force Federalism: States as Laboratories of Immigration Reform," 62 *Hastings L. J.* 1673, 1714 (2011).

91. *See* ibid.

92. Lewis, Strange, and Downey, *supra* note 24.

93. *See* Swati Agrawal, "Trusts Betrayed: The Absent Federal Partner in Immigration Policy," 33 *San Diego L. Rev.* 755, 759 (1996).

94. "Arizona v. United States," *New York Times* (Apr. 25, 2012), http://www. nytimes.com/2012/04/26/opinion/arizona-v-united-states.html?_r=1.

95. Section 2(B) provides that officers who conduct a stop, detention, or arrest must in some circumstances make efforts to verify the person's immigration status with the federal government.

96. Section 3 makes failure to comply with federal alien registration requirements a state misdemeanor.

97. Section 5(C) makes it a misdemeanor for an unauthorized alien to seek or engage in work in the state.

98. Section 6 authorizes officers to arrest without a warrant a person whom "the officer has probable cause to believe . . . has committed any public offense that makes the person removable from the United States."

99. "Arizona v. United States," *New York Times* (Apr. 25, 2012), http://www. nytimes.com/2012/04/26/opinion/arizona-v-united-states.html?_r=1.

100. Ibid.

101. Ibid.

102. Ruthann Robson, "Oral Argument in Arizona v. United States," Constitutional Law Prof Blog (Apr. 25, 2012), http://lawprofessors.typepad.com/con-law/2012/04/oral-argument-in-arizona-v-united-states.html.

103. *U.S. v. Arizona*, 132 S. Ct. 2492.

104. Ibid. (slip op., at 25).

105. Ibid. (slip op., at 24).

106. Editorial Board, "Supreme Court Ruling on Arizona Law Must Lead to 'Civil Discourse' on Illegal Immigration," *Christian Science Monitor* (Jun. 25, 2012), http://www.csmonitor.com/Commentary/the-monitors-view/2012/0625/Supreme-Court-ruling-on-Arizona-law-must-lead-to-civil-discourse-on-illegal-immigration.

107. *U.S. v. Arizona*, 132 S. Ct. 2492 (slip op., at 25).

Chapter Five

1. USCIS Strategic Plan, *supra* chap. 3, note 5.

2. Congress and the president may allocate a separate number for refugee admissions.

3. "How the United States Immigration System Works: A Fact Sheet," Immigration Policy Center (Nov. 4, 2010), http://www.immigrationpolicy.org/just-facts/how-united-states-immigration-system-works-fact-sheet.

4. USCIS Strategic Plan, *supra* chap. 3, note 5.

5. Ibid.

6. Graeme Boushey and Adam Luedtke, "Immigrants Across the U.S. Federal Laboratory: Explaining State-level Innovation in Immigration Policy," *State Politics & Policy Quarterly* 11: 390–414 (2011).

7. Ibid.

8. Ibid.; Brittney M. Lane, "Testing the Borders: The Boundaries of State & Local Power to Regulate Illegal Immigration," 39 *Pep. L. Rev.* 483, 498 (2012).

9. Michael J. Wishnie, "Proportionality: The Struggle for Balance in U.S. Immigration Policy," 72 *U. Pitt. L. Rev.* 431, 438 (2010).

10. Editorial Board, *supra* chap. 4, note 106.

11. Prosecutorial discretion is a legal principle that allows the government to not enforce the law to its fullest extent in any particular case.

12. *U.S. v. Arizona*, 132 S. Ct. 2492 (slip op., at 4–5). Note that the Court uses "unauthorized" workers and does not use the term "illegal."

13. *See* earlier discussion in chapter 2.

14. *See*, e.g., U.S. Const. art. i, § 8, cl. 3; Thomas A. Saenz, "A New Nullification: Arizona's S.B. 1070 Triggers a National Constitutional Crisis," 21 *Berkeley La Raza L. J.* 5, 6 (2011).

15. *See* Saenz, *supra* note 14, at 6.

16. Ibid.

17. Boushey and Luedtke, *supra* note 6.

18. Ibid.

19. *See* Michaud, *supra* chap. 4, note 27, at 1090–91.

20. *See* Chin, *supra* chap. 4, note 83.

21. *See* Cunningham-Parmeter, *supra* chap. 4, note 90.

22. Ibid.

23. Ibid. We recognize the roles of the DOS, DHS, and even the DOJ but nevertheless characterize the federal scheme as a "single entry attempt" because each of these departments is acting under one federal scheme. *See generally* chapter 8.

24. William Riker, *Federalism: Origin, Operation, Significance* (1964).

25. Boushey and Luedtke, *supra* note 6.

26. *See*, e.g., Eduardo Porter, "Illegal Immigrants Are Bolstering Social Security with Billions," *New York Times* (Apr. 5, 2005); Alfonso Serrano, "Why Undocumented Workers Are Good for the Economy," *TIME* (Jun. 14, 2012), http://business.time.com/2012/06/14/the-fiscal-fallout-of-state-immigration-laws/.

27. *See* Cunningham-Parmeter, *supra* chap. 4, note 90; Randy Capps and Michael Fix, "Undocumented Immigrants: Myths & Reality" (2005), 1; Porter, *Illegal Immigrants Are Bolstering Social Security with Billions*, *supra* note 26.

28. *See* Cunningham-Parmeter, *supra* chap.4, note 90; Capps and Fix, *supra* note 27; Porter, *supra* note 27.

29. *See* Serrano, *supra* note 26.

30. See, *e.g.*, Support Our Law Enforcement & Safe Neighborhoods Act, S. 1070, 49th Leg., 2d Sess. (Az. 2010) (amended by H.R. 2162, 49th Leg., 2d Sess. (Az. 2010)).

31. Ibid.

32. *See* Randal C. Archibold and Megan Thee-Brenan, "Poll Finds Serious Concern among Americans about Immigration," *New York Times* (May 4, 2010) (summarizing that roughly two-thirds of Americans hold this belief).

33. Editorial Board, *supra* chap. 4, note 106.

34. Ibid.

35. University of Miami political science professor Casey Klofstad notes that the media attributes President Obama's reelection to the Latino vote. Casey A. Klofstad, "Pre-Election Polls Got It Wrong in Florida," *Latino Decisions* (Nov.

14, 2012), http://www.latinodecisions.com/blog/2012/11/14/pre-election-polls-got-it-wrong-in-florida/.

36. Dan Balz, "Obama & Romney on the Issues: Immigration," *Washington Post* (Oct. 5, 2012), http:// www.washingtonpost.com/politics/decision2012/obama-and-romney-on-the-issues-immigration/2012/10/05/869e516e-0f0a-11e2-bd1a-b868e65d57eb_story.html.

37. Cameron Joseph, "McCain, Hatch, Rubio Offer Optimism on Immigration on Return for Lame Duck," *The Hill* (Nov. 13, 2012), http://thehill.com/homenews/senate/267763-rubio-mccain-hatch-ready-to-negotiate-on-pathway-to-citizenship.

38. "Is Amnesty a Good Solution to Illegal Immigration?," ProCon.Org (last updated May 22, 2009), http://immigration.procon.org/view.answers.php?questionID=000771.

39. We note here that the INA already has several provisions that allow for what may fairly be characterized as amnesty—cancellation of removal for non-permanent residents, registry, adjustment of status for visa overstayers, etc.

40. *See*, e.g., "Immigration Bill Will Not Offer Pathway to Citizenship, GOP Says," *Fox News Latino* (Jun. 30, 2013), http://www.upi.com/Top_News/US/2013/10/20/The-Issue-Supporters-want-immigration-reform-back-in-the-limelight/UPI-91091382259840/; *see also* Mark Hugo Lopez, Paul Taylor, Cary Funk, and Ana Gonzalez-Barrera, *On Immigration Policy, Deportation Relief Seen As More Important Than Citizenship: A Survey of Hispanics and Asian-Americans*, PewResearch Hispanic Trends Project (Dec. 19, 2013), http://www.pewhispanic.org/2013/12/19/on-immigration-policy-deportation-relief-seen-as-more-important-than-citizenship/.

41. *See*, e.g., Ashby Jones, "Samoans' Lawsuit Seeks Automatic U.S. Citizenship," *Wall Street Journal* (Jul. 13, 2012), http://online.wsj.com/article/SB10001424052702303644004577523291350498870.html?KEYWORDS=ashby+jones; *see also* Haw. Const. art. II, § 1(right to vote); Wash. Const. art. III, § 25 (right to hold office); Wash. Rev. Code § 2.36.070 (right to serve as juror); Haw. Rev. Stat. § 134-2(d) (right to bear arms). Importantly, however, a national is not subject to the grounds of inadmissibility. The grounds of inadmissibility are laid out in INA § 212 and in every instance reference made is to an "alien." Under INA § 101(a)(3) the term "alien" is defined as "any person not a citizen or national of the United States." Thus, a proper reading would infer that

nationals are not subject to the grounds of inadmissibility. See also *Matter of Ah San*, 15 I & N. Dec. 315 (1975) ("Most of the inhabitants of these possessions are nationals of the United States and as such they are not subject to the exclusion provisions of our immigration laws") (as reported by S. Comm. on the Judiciary, Apr. 20, 1950).

42. Undoubtedly, many will claim that any immigration reform conferring only U.S. nationality rather than full citizenship is unfair. To such a claim, the authors would query, it is unfair to whom?

43. Consequently, a noncitizen national may only file petitions for those family members described in the second-preference category.

44. *Matter of Ah San*, 15 I. & N. Dec. 315 (BIA 1975).

45. Ibid.

46. Ibid.

47. *Matter of B—*, 6 I. & N. Dec. 555 (BIA 1955).

48. Ibid.

49. Ibid. "Since she does not qualify as a citizen of the United States the petitioner is not eligible to file a visa petition for nonquota status . . . because in both instances the relationship existing must be between that of a citizen parent and an alien child."

50. *Matter of B—*, 6 I. & N. Dec. 555.

51. Ibid. "She will be regarded as eligible to file a petition for a preference [relative] . . . and the visa petition will be approved for . . . preference status for the minor beneficiaries."

52. Michael J. Wishnie, "Proportionality: The Struggle for Balance in U.S. Immigration Policy," 72 *U. Pitt. L. Rev.* 431, 443–44 (2010).

53. The proposed Senate bill, however, has found labor union support. *See*, e.g., Parker and Martin, *supra* chap. 2, note 17.

54. *See* Alan Gomez, "CBO: Senate Bill Could Cut Illegal Immigration by 50%," *USA Today* (Jul. 3, 2013), http://www.usatoday.com/story/news/politics/2013/07/03/immigration-senate-illegal-budget/2486353/.

55. *See* ibid. *But see* Ezra Klein, "CBO: Immigration Reform Is a Free Lunch," *Washington Post* (June 18, 2013) http://www.washingtonpost.com/blogs/wonkblog/wp/2013/06/18/cbo-immigration-reform-is-a-free-lunch/.

56. Ibid.

57. "American Roots in the Immigrant Experience: Immigrants & Children of

Immigrants Comprise Nearly One Quarter of the U.S. Population," Immigration Policy Center (Oct. 19, 2009), http://www.immigrationpolicy.org/sites/default/files/docs/American_Roots_in_the_Immigrants_Experience_101909.pdf.

Chapter Six

1. CBP.gov, "Southwest Border Fence Construction Progress," U.S. Department of Homeland Security, http://www.cbp.gov/xp/cgov/border_security/ti/ti_news/sbi_fence/.
2. Secure Fence Act of 2006, H.R. 6061, 109th Cong. (2006).
3. *See* Stephen Dinan, "Border Patrol Agents Have 'Serious Concerns' about Senate Immigration Bill," *Washington Times* (Jun. 28, 2013), http://www.washingtontimes.com/news/2013/jun/28/border-patrol-agents-have-serious-concerns-about-s/.
4. Secure Fence Act of 2006, H.R. 6061, 109th Cong. (2006).
5. Ibid.
6. *See* David S. Addington, "Encouraging Lawful Immigration and Discouraging Unlawful Immigration," Heritage Foundation (Mar. 27, 2013), http://www.heritage.org/research/reports/2013/03/encouraging-lawful-immigration-and-discouraging-unlawful-immigration.
7. *See*, e.g., "Senate Considering Environmentally Harmful Border Provisions as Part of Immigration Bill," Sky Island Alliance, http://skyislandalliance.org/border-law.htm.
8. *See* Randal C. Archibold, "Border Plan Will Address Harm Done at Fence Site," *New York Times* (Jan. 16, 2009), http://www.nytimes.com/2009/01/17/us/17border.html?ref=borderfenceusmexico&_r=0.
9. *See*, e.g., Senator Chuck Grassley, "Press Release: The Southern Border Security Commission: Comprehensive Immigration Reform" (Jun. 12, 2013), http://www.grassley.senate.gov/news/Article.cfm?customel_dataPageID_1502=46219.
10. With this thought in mind, we should not forget the lessons of the Maginot Line. We also must take careful note that many of the people unlawfully present today are those who have overstayed their visas, rather than those who have unlawfully crossed the border.
11. Secure Fence Act of 2006, H.R. 6061, 109th Cong. (2006).

12. *See generally* CBP.gov, "U.S. Border Security," U.S. Dep't of Homeland Security, http://www.cbp.gov/xp/cgov/border_security/border_patrol/.

13. *See generally* ibid.

14. Homeland Security, "Written Testimony of U.S. Customs and Border Protection Border Patrol Chief Michael Fisher, Office of Field Operations Assistant Commissioner Kevin McAleenan, and Office of Technology Innovation and Acquisition Assistant Commissioner Mark Borkowski for a House Committee on Homeland Security, Subcommittee on Border and Maritime Security 'Measuring the Outcomes to Understand the State of Border Security,'" Department of Homeland Security, http://www.dhs.gov/news/2013/03/20/written-testimony-cbp-house-homeland-security-subcommittee-border-and-maritime.

15. Ibid.

16. Ed Pilkington, "US Immigration Deal Envisages Use of Military Surveillance at Southern Border," *Guardian* (Jun. 25, 2013), http://www.guardian.co.uk/world/2013/jun/25/us-immigration-amendment-surveillance.

17. CBP.gov, "U.S. Border Patrol," U.S. Dep't of Homeland Security, http://www.cbp.gov/xp/cgov/border_security/border_patrol/.

18. Press Release, U.S. Customs & Border Protection, "CBP Makes History with the Launch of Predator B" (Sept. 29, 2005), *see also* Richard M. Thompson II, Cong. Research Serv., "Drones in Domestic Surveillance Operations: Fourth Amendment Implications and Legislative Responses" (Sept. 6, 2012), 1. While drones are controversial and there is a potential for abuse, there should be a clear rule of engagement and an explanation of these rules to the public. Additionally, the administration should have to provide Congress with an annual report on the use and the effectiveness of drones.

19. See Homeland Security, *supra* note 14.

20. The Fourth Amendment guarantees that: "The right of the people to be secure in their persons, houses, papers, and effects, against unreasonable searches and seizures, shall not be violated, and no Warrants shall issue, but upon probable cause, supported by Oath or affirmation, and particularly describing the place to be searched, and the persons or things to be seized." U.S. Const. amend. IV.

21. *See Katz v. United States*, 389 U.S. 347 (1967) (employing "reasonable expectation of privacy" test); *California v. Ciraolo*, 476 U.S. 207 (1986) (finding that the use of a private plane to identify defendant's marijuana operation in

his backyard did not violate the Fourth Amendment); *Florida v. Riley*, 448 U.S. 445 (1989) (finding that the use of a helicopter to observe defendant's marijuana operation did not violate his Fourth Amendment rights because the helicopter was legally within navigable airspace); *Kyllo v. United States*, 533 U.S. 27 (2001) (limiting the ability of law enforcement to use thermal imaging devices to detect activity within the home).

22. *Katz*, 389 U.S. at 360–61 (Harlan, J., concurring).

23. Anthony Kimery, "Legal Aspects of Using Drones for Domestic Surveillance Explored in Congressional Report," *Homeland Security Today* (Apr. 8, 2013), http://www.hstoday.us/single-article/legal-aspects-of-using-drones-for-do-mestic-surveillance-explored-in-congressional-report/2ea2c36e-6f248a0c6e815d2b8f65c91a.html.

24. *Ferguson v. City of Charleston*, 532 U.S. 67 (2001).

25. CBP Canine Program, http://www.cbp.gov/xp/cgov/Border_Security/canine.

26. *See* Homeland Security, *supra* note 14.

27. Ibid.

28. INA §§ 287(g) (1)–(2).

29. INA §§ 287(g)(1)–(4).

30. Ibid.

31. Stephen H. Legomsky and Cristina M. Rodriguez, *Immigration and Refugee Law and Policy*, 1275 (5th ed. 2009).

32. The fact that many people seek voluntary departure from ICE to avoid an order of removal—and are consequently never placed into removal proceedings—may explain why the number here is only 41 percent.

33. *See* Legomsky and Rodriguez, *supra* note 31.

34. *See*, e.g., Audrey Hudson, "Chertoff Warns Meddling 'Sanctuary Cities,'" *Washington Times* (Sept. 6, 2007).

35. *See* Legomsky and Rodriguez, *supra* note 31, at 1279; INA § 287(g)(5).

36. J. J. Hensley, "Judge: Maricopa County Sheriff's Office, ACLU Must Resolve Biased Policing Issue," *AZ Central* (Jun. 14, 2013), http://www.azcentral.com/news/arizona/articles/20130614maricopa-county-sheriff-aclu-biased-policing.html.

37. *See* Legomsky and Rodriguez, *supra* note 31, at 1279.

38. Andrea Noble, "D.C. lags Virginia, Maryland in Immigration Deportations for Secure Communities," *Washington Times* (May 9, 2013), http://www.washingtontimes.com/news/2013/may/9/dc-lags-virginia-maryland-in-immi-grant-deportation/?page=all.

39. *See* Legomsky and Rodriguez, *supra* note 31, at 1281.

40. *Interpreter Releases* 90, no. 1 (2013), 10.

41. Ibid.

42. ICE, "Frequently Asked Questions (FAQs)," U.S. Department of Homeland Security, http://www.ice.gov/secure_communities/faq.htm.

43. Ibid.

44. Ibid.

45. Immigration Policy Center, "Secure Communities: A Fact Sheet," American Immigration Council, http://www.immigrationpolicy.org/just-facts/secure-communities-fact-sheet.

46. "Border Enforcement Security Task Force (BEST)," U.S. Department of Homeland Security, ICE, http://www.ice.gov/best/.

47. Ibid.

48. Ibid.

49. Ibid.

50. Ibid.

51. "Sixty-nine percent of Americans favor the use of military on the border." *Rasmussen*, Apr. 3–4, 2013, http://www.rasmussenreports.com/public_content/politics/general_politics/april_2013/69_favor_use_of_u_s_military_on_border_to_keep_mexican_drug_violence_out. The Posse Comitatus Act of 1878 prohibits the use of U.S. military forces to perform the tasks of civilian law enforcement unless explicitly authorized by Congress, but it does not prohibit acting in support of civilian law enforcement. However, it limits but does not eliminate the power of the president to declare martial law. *See*, e.g., H. CON. RES. 274 (Oct. 25, 2005).

52. Michael D. Doubler, "Operation Jump Start: The National Guard on the Southwest Border, 2006–2008," http://www.nationalguard.mil/features/Border/factsheets/NGB_JumpStart.pdf.

53. *See* ibid.

54. *See* ibid.

55. *See* ibid.

56. "Fact Sheet: Southwest Border Next Steps," U.S. Department of Homeland Security, http://www.dhs.gov/ynews/releases/pr_1277310093825.shtml.

57. *See* ibid.

58. Brian R. Wahlquist, "Slamming the Door on Terrorists and the Drug Trade While Increasing Legal Immigration: Temporary Deployment of the United

States Military at the Borders," 19 *Geo. Immigr. L. J.* 551, 552 (2005).

59. 18 U.S.C.A. § 1385 (2012).

60. 10 U.S.C.A. § 375.

61. 19 *Geo. Immigr. L. J.* 551, 574 (2005).

62. We do not mean to belittle an individual's right to seek relief before a court; we are merely pointing out the need for increased personnel to relieve the strain on our overburdened court system.

Chapter Seven

1. *See* Legomsky and Rodriguez, *supra* chap. 6, note 31, at 1158.

2. *See* GAO-05-259 (Feb. 18, 2008). Employment Eligibility Verification, Form I-9 is a one-page form that employees complete verifying identity as well as the right to work in the United States. The form itself has three parts. The first section includes basic biographical information on the employee, and it asks the employee to certify that he is a citizen, permanent resident, or authorized to work under another status. The second section is completed by an employer who must verify the employee's identity and his right to work in the United States. The third section is reserved for employers who must periodically update the I-9 form if the worker is not authorized to permanently work in the United States.

3. "Overview," U.S. Dep't of Homeland Security, ICE, http://www.ice.gov/about/overview/.

4. *See* ibid.

5. *See* ibid.

6. *See* ibid.

7. *See* ibid.

8. *See* ibid.

9. *See* ibid.; U.S. Immigration and Customs Enforcement, News Releases, "Detroit-area Manager Charged Criminally for Hiring Illegal Aliens," http://www.ice.gov/news/releases/1111/111129detroit.htm.

10. "DHS's Progress in 2011: Identity Verification," U.S. Department of Homeland Security, www.dhs.gov/xabout/2011-dhs-accomplishments-identity-verification.shtm.

11. "E-verify Receives High Ratings in Customer Survey," U.S. Citizenship

and Immigration Services, http://www.uscis.gov/portal/site/uscis/menu-item.5af9bb95919f35e66f614176543f6d1a/?vgnextoid=1671ed7ebecfc310V gnVCM100000082ca60aRCRD&vgnextchannel=68439c7755cb9010Vgn-VCM10000045f3d6a1RCRD.

12. *See* Legomsky and Rodriguez, *supra* chap. 6, note 31, at 1171.

13. *See* ibid., at 1158.

14. INA §§ 274A(a)(1)(A) & (2).

15. *See* Legomsky and Rodriguez, *supra* chap. 6, note 31, at 1160.

16. *Mester Manufacturing Co. v. INS*, 879 F.2d 561, 567 (9th Cir. 1989).

17. *See* ibid.

18. See *New El Rey Sausage Co. v. United States INS*, 925 F.2d 1153, 1157–58 (9th Cir. 1991).

19. Ibid.

20. *Collins Foods International, Inc. v. INS*, 948 F.2d 549, 555 (9th Cir. 1991).

21. *See* ibid.

22. 8 C.F.R. § 274a.1(l)(1).

23. INA §§ 274A(a)(1)(B)(i) & (b).

24. INA § 274A(b)(6).

25. Charles M. Miller, Marcine A. Seid, S. Christopher Stowe, Jr., *Immigration Compliance Auditing for Lawyers* (ABA 2011), 28. The exceptions include (1) persons hired before November 7, 1986; (2) persons employed for domestic work in a private home that is "sporadic, irregular, or intermittent"; (3) persons who are independent contractors and their employees, unless the contract was entered into, renegotiated, or extended after November 6, 1986, to obtain the services of unauthorized aliens; and (4) persons who, though providing services to the employer under contract with an independent contractor, are employees of that contractor. Ibid. (citing 8 C.F.R. §§ 274a.7(a), .1(h), .5). Self-employed persons generally do not need to complete an I-9 form. *See* ibid.

26. INA § 274A(b)(1)(B)(i)–(ii).

27. INA § 274A(b)(1)(C)–(D).

28. *See*, e.g., INA § 274(b).

29. INA § 274A(b)(1)(A).

30. INA § 274A(b)(2).

31. *See*, e.g., 8 CFR 274a.12.

32. "USCIS Redesigns Employment Authorization Document and Certificate of Citizenship to Enhance Security and Combat Fraud," U.S. Citizenship and Immigration Services (Oct. 25, 2011), http://www.uscis.gov/portal/site/uscis/menuitem.5af9bb95919f35e66f614176543f6d1a/?vgnextchannel=68439c7755 cb9010VgnVCM10000045f3d6a1RCRD&vgnextoid=338ce8ba05b33310Vgn-VCM100000082ca60aRCRD.

33. "E-Verify," U.S. Department of Homeland Security, U.S. Citizenship and Immigration Services, http://www.dhs.gov/files/programs/gc_1185221678150.shtm.

34. *See* ibid. Executive Order 12989, which took effect in 2009, mandates the electronic verification of all employees working on any federal contract. Ibid.

35. *See* ibid.

36. "History & Milestones," U.S. Department of Homeland Security, U.S Citizenship and Immigration Services, http://www.uscis.gov/portal/site/uscis/menuitem.eb1d4c2a3e5b9ac89243c6a7543f6d1a/?vgnextoid=84979589cdb762 10VgnVCM100000b92ca60aRCRD&vgnextchannel=84979589cdb76210Vgn-VCM100000b92ca60aRCRD.

37. "E-Verify and Form I-9," U.S. Department of Homeland Security, U.S. Citizenship and Immigration Services, http://www.uscis.gov/portal/site/uscis.

38. *See* "E-verify," *supra* note 33.

39. "The Verification Process," E-Verify, U.S. Department of Homeland Security, U.S. Citizenship and Immigration Services, http://www.uscis.gov/portal/site/uscis.

40. "M-775, E-Verify User Manual for Employers," U.S. Citizenship and Immigration Services (May 2011), 45, www.dhs.gov/E-Verify.

41. Catherine P. Wells, "The Modification and Expansion of the Employment Eligibility Verification Process," *Aspatore Special Report* (2009), 47.

42. Gregory H. Siskind, *The Employer's Immigration Compliance Desk Reference* (2009), 112.

43. Ibid.

44. "IMAGE," U.S. Department of Homeland Security, ICE, http://www.ice.gov/image.

45. "IMAGE Flyer," U.S. Department of Homeland Security, U.S. Immigration and Customs Enforcement, http://www.ice.gov/doclib/image/pdf/image-flyer.pdf.

46. *See* Legomsky and Rodriguez, *supra* chap. 6, note 31, at 1171.

47. Ibid.

48. Ibid.

49. Ibid.

50. INA § 274B(a)(1).

51. INA § 274B(a)(6).

52. INA § 274B(a)(3).

53. INA § 274B(a)(4).

54. INA §274B(a)(2).

55. INA § 274B(a)(2)(A).

56. INA § 274B(a)(2)(B).

57. INA § 274B(a)(2)(C).

58. *See* Legomsky and Rodriguez, *supra* chap. 6, note 31, at 1173.

59. Ibid.

60. INA § 274B(c)(1).

61. INA § 274B(c)(1) & (2).

62. INA § 274B(c)(1).

63. *See* Legomsky and Rodriguez, *supra* chap. 6, note 31, at 1171.

64. Ibid.

65. Ibid.

66. *See* ibid., at 1172.

67. Ibid.

68. 42 U.S.C.A. § 2000e-2(a)(1) & (b); see also *Espinoza v. Farah Manufacturing Co.*, 414 U.S. 86 (1973).

69. *See* Legomsky and Rodriguez, *supra* chap. 6, note 31, at 1172.

70. 42 U.S.C.A. § 1981.

71. *Bhandari v. First National Bank*, 829 F.2d 1343 (5th Cir. 1987); *Anderson v. Conboy*, 156 F.3d 167 (2d Cir. 1998).

72. *See* Legomsky and Rodriguez, *supra* chap. 6, note 31, at 1172.

73. Ibid. at 1175.

74. See *McDonnell Douglas Corp. v. Green*, 411 U.S. 792 (1973).

75. See *Griggs v. Duke Power Co.*, 401 U.S. 424 (1971).

76. *See* Legomsky and Rodriguez, *supra* chap. 6, note 31, at 1175.

77. Ibid.

78. Ibid.

79. *See* ibid. at 1175–76.

80. *See* Legomsky and Rodriguez, *supra* chap. 6, note 31, at 1176.

81. Ibid.

82. Ibid.

83. ICE, "Two Companies Admit to Hiring Illegal Aliens, Each Forfeit $2 Million," News Releases, U.S. Dep't of Homeland Security, http://www.ice.gov/news/releases/1201/120124houston.htm.

84. ICE, "Four Arrested for Employing Illegal Aliens," News Releases, U.S. Department of Homeland Security, http://www.ice.gov/news/releases/1202/120224gulfport.htm. "In fiscal year 2011, HSI initiated audits involving 2,496 employers nationwide—surpassing the record number conducted in all of fiscal year 2010." Ibid.

85. ICE, "St. Louis Industrial Supply Company Sentenced for Employing Illegal Aliens," News Releases, U.S. Department of Homeland Security, http://www.ice.gov/news/releases/1201/120117stlouis.htm

86. ICE, "Fact Sheet: Form I-9 Inspection Overview," Worksite Enforcement, U.S. Department of Homeland Security (Dec. 1, 2009), www.ice.gov/news/library/factsheets/i9-inspection.htm.

87. ICE, "Seven Companies Notified of Potential Debarment for Unlawful Employment Practices," News Releases, U.S. Department of Homeland Security, http://www.ice.gov/news/releases/0809/080912washington1.htm.

88. *See* ibid.

89. *See* Giovanni Peri, *The Impact of immigrants in Recession and Economic Expansion*, Migration Policy Institute (2010), 5.

90. *See* ibid.

91. *See* Federal Reserve Bank of Dallas, *From Brawn to Brains: How Immigration Works for America* (2010), 1, 14.

Chapter Eight

1. "Visas," U.S. Dep't of State, http://travel.state.gov/visa/.

2. *See* ibid.; *see* Legomsky and Rodriguez, *supra* chap. 6, note 31, at 470.

3. A tourist visa is an excellent example of an instance where a visa petition is not needed or even available. *See*, e.g., INA § 101(a)(15)(B).

4. *See*, e.g., 8 C.F.R. § 217.2(a).

5. "Temporary Workers," U.S. Department of State, http://travel.state.gov/visa/temp/types/types_1275.html.

6. Ibid.

7. *See*, e.g., INA § 101(a)(15).

8. *See*, e.g., *Temporary Workers*, U.S. Department of State; *see also*, e.g., INA § 101(a)(15)(K).

9. "Temporary (Nonimmigrant) Workers," U.S. Citizenship and Immigration Services, http://www.uscis.gov/portal/site/uscis/menuitem.eb1d4c2a3e5b9ac89243c6a7543f6d1a/?vgnextoid=13ad2f8b69583210VgnVCM100000082ca60aRCRD&vgnextchannel=13ad2f8b69583210VgnVCM100000082ca60aRCRD.

10. "Visas," U.S. Department of State, http://travel.state.gov/visa/.

11. "Temporary (Nonimmigrant) Workers," U.S. Citizenship and Immigration Services. It should be noted here that we are not speaking about changing status or adjusting status in the United States but only of the visa process for a foreign national seeking admission from abroad.

12. *See* ibid.

13. *See generally* ibid.

14. "Visa Wait Times—for Interviewing Appointments & Processing," U.S. Department of State, http://travel.state.gov/visa/temp/wait/wait_4638.html.

15. "Admission into United States," U.S. Department of Homeland Security (Dec. 17, 2010), http://www.cbp.gov/xp/cgov/travel/id_visa/legally_admitted_to_the_u_s.xml.

16. Ibid.

17. Ibid.

18. Ibid.; *see also* INA § 235.

19. INA §101(a)(15)(H).

20. *See* ibid.

21. "H-2B Certification for Temporary Non-Agricultural Work," U.S. Department of Labor, http://www.foreignlaborcert.doleta.gov/h-2b.cfm.

22. "H-2 Visa Temporary Workers," http://www.immigration.com/visa/h-2-visa/h-2-visa-temporary-workers.

23. "H-2B Program," International Recruiting Solutions, http://www.intrecsolutions.com/lang-en/solutions/79-h2b.html.

24. We also support setting aside additional green cards for foreign graduates with advanced degrees.

25. *See*, e.g., Stephen Dinan, "Homeland Security Loses Track of 1 Million Foreigners; Report Could Hurt Immigration Deal," *Washington Times* (Jul.

30, 2013), http://www.washingtontimes.com/news/2013/jul/30/homeland-security-loses-track-of-1-million-foreign/; Mark Krikorian, "Holding Foreign Visitors to Their Promises," *National Review Online* (Nov. 26, 2013), http://www.nationalreview.com/corner/364893/holding-foreign-visitors-their-promises-mark-krikorian.

26. GAO-12-287T, at 8.

27. Ibid.

28. Ibid.

29. Richard M. Stana, Director Homeland Security and Justice Issues, "Statement: Visa Security: Additional Actions Needed to Strengthen Overstay Enforcement and Address Risks in the Visa Process" (Sep. 13, 2011).

30. *See* Australian Government, Department of Immigration and Citizenship, Community Status Resolution Service, http://www.immi.gov.au/managing-australias-borders/compliance/community-status-resolution/_pdf/csrs-english.pdf.

31. Australian Government, Department of Immigration and Citizenship, Visas, Immigration and Refugees, http://www.immi.gov.au/visas/bridging. For example, the Australian government offers three types of bridging visas: (A) one that allows a person to stay in Australia while the extension of that person's substantive visa is being processed; (B) one that allows a person to travel outside of Australia and then return while his substantive visa is pending; and (C) one that allows a person to stay in Australia while an application for a visa is pending and the person does not have a substantive visa. Ibid.

32. Alberto R. Gonzales, "An Immigration Crisis in a Nation of Immigrants: Why Amending the Fourteenth Amendment Won't Solve Our Problems," 96 *Minn. L. Rev.* 6, 1859 (2012).

33. Joseph A. Vail, *Essentials of Removal and Relief* at 92 (citing 8 C.F.R. 264.1); *see supra* chap. 1, note 100.

34. *See* ibid.

35. *See* ibid.

36. *See* ibid. at 93 (citing INA §237(a)(3)).

37. "For International Visitors," http://www.cbp.gov/xp/cgov/travel/id_visa/nseers/imp_nseers_info.xml.

38. *See*, e.g., Raymond R. Parmer, Director, Office of International Affairs, U.S. Immigration and Customs Enforcement, Department of Homeland Security, statement regarding a hearing on "Visa Security and Passenger Pre-Screening

Efforts in the Wake of Flight 253," Before the U.S. House of Representatives, Committee on Homeland Security, Subcommittee on Border, Maritime and Global Counterterrorism (Mar. 11, 2010).

39. *See* ibid.

40. *See* ibid.

Chapter Nine

1. Also known as the McCarran-Walter Act, the Immigration and Nationality Act (INA) was enacted into law on June 27, 1952, Pub. L. 82-414, 66 Stat. 163 (June 27, 1952), and has been amended many times since then.

2. Prior to 1952 other statutes combined to govern U.S. immigration law. *See*, e.g., the Naturalization Act of 1790, the Aliens Act of 1798, the Immigration Act of 1891, the Immigration Act of 1924.

3. While many believe that we have a "broken" immigration system, no other country in the world receives as many immigrants and nonimmigrants annually as does the United States.

4. Pelofsky and Allen, *supra* chap. 3, note 11.

5. *See*, e.g., 22 C.F.R. part 42, subparts G and H. The Department of State administers consular processing.

6. *See*, e.g., INA § 245. The United States Citizenship and Immigration Services, within the Department of Homeland Security, administers adjustment of status.

7. *2012 Yearbook of Immigration Statistics*, U.S. Department of Homeland Security, Office of Immigration Statistics, Table 7, https://www.dhs.gov/yearbook-immigration-statistics-2012-legal-permanent-residents.

8. Likewise, an alien seeking to acquire lawful permanent resident status at a U.S. consulate must also be able to clear the various grounds of inadmissibility.

9. The ground of inadmissibility found at INA § 212(a)(6)(A)(i) is discussed further in this chapter.

10. *See* INA § 101(a)(13)(A) for a definition of "admitted," which includes "the lawful entry of the alien into the United States after inspection and authorization by an immigration officer."

11. The parole provision is found at INA § 212(d)(5) and is authorized for humanitarian reasons and significant public benefit. Parole is not regarded as an admission.

12. The alien must also apply for adjustment, be eligible to receive an immigrant

visa, and be admissible for permanent residence, and there must be an immigrant visa available at the time the application is filed. INA § 245(a)(1)–(3). VAWA self-petitioners are exempted from the requirement of "inspected and admitted or paroled" into the United States. INA § 245(a).

13. Note that INA § 245(a) not only requires that the alien be admissible but also that the alien be eligible to receive an immigrant visa. Conveniently, INA § 245(c) lists those aliens who are not eligible to receive an immigrant visa under INA § 245(a). Immediate relatives are specifically exempted from at least one category of the disqualified aliens listed. *See*, e.g., INA § 245(c)(2). As a result, an immediate relative alien could adjust status in the United States under INA § 245(a) despite being subject to deportation under INA § 237(a)(1)(C)(i) as a visa overstay or violator. Aliens who fail to maintain lawful status through no fault of their own or for technical reasons are also exempt from the list of disqualified aliens. Ibid. INA § 245(k) may also exempt certain employment-based immigrants.

14. *See*, e.g., Pub. L. 103-317, 108 Stat. 1724, 1765–66 (Aug. 26, 1994), § 506(b).

15. *See* Memorandum from David Martin, INS General Counsel, to Michael L. Aytes, Assistant Commissioner, Office of Benefits (Feb. 19, 1997), reprinted in Interpreter Releases 74, no. 11 (Mar. 24, 1997), app. II at 516–22. While no § 212(a)(6)(A)(i) ground of inadmissibility existed in 1994, that ground was passed in 1996 and the Martin memo later clarified that § 245(i) implicitly waives § 212(a)(6)(A)(i).

16. See former INA § 245(i)(1)(A).

17. *See* Legomsky and Rodriguez, *supra* chap. 6, note 31. Also note that there were over thirty-six million officially recorded nonimmigrant admissions into the United States in fiscal year 2009 compared with only slightly over one million immigrant admissions. *See* discussion in chapter 1 herein. Moreover, remember that adjustment of status accounted for only roughly 53 percent of all lawful immigration. *See* earlier discussion in chapter 9. Consequently, the consulates were further burdened with an additional 47 percent of the one million immigrant admissions in addition to administering the nonimmigrant admissions. Clearly, the consulates are carrying a heavy, and some might argue unnecessary, workload.

18. See former INA § 245(i). There were some, limited exceptions to the $1,000 remittance requirement. Ibid.

19. *See*, e.g., Pub. L. 103-317, 108 Stat. 1724, 1765–66 (Aug. 26, 1994). *See also Immigration & Nationality Act,* AILA (2010 ed.) § 245(i), n. 158.

20. *See*, e.g., Pub. L. 105-119, 111 Stat. 2440, 2458 (Nov. 26, 1997), amending former INA § 245(i).

21. Ibid.

22. The required visa petition is a petition for classification under INA § 204.

23. An application for labor certification is required for aliens seeking to immigrate under the employment-based second- and third-preference categories. INA § 212(a)(5)(D). Labor certification is required to ensure that U.S. workers are not displaced by alien workers. *See*, e.g., INA § 212(a)(5)(A)(i)(I)–(II).

24. *See*, e.g., Pub. L. 105-119, 111 Stat. 2440, 2458 (Nov. 26, 1997), amending former INA § 245(i); see also former INA § 245(i)(1)(B).

25. Ibid.

26. Any alien seeking to adjust status under INA § 245(i) based on a petition or application for labor certification filed after January 14, 1998, but on or before April 30, 2001, must demonstrate physical presence in the United States on December 21, 2000 (the date of the enactment of the LIFE Act Amendments of 2000).

27. *See*, e.g., LIFE Act Amendments, § 1502, Pub. L. 106-554 (2000).

28. Several bills have been introduced in Congress to extend INA § 245(i), but each bill has failed—no doubt largely influenced by the aftermath of September 11, 2001. Proposed immigration reform should be mindful of September 11, but not so mindful that efficiency in U.S. immigration law becomes a victim to September 11 as well.

29. *See*, e.g., "It's Time to Bring Back Section 245(i)," Immigration Blog (May 2, 2011) http://myimmigrationlawyer.blogspot.com/2011/05/its-time-to-bring-back-section-245i.html.

30. The alien may not be "inadmissible under section 212(a)(3)(E) or under section 212(a) insofar as it relates to criminals, procurers and other immoral persons, subversives, violators of the narcotic laws or smugglers of aliens," INA § 249.

31. INA § 249.

32. *See*, e.g., Registry Act of March 2, 1929, 45 Stat. 1512.

33. *See*, e.g., *Beltran-Tirado v. INS*, 213 F.3d 1179, 1181 (9th Cir. 1993). The entrance requirement in the registry provision was last updated as part of the

1986 Immigration Reform and Control Act (IRCA), Pub. L. 99-603, 100 Stat. 3359 (Nov. 5, 1986).

34. Currently one must show more than forty years of continuous residence to take advantage of the registry provision. In comparison, one only had to show between fourteen and fifteen years of continuous residency when registry was last updated in 1986.

35. INA § 249(a).

36. Ibid.

37. "It is the combined wisdom of every Congress during the past 70 years that persons who have somehow managed to live and work in the U.S. for many years, and who are not criminals, should be allowed to obtain permanent residence." Carl Michael Shusterman, "Registry: A Time-Tested Part of Our Immigration Laws," http://www.avvo.com/legal-guides/ugc/registry-a-time-tested-part-of-our-immigration-laws-1.

38. When first passed in 1929, the cutoff date for registry only went back five years. Registry Act of March 2, 1929, 45 Stat. 1512. When last updated in 1986, the cutoff date went back fourteen years. IRCA, Pub. L. 99-603, 100 Stat. 3359. Presently, the cutoff date goes back more than forty years. INA § 249(a). A reasonable cutoff date might be something significantly less than forty-plus years.

39. A fixed period of time establishing eligibility will evenly preserve the usefulness of the registry provision and further relieve Congress of the burden of having to periodically revise the cutoff date.

40. As discussed earlier, INA § 245(i) imposes a $1,000 fine. Our proposed new ground of inadmissibility, INA § 212(a)(6)(H), would also impose a monetary fine. Moreover, INA §§ 216 and 216A impose conditions subsequent on certain aliens. Consequently, neither fines nor conditions subsequent are novel ideas.

41. The required skills might be similar to those required by INA § 312 for naturalization purposes.

42. The Development, Relief, and Education for Alien Minors (DREAM) Act which seeks to provide relief for eligible alien youth and young adults.

43. *See*, e.g., U.S. Senate, Development, Relief, and Education for Alien Minors Act of 2009, S. 729, 111th Cong., 1st session; U.S. House of Representatives, American Dream Act, H.R. 1751, 111th Cong., 1st session. The DREAM Act would also have good moral character and high school diploma or GED

requirements. The DREAM Act also imposes certain conditions subsequent, such as pursuing higher education or honorable service in the military. The House of Representatives passed the DREAM Act on December 8, 2010, but the bill failed to reach the sixty-vote threshold necessary for it to advance to the Senate floor (55 yeas–41 nays). On May 11, 2011, Senate Majority Leader Harry Reid reintroduced the DREAM Act in the Senate.

44. Proposals for the DREAM Act have not yet clearly answered whether an alien who only resided part-time in the United States since entering before the age of sixteen would be eligible to take advantage of the DREAM Act. In the above hypothetical, must the alien demonstrate residence for only the preceding five years or for the entire past twenty years? Allowing a thirty-four-year-old alien to take advantage of the DREAM Act by only showing continuous residency for the preceding five years, for example, because in fact the alien largely lived abroad while still a minor would seem to circumvent the intent of the DREAM Act, which is aimed at providing relief to alien minors living in the United States through no fault of their own.

45. One might further assume that any alien applying under the DREAM Act would be required to show residency in the United States from the time the alien entered the country while under the age of sixteen, with such period of residency not less than five years. *See*, e.g., the discussion of DACA in chapter 10.

46. Moreover, an updated registry provision with a fixed date would be a permanent fixture, unlike the DREAM Act, which by its own terms would be "a remedy of constantly decreasing utility" because children who are currently not now at least twelve years old (i.e., "at the time the law is enacted") will likely continue to be brought into the United States through no fault of their own.

47. Moreover, INA § 291 puts the burden on the alien to establish "time, place, and manner of his entry into the United States." If that burden is not met, the alien "shall be presumed to be in the United States in violation of law."

48. *See*, e.g., INA § 235(a)(1) (an alien present in the United States who has not been admitted or who arrives in the United States . . . shall be deemed for purposes of this Act an applicant for admission). As discussed earlier, INA § 245(i), when applicable, trumps § 212(a)(6)(A)(i) and allows the alien to undergo the necessary inspection and admission without leaving the United States.

49. INA § 212(a)(9)(B)(i)(I). The alien must have left prior to the commence-

ment of removal proceedings. Ibid. Exceptions to the § 212(a)(9)(B) ground of inadmissibility include minor children, asylees, battered women and children. INA § 212(a)(9)(B)(iii).

50. INA § 212(a)(9)(B)(i)(II). Here there is no similar language avoiding inadmissibility if the alien departs prior to the commencement of removal proceedings, but the same exceptions that apply to (B)(i)(I) also apply to (B)(i)(II). INA § 212(a)(9)(B)(iii).

51. For a more extensive discussion of the INA § 212(a)(9)(B)(v) waiver, see David N. Strange, "The Waiver of Inadmissibility Pursuant to Section 212(a)(9)(B)(v) of the Immigration and Nationality Act: A Case Study," 41 *Tex. Tech L. Rev. Addendum* 49 (2009).

52. Ibid. *See also* INA § 212(a)(9)(B)(v).

53. Note that the alien is simply inadmissible (i.e., there is no period of inadmissibility identified). In effect, this renders the alien forever inadmissible, or at least until he cures the ground of inadmissibility (assuming that there are no other grounds of inadmissibility attached to the alien).

54. INA § 212(a)(9)(C)(ii). There is also a waiver to the § 212(a)(9)(C) ground of inadmissibility for battered self-petitioners who can show a connection between the alien's battering or subjection to extreme cruelty and the alien's removal or departure, subsequent reentry or reentries, or attempted reentry. INA § 212(a)(9)(C)(iii).

55. *See*, e.g., *Matter of Briones*, 24 I. & N. Dec. 355 (BIA 2007).

56. Please note that these three provisions are not the only grounds of inadmissibility. The INA encompasses many other additional grounds of inadmissibility. *See*, e.g., INA §§ 211, 212(a, e, f, j, m, n), 222(g), 214(k)(3).

57. Remember that the INA § 212(a)(9)(B)(i)(I) ground of inadmissibility requires unlawful presence for a period of more than 180 days.

58. Ibid.

59. Of course, if periods of unlawful presence amount in the aggregate to more than one year, and the alien then attempts to unlawfully reenter the United States, the INA § 212(a)(9)(C)(i)(I) ground of inadmissibility is triggered.

60. Chapter 1 describes immediate relative aliens.

61. This, again, is because immediate relatives are specifically exempted from the list of disqualified aliens found at INA § 245(c).

62. Compare with Australia's requirement that a person who has been excluded

for overstaying a visa cannot be granted a new nonimmigrant visa unless that person repays any debt owed to the Australian government, including the costs of removal. Australian Government, Department of Immigration and Citizenship, "Fact Sheet 86—Overstayers and Other Unlawful Non-citizens," http://www.immi.gov.au/media/fact-sheets/86overstayers-and-other-unlawful-non-citizens.htm.

63. *See*, e.g., USCIS Interoffice Memorandum, "Consolidation of Guidance Concerning Unlawful Presence for Purposes of Sections 212(a)(9)(B)(i) and 212(a)(9)(C)(i)(I) of the Act," Donald Neufeld, Acting Associate Director, Domestic Operations Directorate, Lori Scialabba, Associate Director Refugee, Asylum and International Operations Directorate, and Pearl Chang, Acting Chief, Office of Policy and Strategy (May 6, 2009).

64. *See*, e.g., *Matter of Briones*, 24 I. & N. Dec. 355 (BIA 2007).

65. *See also* David A. Martin, "Waiting for Solutions: Extending the Period of Time for Migrants to Apply for Green Cards Doesn't Get at the Real Problem," *Legal Times* (May 28, 2011), 66. We also think it important to point out that while INA §212(a)(9)(C)(i)(II) deals with aliens who have previously been ordered removed, INA § 241(a)(5) allows for the automatic reinstatement of orders of removal against aliens unlawfully reentering (without the right to see an immigration judge), and we further note that INA §212(a)(9)(A) also addresses aliens previously ordered removed and is another ground of inadmissibility for intending immigrants.

66. *See generally* Mike Riggs, "Obama Finally Does Something Right on Immigration," Reason.com (Jan. 7, 2012), http://reason.com/archives/2012/01/07/obama-finally-does-something-right-on-im.

67. *See*, e.g., INA § 212(a)(6)(A)(i).

68. Ibid.; INA § 212(a)(9)(B). *See also* discussion in chapter 9.

69. "Progress on Immigration," *New York Times* (Apr. 22, 2007), http://www.nytimes.com/2007/04/22/opinion/22sun1.html.

70. *See* Provisional Unlawful Presence Waivers of Inadmissibility for Certain Immediate Relatives, 78 Fed. Reg. 536, 536 (Jan. 3, 2013) (to be codified at 8 C.F.R. pts. 103 & 212).

71. Ibid.

72. Ibid.

73. *See* INA § 101(a)(48) (supp. II, 1996); Rachel E. Rosenbloom, "Will *Padilla*

Reach Across the Border?," 45 *New Eng. L. Rev.* 327, 337, and note 54 (2011); Nancy Morawetz, "Understanding the Impact of the 1996 Deportation Laws and the Limited Scope of Proposed Reforms," 113 *Harv. L. Rev.* 1936, 1939 (2000).

74. *See* INA § 101(a)(43)(B) (supp. II, 1996); Morawetz, *supra* note 73, at 1939 (giving an example of a misdemeanor crime of petty theft under New York state law becoming an aggravated felony under the immigration laws); Rosenbloom, *supra* note 73, at 337 and n. 54 ("Congress drastically expanded the scope of the term 'aggravated felony' in 1996 to include many crimes that are neither aggravated nor felonies").

75. Tova Indritz, "Ch. 6 Immigration Consequences of Criminal Convictions," in *Cultural Issues in Criminal Defense,* 241, 273, ed. by Linda Friedman Ramirez, 3d ed. (2010) (collecting cases from various jurisdictions).

76. J. McGregor Smyth, Jr., "From Arrest to Reintegration: A Model for Mitigating Collateral Consequences of Criminal Proceedings," 24 *Crim. Just.* (Fall 2009), reprinted in *Padilla and Beyond*, 9, 10 (A.B.A. Crim. Just. Section Pub. 2010); INA § 237(a)(2)(A)(ii).

77. *See* Legomsky and Rodriguez, *supra* chap. 6, note 31, at 575 ("From its humble origins, however, the aggravated felony definition has grown into a colossus. A series of amendments have steadily expanded its reach, to the point where an 'aggravated felony' need not be 'aggravated' and . . . need not be a felony."). *See also* Stephen Lee, "De Facto Immigration Courts," 101 *Cal. L. Rev.* 553 (2013).

78. *See* INA § 237(a)(2)(A)(iii); ibid., § 240(a)(3) (cancellation of removal for certain lawful permanent residents unavailable to "aggravated felons"); ibid., § 208(b)(2)(B)(i) (asylum unavailable to a refugee convicted of an aggravated felony); Indritz, *supra* note 75, at 299–301.

79. *Carachuri-Rosendo v. Holder*, 560 U.S., 130 S. Ct. 2577, 2582 (2010).

80. Ibid.

81. *See* 130 S. Ct. at 2585.

82. *See* ibid.

83. Ibid., 130 S. Ct. at 2584 & n. 9 (citing conflicting decisions from several federal circuits).

84. Congress may decide to treat attempt or conspiracy offenses as requiring something less than a felony offense that carries with it a term of sentence of at least one year. See INA § 101(a)(43)(U).

85. The Supreme Court describes aggravated felony as a "category of crimes singled out for the harshest deportation consequences." *Carachuri-Rosendo*, 130 S. Ct. at 2580.

86. President Obama's decision not to remove certain eligible children is a prime example.

Chapter Ten

1. However, we should be careful in calling these children "innocent." While they certainly had no mens rea in coming to the United States initially, their continued unlawful presence itself is by no means innocent under the INA.

2. Jeffrey Passel and D'Vera Cohn, "Unauthorized Immigrant Population: National and State Trends, 2010," Pew Research Hispanic Center (Feb. 1, 2011), http://www.pewhispanic.org/2011/02/01/ii-current-estimates-and-trends/.

3. Ibid.

4. See generally *Plyler v. Doe*, 457 U.S. 202 (1982).

5. National Conference of State Legislatures, "Allow In-State Tuition for Undocumented Students" (Jul. 2013), http://www.ncsl.org/issues-research/educ/undocumented-student-tuition-state-action.aspx.

6. "Undocumented Students," National Association of Secondary School Principals, http://www.nassp.org/Content.aspx?topic=Undocumented_Students.

7. Immigration Policy Center, "Deferred Action for Childhood Arrivals: A Q&A Guide (Updated)," American Immigration Council, http://www.immigrationpolicy.org/just-facts/deferred-action-childhood-arrivals-qa-guide-updated.

8. *See* ibid.

9. Alejandro Mayorkas, "Deferred Action for Childhood Arrivals: Who Can Be Considered?," The White House (Aug. 15, 2012), http://www.whitehouse.gov/blog/2012/08/15/deferred-action-childhood-arrivals-who-can-be-considered.

10. Ibid.

11. A group of ICE employees sued the government in 2012 to put an end to DACA. In essence, the group argued that DACA violates federal law and forces ICE employees to break the law by not arresting certain immigrants who arrived in the country as minors. The case was ultimately dismissed on jurisdictional grounds. *See*, e.g., Elizabeth Llorent, "Judge Dismisses ICE Agents' Lawsuit Challenging Obama's Deferred Action," *Fox News Latino* (Aug. 1, 2013), http://latino.foxnews.com/latino/politics/2013/08/01/judge-dismisses-

immigration-agents-lawsuit-against-obama-program-to-suspend/.

12. Linda Bentley, "Obama Now Denying Benefits for Deferred Action Individuals," *Sonoran News.com* 18, no. 36 (Sept. 5–11, 2012), http://www.sonoran-news.com/archives/2012/120905/news-obama.html.

13. "ICE Agents Sue Homeland Security Over Obama Amnesty," Federation for American Immigration Reform (Aug. 27, 2012), http://www.fairus.org/legislative-updates/fair-legislative-update-august-27-2012.

14. Bentley, "Obama Now Denying Benefits", *supra* note 12.

15. Muzaffar Chishti and Faye Hipsman, "Sequester Affects Immigration Enforcement—and Invites Attention to Detention Policy," Migration Information Source (Mar. 15, 2013), http://www.migrationinformation.org/Feature/display.cfm?id=937.

16. *See* http://www.defineamerican.com/.

17. *See, e.g.,* "The Ridenhour Prize for Truth Telling, 2013," The Ridenhour Prizes, http://www.ridenhour.org/prizes_truth-telling_2013.html.

18. *See* INA § 212(a)(9)(B). Based on his own admissions, it appears that he would also be inadmissible under INA § 212(a)(6)(C)(ii) for having made a false claim to U.S. citizenship.

19. *Matter of Hranka*, 16 I&N Dec. 491 (BIA 1978). In *Hranka*, the BIA also based its decision in part on a showing of rehabilitation. Admittedly, this advocate may have a difficult time showing rehabilitation.

20. *See, e.g.,* INA § 212(a)(9)(B)(iii)(I) explaining that the waiver is only necessary for those who accrued unlawful presence for a specific period after reaching the age of 18. *See*, also, INA § 212(a)(6)(C)(ii) laying out the false claim to citizenship ground of inadmissibility. Moreover, immigrant intent will certainly be an issue, but see *Matter of Hosseinpour*, 15 I. & N. Dec. 191, 192 (BIA 1975).

21. *Plyler v. Doe,* 457 U.S. 202 (1982); *see also* previous discussion in chapter 3.

22. "Undocumented Students: DREAMer's Pathway to College," Choose Your Future, http://www.chooseyourfuture.org/college/undocumented-students.

23. Ibid.

24. "Can I Join The Army?," http://army.com/info/usa/eligibility.

25. "Immigrants in the Military—Fact Sheet," One America, http://weareoneamerica.org/immigrants-military-fact-sheet.

26. *See* ibid.

27. U.S. Army, "U.S. Immigration Reaches out to Military Soldiers & Spouses, http://www.army.mil/article/20610/us-immigration-reaches-out-to-military-soldiers-and-spouses/.

28. "Diversity in the Military," Military.com, http://www.military.com/Recruiting/Content/0,13898,diversity_main,,00.html.

29. Matthew Larotonda, "Panetta to Navy Grads: Military Is Evolving in Strategy, Diversity," *ABC News* (May 29, 2012), http://abcnews.go.com/blogs/politics/2012/05/panetta-to-navy-grads-military-is-evolving-in-strategy-diversity/.

30. "Diversity in the Military," Military.com, http://www.military.com/Recruiting/Content/0,13898,diversity_main,,00.html.

31. Recruiting has been slightly boosted by the country's economic downturn, but it historically slows down in years of economic stability. "Recruiting Assistance Programs," U.S. Army, http://www.2k.army.mil/faqs.htm#avgbonus.

32. "Demographics 2010 Profile of the Military Community," http://www.militaryonesource.mil/12038/MOS/Reports/2010_Demographics_Report.pdf.

33. We recognize that the percentage might change every year with new high school graduating classes, but we also point out that not every new undocumented high school graduate will seek to join the military.

34. "U.S. Immigration Reaches out to Military Soldiers & Spouses," U.S. Army, http://www.army.mil/article/20610/us-immigration-reaches-out-to-military-soldiers-and-spouses/.

35. *See* ibid.

36. "Joining the Military, Military Entrance Requirements," Popular Military, http://www.popularmilitary.com/military-requirements.htm.

37. "Immigrants in the Military—Fact Sheet," One America, http://weareoneamerica.org/immigrants-military-fact-sheet.

Chapter Eleven

1. *See* Gonzales, *supra* chap. 8, note 32.

2. *See* ibid.

3. Robert A. Blecker, "The North American Economies after NAFTA: A Critical Appraisal," *International Journal of Political Economy* (2005), http://www.carnegieendowment.org/pdf/Blecker_NAFTA_paper_final.pdf.

4. J. J. Audley et al., eds., *NAFTA's Promise and Reality: Lessons from Mexico for the Hemisphere*, Carnegie Endowment for International Peace (Washington, D.C. 2004), 12, 17, http://www.carnegieendowment.org/files/nafta1.pdf.

5. David Bacon, "Illegal People: How Globalization Creates Migration and Criminalizes Immigrants," 63 *Ind. & Lab. Rel. Rev.* 357 (2008).

6. Ibid.

7. Héctor E. Sánchez, "Disposable Workers: Immigration After NAFTA and the Nation's Addiction to Cheap Labor," Labor Council for Latin American Advancement (Oct. 2011), 2, http:// longislandfed.org/sites/longislandfed.org/files/disposable_workers_0.pdf.

8. Jillian H. Hishaw, "Mississippi is Burning Georgia's Peaches Because Alabama is No Longer a Sweet Home: A Legislative Analysis of Southern Discomfort Regarding Illegal Immigration," 58 *S.D. L. Rev.* 30, 38 (2013).

9. Andres Oppenheimer, "Everyone Is Upbeat on Mexico—Except Mexicans," *Miami Herald* (Mar. 2, 2013), http://www.miamiherald.com/2013/03/02/3262162/everybody-is-upbeat-on-mexico.html.

10. Ibid.

11. Gus Taylor, "Energy Links Seen Boosting U.S. Ties to Mexico," *Washington Times* (Feb. 28, 2013), http://www.washingtontimes.com/news/2013/feb/28/energy-links-seen-boosting-us-ties-mexico/.

12. U.S. Customs and Border Protection, http://www.cbp.gov/.

13. "Merida Initiative," U.S. Department of State, http://www.state.gov/j/inl/merida/.

14. Ibid.

15. Ibid.

16. The White House, http://www.whitehouse.gov.

17. "Universal Background Checks—Key Facts to Consider," n. ii., National Shooting Sports Foundation, http://nssf.org/factsheets/PDF/UBC.pdf.

18. *See*, e.g., previous discussion of the BEST Program.

19. David T. Johnson, Assistant Secretary of State, Bureau of International Narcotics and Law Enforcement Affairs, Statement before the Subcommittee on the Western Hemisphere of the House Foreign Affairs Committee, "Guns, Drugs and Violence; The Merida Initiative & the Challenge in Mexico" (Mar. 18, 2009), http://www.state.gov/j/inl/rls/rm/120679.htm.

20. "Project Gunrunner," Bureau of Alcohol, Tobacco, Firearms and Explosives, http://www.atf.gov/firearms/programs/project-gunrunner/.

21. Ibid.

22. Committee on Oversight & Government Reform, http://www.oversight. house.gov/.

23. Charlie Savage, "Report by House Democrats Absolves Administration in Gun Trafficking Case," *New York Times* (Jan. 31, 2012), http://www.nytimes. com/2012/01/31/us/politics/operation-fast-and-furious-report-by-demo-crats-clears-obama-administration.html?scp=7&sq=department%20of%C-20justice,%C20fast%C20and%C20furious%program&st=cse.

24. "Thirty Years of America's Drug War: A Chronology," PBS, http://www.pbs. org/wgbh/pages/frontline/shows/drugs/cron/.

25. *See* H.R. 5729 (99th), Anti-Drug Abuse Act of 1986.

26. Alyssa L. Beaver, "Getting a Fix on Cocaine Sentencing Policy: Reforming the Sentencing Scheme of the Anti-Drug Abuse Act of 1986," *Fordham L. Rev.* 78 (2010), 2543–45, 2549, http://fordhamlawreview.org/assets/pdfs/Vol_78/ Beaver_April_2010.pdf.

27. "President Obama Signs the Fair Sentencing Act," The White House, http:// www.whitehouse.gov/blog/2010/08/03/president-obama-signs-fair-sentenc-ing-act.

28. "War on Drugs," Report of the Global Commission on Drug Policy (June 2011), http://www.globalcommissionondrugs.org/wpcontent/themes/gcdp_ v1/pdf/Global_Commission_Report_English.pd.

29. "Marijuana Legalization and Regulation," We are the Drug Policy Alliance, http://www.drugpolicy.org/marijuana-legalization-and-regulation.

30. Ibid.

31. *See* "2011 National Drug Control Strategy," The White House, Office of National Drug Control Policy, http://www.whitehouse.gov/ondcp/nation-al-drug-control-strategy.

32. "Drug Courts," National Institute of Justice, Office of Justice Programs, http://www.nij.gov/topics/courts/drug-courts/welcome.htm.

33. "Drug Courts," National Criminal Justice Reference Service, https://www. ncjrs.gov/spotlight/drug_courts/Summary.html.

34. *See* "Drug Courts," National Institute of Justice, Office of Justice Programs, http://www.nij.gov/topics/courts/drug-courts/welcome.htm.

35. Ibid.

36. Ibid.

37. "Drug Courts," National Criminal Justice Reference Service, https://www.ncjrs.gov/spotlight/drug_courts/Summary.html.

38. *See* "Drug Courts," National Institute of Justice, Office of Justice Programs, http://www.nij.gov/topics/courts/drug-courts/welcome.htm.

Epilogue

1. *See*, e.g., Julia Preston, "Legal Immigrants Seek Reward for Years of Following the Rules," *New York Times* (Jul. 15, 2013).

2. *See*, e.g., Aguilar, *supra* Preface, Note 6.

Appendix 1

1. INA § 101(a)(15)(A)(i).

2. INA § 101(a)(15)(A)(ii).

3. INA § 101(a)(15)(A)(iii).

4. *See supra* chap. 1, note 12.

5. INA § 101(a)(15)(B).

6. Ibid. See also *International Bricklayers and Allied Craftsmen v. Meese*, 616 F.Supp. 1387 (N.D. Cal 1985).

7. Ibid. See also *Islamic and Educational Center Ezan of Greater Des Moines v. Napolitano*, 826 F.Supp.2d 1122 (S.D. Iowa 2011).

8. Ibid.

9. *See supra* chap. 1, note 12.

10. INA § 101(a)(15)(C).

11. Ibid.; 8 C.F.R. § 214.1(a)(1)(ii).

12. *See supra* chap. 1, note 12.

13. INA § 101(a)(15)(D).

14. INA § 101(a)(15)(D)(i).

15. INA § 101(a)(15)(D)(ii).

16. Ibid.

17. INA § 101(a)(15)(E).

18. INA § 101(a)(15)(E)(i).

19. INA § 101(a)(15)(E)(ii). "Under the treaty investor criteria, no particular dollar amount is required for an investment to be deemed substantial; however, . . . [it] must be of an amount normally considered necessary to establish a viable enterprise of the nature contemplated." *Matter of Walsh and Pollard*, 20

I. & N. Dec. 60 (BIA 1988) Interim Decision 3111, WL 312511.

20. INA § 101(a)(15)(E)(iii).

21. *See supra* chap. 1, note 12.

22. *See* INA § 101(a)(15)(F) generally.

23. INA § 101(a)(15)(F)(i). Accredited academic institutions include colleges, universities, seminaries, conservatories, high schools, and elementary schools.

24. INA § 101(a)(15)(F)(ii).

25. INA § 101(a)(15)(F)(iii).

26. *See supra* chap. 1, note 12.

27. *See* INA § 101(a)(15)(G), generally.

28. INA § 101(a)(15)(G)(i).

29. Ibid.

30. INA § 101(a)(15)(G)(ii).

31. INA § 101(a)(15)(G)(iii).

32. INA § 101(a)(15)(G)(iv).

33. INA § 101(a)(15)(G)(v).

34. *See supra* chap. 1, note 12.

35. *See* INA § 101(a)(15)(H) generally; 8 C.F.R. § 214.2(h)(1)(i)

36. In order to qualify under the H-1C classification, the alien must meet the requirements of INA § 212(m)(1). The alien is also subject to the restrictions of INA § 212(m)(3)–(7).

37. 8 C.F.R. §§ 214.2(h)(1)(i), (2)(i)(A).

38. 8 C.F.R. § 214.2(h)(4)(v)(A).

39. *See supra* chap. 1, note 12.

40. INA § 101(a)(15)(H)(i)(b); a specialty occupation, for purposes of the H-1B visa, is one described in INA § 214(i).

41. Ibid.; 8 C.F.R. 214.2(h)(1)(ii)(B)(3).

42. INA § 214(g)(4).

43. INA § 214(g)(1)(A)(vii). The numerical limitation only applies to the principal alien receiving the H-1B visa and not to the alien's spouse or children. Similarly, the limitation does not apply to aliens who (1) are employed or have been offered employment at an institution of higher education (as defined in 20 U.S.C.A. § 1001(a)), or (2) are employed or have been offered employment at a non-profit research organization or government research organization, or (3) have earned a master's degree or higher degree from a U.S. institution of higher education (INA § 214(g)(5)(A)–(C)).

44. *See supra* chap. 1, note 12.

45. INA §§ 101(a)(15)(H)(i)(b1) and 214(g)(8)(A). This category is subject to numerical limitations of 1,400 for nationals of Chile and 5,400 for nationals of Singapore for any fiscal year. There are also restrictions and time limitations further laid out in INA § 214(g)(8).

46. INA § 101(a)(15)(H)(ii)(a); 8 C.F.R. § 214.2(h)(5)(iv)(A). For an extensive description of what is included in "agricultural labor or service," *see* 29 U.S.C.A. § 203(f) and 26 U.S.C.A. § 3121(g). Seasonal work is defined in 8 C.F.R. § 214.2(h)(5)(iv)(A) as "[e]mployment . . . where the employer's need to fill the position with a temporary worker will, except in extraordinary circumstances, last no longer than one year."

47. INA § 214(g)(1)(B). The apportionment of the visa is set at half (33,000) for the first six months and the remaining half for the following six months (INA § 214(g)(10)).

48. INA § 214(g)(2).

49. INA § 101(a)(15)(H)(ii)(b); 8 C.F.R. § 214.2(h)(6)(i)(A).

50. Ibid.

51. INA § 214(g)(1)(B); INA § 214 (g)(1)(B).

52. *See supra* chap. 1, note 12. For a thorough explanation of the H-2B process for both the alien and employer, *see* 8 C.F.R. § 214.2(h).

53. INA § 101(a)(15)(H)(iii).

54. *See supra* chap. 1, note 12.

55. *USCIS Adjudicator's Field Manual* (AFM), chap. 31.9.

56. *See supra* chap. 1, note 12.

57. A "bona fide representative" is an alien who represents or stands for a number or class of persons in a real, actual and genuine capacity. See *Black's Law Dictionary* (6th ed. 1990), 117, 1302.

58. INA § 101(a)(15)(I).

59. Ibid. For information on which countries retain reciprocity with the United States, *see* U.S. Department of State Visa Reciprocity Table, http://travel.state.gov/visa/fees/fees_3272.html.

60. INA § 101(a)(15)(I).

61. *See supra* chap. 1, note 12.

62. INA § 101(a)(15)(J).

63. Ibid. The further restrictions, such as an assurance from the alien that he

will return to his country of nationality upon completion of the program, are contained in INA § 212(j).

64. INA § 101(a)(15)(K)(i).

65. INA § 101(a)(15)(K)(ii). The K-2 visa preference is also subject to the regulations of INA § 214(r).

66. INA § 101(a)(15)(K)(iii). Although the provision allowing minor children to follow or join the alien parent is specified in only one subsection of the INA, the admissions are divided into two separate visas, K-2 for the children following a K-1 visa holder and K-4 for children following the K-3 visa holder. *See*, e.g. 8 C.F.R. § 214.2(k).

67. INA § 101(a)(15)(L).

68. Ibid.

69. Ibid.

70. 8 C.F.R. § 214.2(l)(16).

71. *See supra* chap. 1, note 12.

72. INA § 101(a)(15)(M)(i).

73. INA § 101(a)(15)(M)(ii). *See also* 8 C.F.R. § 214.2(m)(3).

74. INA § 101(a)(15(M)(iii).

75. *See supra* chap. 1, note 12. Interestingly, the M-3 visa had a total of three admissions from 2005–2009, all of which occurred in 2007. See United States Department of Homeland Security, *Yearbook of Immigration Statistics: 2009* (Washington, D.C.: Office of Immigration Statistics, 2010), Table 25.

76. INA § 101(a)(15)(N)(i).

77. 8 C.F.R. § 214.2(n).

78. INA § 101(a)(15)(N)(ii).

79. INA § 101(a)(15)(O)(i).

80. Ibid.

81. INA § 101(a)(15)(O)(ii).

82. INA § 101(a)(15)(O)(iii).

83. *See supra* chap. 1, note 12.

84. INA § 101(a)(15)(P)(i)–(iii). *See also* 8 C.F.R. § 214.2(p)(1)(i).

85. INA § 101(a)(15)(P)(iv). Recipients of the P-1 visa must also meet the requirements of INA § 214(c)(4)(A) for professional and amateur athletes and coaches and INA § 214(c)(4)(B) for performers and entertainers.

86. *See supra* chap. 1, note 12.

87. INA § 101(a)(15)(Q). An international cultural exchange program is one de-

signed to provide an opportunity for the American public, or a segment of the public, to learn about foreign cultures and for an alien or aliens to learn about American culture. *See*, e.g., 8 C.F.R. § 214.2(q)(3).

88. 8 C.F.R. § 214.2(q)(1)(i).

89. 8 C.F.R. § 214.2(q)(1)(ii). In order to participate in this program, the alien must have been physically present for at least three months immediately prior to submitting the application in either Northern Ireland, Louth, Monaghan, Cavan, Leitrim, Sligo, or Donegal. Additionally, the alien must be between the ages of eighteen and thirty-five. *See* 8 C.F.R. § 214.2(q)(15)(ii)(A). Interestingly, the Q-2 category provided for dependents to follow the principal beneficiary in Q-3 status. The Q1 category does not provide for any such dependent status, therefore a dependent of a Q-1 visa holder must qualify under a separate visa classification. *See* 8 C.F.R. § 214.2(q)(1)-(11). The Irish peace process cultural and training program ended on October 1, 2008, and therefore is no longer in effect. *See* Pub. L. 108-449, 118 Sta. 3469 (Dec. 10, 2004).

90. INA § 101(a)(15)(R).

91. INA § 101(a)(15)(R)(i)-(ii). *See also* INA § 101(a)(27)(C).

92. Ibid.

93. *See supra* chap. 1, note 12.

94. INA § 101(a)(15)(S)(i)–(ii).

95. 8 C.F.R. § 214.2(t)(1)–(3).

96. INA § 101(a)(15)(S)(i). *See also* INA § 214(k)(1).

97. INA § 101(a)(15)(S)(ii).

98. INA § 214(k)(1).

99. INA § 101(a)(15)(S)(ii)(IV). The family of the visa beneficiary is granted S-7 status if the attorney general (in the case of an S-5 beneficiary) or both the attorney general and secretary of state (in the case of an S-6 beneficiary) find it "appropriate." *See* INA § 101(a)(15)(S)(ii)(IV). S-visa status is not initiated by an intending nonimmigrant; rather a law enforcement authority must initiate the process. *See* 9 FAM 41.83 N3.

100. INA § 101(a)(15)(T)(i). Sex trafficking (using a person for a commercial sex act) and involuntary servitude or slavery are the severe forms of trafficking defined in § 103 of the Victims of Trafficking and Violence Protection Act of 2000, Pub. L. 106-386, 114 Sta. 1464 (Oct. 28, 2000).

101. INA § 101(a)(15)(T)(ii). The member of the family that may accompany or

follow to join the victim of trafficking is dependent on the age of the victim and the relationship the victim has to the intending family member. *See* INA § 101(a)(15)(T)(ii).

102. INA § 101(a)(15)(U)(i).

103. INA § 101(a)(15)(U)(i)(I). Criminal activities that qualify for the U visa include: rape; torture; trafficking; incest; domestic violence; sexual assault; abusive sexual contact; prostitution; sexual exploitation; stalking; female genital mutilation; being held hostage; peonage; involuntary servitude; slave trade; kidnapping; abduction; unlawful criminal restraint; false imprisonment; blackmail; extortion; manslaughter; murder; felonious assault; witness tampering; obstruction of justice; perjury; fraud in foreign labor contracting; or any attempt or conspiracy to commit any of these crimes. *See* INA § 101(a)(15)(U)(iii).

104. INA § 101(a)(15)(U)(i)(II).

105. INA § 101(a)(15)(U)(i)(III).

106. INA § 101(a)(15)(U)(i)(IV). The criminal activity "occurring in the U.S." includes Indian territories, military bases, and the outlying territories or possessions of the United States. *See* INA § 101(a)(15)(U)(i)(IV).

107. INA § 101(a)(15)(U)(ii).

108. The child must meet the requirements of INA § 203(d).

109. INA § 101(a)(15)(V).

110. Ibid.

111. *See* Department of State: Nonimmigrant (V) Visa for Spouse and Children of Lawful Permanent Resident (LPR) notice, http://travel.state.gov/visa/immigrants/types/types_1493.html.

112. *See supra* chap. 1, note 12.

113. 22 C.F.R. § 214.6(d)(1)–(2). See also INA § 214(e). The professions from which the alien seeking admittance under TN classification must participate are found in Appendix 1603.D.1 to Annex of the NAFTA.

114. For purposes of the TD visa, a dependent is a spouse or unmarried minor child. *See* 22 C.F.R. § 214.6(j)(1).

115. 22 C.F.R. § 214.6(j).

116. *See supra* chap. 1, note 12.

117. For an overview of the various and complex regulations and requirements for the different NATO visas, *see* 8 C.F.R. §§ 214.2(s), 316.20(b), and 319.5 and 22 C.F.R. §§ 41.1(d), 41.1(e), 41.25, and 42.32(d)(5).

118. *See supra* chap. 1, note 12.

119. *See* Pub. L. 99-603, 100 Sta. 3359 (Nov. 6, 1986).

120. The U.S. Department of State, Bureau of Consular affairs has a complete list of the current countries designated as Visa Waiver Program countries at http://travel.state.gov/visa/temp/without/without_1990.html.

121. INA § 217(a). Generally, any nonimmigrant who is not in possession of a valid nonimmigrant visa or border crossing card is inadmissible. *See* INA § 212(a)(7)(B)(i)(II).

122. *See* 8 C.F.R. § 214.1(a)(2).

123. *See supra* chap. 1, note 12.

Appendix 3

1. Currently, § 212(a)(6)(H) does not exist. It is proposed herein as a new ground of inadmissibility.

Appendix 4

1. Current INA § 249 does not mention terrorist activities.

INDEX